Collaborating to Manage

Collaborating to Manage

A Primer for the Public Sector

Robert Agranoff

Georgetown University Press
Washington, DC

Library of Congress Cataloging-in-Publication Data

Agranoff, Robert.
   Collaborating to manage : a primer for the public sector / Robert Agranoff.
      p. cm.
   Includes bibliographical references and index.
   ISBN 978-1-58901-916-4 (pbk. : alk. paper)
    1. Public-private sector cooperation—United States. 2. Intergovernmental cooperation—United States. 3. Local government—United States. 4. Public administration—United States. I. Title.
   JK421.A557   2012
   658′.044—dc23

15 14 13 12   9 8 7 6 5 4 3 2   First printing

Contents

APPENDIXES

Illustrations

BOXES

Preface

THIS BOOK SEEKS TO CAPTURE the basic ideas and approaches for public managing across agency and organization boundaries in an era of governance where governments form partnerships with external organizations and they work together to deal with difficult public problems. The book examines the current and emergent approaches and techniques in intergovernmental grants and regulation management, purchase-of-service contracting, networking, public and/or nonprofit partnerships, and other such lateral arrangements in the context of the changing public agency. Rather than subscribing to the assumption that extant theories of the state are virtually emptying out or otherwise disappearing, the book maintains a focus on the changing role of the public agency and its interlocutors in the light of externalization. It takes a deeper look at public management in an era of shared public program responsibility, that is, management within the sphere of governance.

The book is geared to professionals who work within and with the new, externally as well as internally geared bureaucracy—the "conductive" public agency—and for students who are pursuing or will pursue careers on one or the other side of public programs in the network era. Thus it looks at contemporary structure and operations on both sides of the permeable boundaries between public agency and nongovernmental organizations, particularly how collaborative managing is used to achieve program results. It is both an introduction to these intractable subjects and a review of current practices for those who toil in these contemporary fields of exchange. Finally, for students who are entering public service, it is a means of alerting them that there is more out there than hierarchy, and that within the public agency there are other aspects of bureaucratic organizing.

The basis of the book's eight substantive or core chapters are expansions of six delivered lectures and three conference papers that were presented between March 2008 and April 2010. They include the Lent Upson Lecture, Wayne State University, Detroit, March 2008; Political Science and Public Administration, Autonoma University, Barcelona, May 2008; School of Business (Mental Health Institute),

University of North Carolina–Chapel Hill, August 2008; John Glenn School of Public Affairs, Ohio State University, November 2008; National Academy of Public Administration, November 2008; Center for Governance and Public Management, ESADE Business School, Barcelona, May 2009; ASPA/EPAG Transatlantic Dialogue at Bucconi University, Milan, July 2008; Center for Constitutional Studies, Madrid, April 2009; and Intergovernmental Relations in 2020 Conference, San Jose, April 2010. The lecture materials and prepared papers provided the basis for a series of approaches that I further develop in the pages that follow on how the public sector is changing, and how this change is having an impact on the ways organizations and management are evolving while still holding on to some of their standard approaches.

In this book's exploration of government and its interlocutors, the reader will find that some important dimensions of collaborative management have been left out or basically overlooked. One is that, other than a discussion of power, the political aspects of many of the decisions and agreements that are reached as administrators operate across boundaries. The fact is that virtually every such action has political overtones, but with few exceptions the decision here was made to hold to managers' operational roles. Another omission here is the general role that civil society—the voluntary or social sector—plays in fostering collaboration. Clearly this element is important in mediating the overarching structures of the market and the state, in building the social capital necessary to bring parties together, and in transmitting important democratic values. Although these are important precursors of how agents can collaborate, they really constitute another subject that has been covered in many volumes during the past decade. Finally, with the exception of several practice-related ideas, a conscious decision was made not to incorporate the bulk of the valuable empirical work on networks and collaboration that has been published in journal articles. This useful body of work contributes less directly to practice and ultimately merits theoretical recognition. The purpose here, however, is to give a more field-based picture of how work is being done collaboratively between governments and nongovernmental organizations.

Acknowledgments

A NUMBER OF ACKNOWLEDGMENTS are due, for without these persons the final product would never have seen the light of day. Colleagues who provided useful comments and suggestions on parts of the manuscript include Xavier Ballart, Cesar Colino, Mark Draves, Richard Elling, Andrew Massey, Jack Meek, Paul Posner, Kurt Thurmaier, Carol Weissert, and Tamyko Ysa. Six persons read the entire manuscript and provided excellent and detailed feedback: two anonymous reviewers, Michael McGuire of the School of Public and Environmental Affairs at Indiana University, Rosemary O'Leary of the Maxwell School at Syracuse University, Beryl Radin of the Public Policy Institute at Georgetown University, and Angel Saz-Carranza of the Center for Public Management at the ESADE Business School. My thanks also go to Beryl Radin for her encouragement and suggestions as series editor. At Georgetown University Press, Don Jacobs deserves a great deal of credit for guiding this project, and thanks are also due to the entire staff. The index was prepared by Ron Sheriff of Bremerton, Washington. Finally, a great deal of support was provided by the School of Public and Environmental Affairs at Indiana University–Bloomington, including four persons who diligently prepared the manuscript: Stephanie Dunbar, Kim Evans, Betsy Hobbs, and Patricia Withred. I would like to recognize the patience and support of my wife, Susan Klein. Finally, because the book focuses on present–future dynamics, it is dedicated to our grandchildren: Lily, Zada, and Zevan.

CHAPTER 1

To Manage Is to Collaborate

THE AIM OF THIS BOOK is to help readers sort their way through the new and emerging ways of coping with the organizational richness that is a result of the cross-boundary government-to-governing changes of recent decades. It is designed to provide a guide to the core concepts regarding how to cope with the demands of this new and interesting and interactive world. The book should not be read as an operating manual but as a way to link thought to action.

Public visibility of the need to operationally coordinate public agencies and services has become prominent since the Hurricane Katrina disaster of 2005. Officials appearing on cable television news programs and in Internet blogs, as well as public administration pontificators, have called for a new emphasis on collaboration among federal, state, and local governments, and also with nongovernmental organizations (NGOs).

At the local level there are hundreds of interagency programs like Strive Together in the Cincinnati and northern Kentucky area. This program links public school superintendents and educators, university administrators, business leaders, and nonprofit and civil society executives into a collaborative devoted to using data-driven exchanges toward improvements in a series of priority outcomes ranging from kindergarten readiness to postsecondary enrollment and completion (www.strivetogether.org).

The Strive Together effort and disaster mitigation have a great deal of surface validity given the scattering of legal authority, funding streams, and delivery capability among disparate agencies and organizations charged with disaster relief and educational outcomes. This could also be the case for approaches to other pressing societal problems. Coordinated attacks on problems require collaborative management, a subject area that the field of public administration has not gone into very deeply. To be sure, many have called for a need to develop skills in bargaining and negotiation, or to learn how to manage with distributed leadership, or to engage in cross-disciplinary planning, but the advice givers rarely trenchantly consider the administrative domains of collaborative management.

What does collaborative management entail? It is an endeavor that has at least 101 definitions, and those who engage in it need to understand what it means. Although at one time collaboration referred to the cross-functional effort of persons working within agencies, it now also refers to those who cross the boundaries of organized entities working in dyadic, triadic, or networked relationships that are transactional in nature. Similarly, at one time management referred to the activity of strategy and direction given to single organizations, whereas today collaborative management refers to similar activities that reach across levels of government and across organizations. Thus, "collaborative management is a concept that describes the process of facilitating and operating in multiorganizational arrangements to solve problems that cannot be solved, or solved easily, by single organizations" (Agranoff and McGuire 2003, 4). As such, it involves purposive relationships that go beyond cooperation, that is, whereby actors work jointly in some helpful fashion. Collaboration is aimed at creating or discovering solutions within given sets of constraints, for example, knowledge, time, money, competition, and/or conventional wisdom (Emerson, Nabatchi, and Balogh 2012; Schrage 1995).

This increasingly important activity does, as mentioned, entail more than actions that include bargaining and negotiations, joint meetings, and formal partnerships or proposals for multiagency change. The field of public administration must go beyond these broad generalizations to break down and communicate the collaborative activities of managers. This book examines theory and practice in this increasingly important arena of collaborative public management. It is not only based on the author's four-plus decades of experiencing and studying in these arenas but also reflects on the literature in this core area, where public and public-serving organizations work across their boundaries. It differs from the author's previous work on human services integration (Agranoff and Pattakos 1979; Agranoff 1991), intergovernmental management (Agranoff 1986; Agranoff and McGuire 2003), and public network processes (Agranoff and McGuire 2001; Agranoff 2007). In this book the work of many researchers and practitioners is reflected, and thus it is designed to lay out the basics of collaborative management.

Collaboration matters a great deal in public management, inasmuch as so much public work is "outside" the bureaucracy, in "conductive" agencies—that is, public bureaucracies that gear their structures and operations to external as well as internal work, a major theme throughout this book. A conductive agency is one that engages in dismantling the boundaries of its structure and functions by connecting with a variety of external organizations and interests to strategically and operationally enhance its performance. Such agencies' work is highly relational; that is, it lies both outside and inside their structures. For example, more and more public services are delivered by NGOs but under public-sector legal constraints and public agency supervision, monitoring, and auditing. As a result, the public management problem then becomes the problem of collaborative management. The knowledge base of collaborative management—that is, the practice–theory interaction—is captured in this volume in order to enhance study and practice.

Three theory-into-practice examples can cast some light on the collaboration knowledge base. First, following the pathbreaking lead of Anselm Strauss (1993, 24), Wagenaar observes that "actions are imbedded in interactions." Wagenaar's (2004, 648) study of interactive bureaucracy suggests that all administrative practice transactions (1) are *situated*, that is, take place in contexts that influence how they are understood and carried out; (2) involve *knowing*, or the application of knowledge in carrying out tasks; (3) are *actions*, the prime vehicle for negotiating in the world; and (4) entail *interaction between parties*, the central focus of work. Although these principles were applied to internal agency work by Wagenaar, they would apply equally to collaborative management, in that it is also always situated, involves the search for and application of knowledge, and requires both interaction and ultimately actions. Thus the practice of collaboration follows a path similar to that of work within hierarchies.

Second, in an interesting work on creative collaboration, Keith Sawyer (2007, 43–55) has found from research and practice that when people are engaged in collaborative endeavors, interpersonal conversation is critical because it leads to *flow*, a state of heightened consciousness, and flow leads to creativity. For Sawyer group flow, whereby persons work together at peak levels of activity, depends on ten conditions: (1) participants have a specific goal in mind, (2) members engage in close or deep listening, (3) participants concentrate deeply, (4) participants possess autonomy from their top management, (5) blended egos emerge as small ideas to build on big ones, (6) all participants play an equal role, (7) familiarity breeds productivity and decision making, (8) there is constant communication, (9) participants extend and build on other ideas, and (10) actors accept the possible risk of failure. These principles of practice, as applied to interorganizational collaboration, point to the kinds of issues that public managers need to think about as they embark on situated interactions designed to solve nettlesome problems.

Third, one important theoretical dimension of collaborative management is interoperability. William Jenkins of the US Government Accountability Office (GAO 2004, 2) uses the Katrina experience to illustrate how "interoperable communications capabilities" reflect "a function of effective incident command planning and operations structure that defines, for different circumstances and types of events, who is in charge and what types of information . . . would need to be communicated." Jenkins's GAO report stresses the immediate need for comprehensive planning, establishment of interoperable communications requirements, assessment of current responsibilities, and state governments' operational planning and training requisites. It would appear that the concept of interoperability—reciprocally communicated planning and program operations—could well be one key from practice for unlocking the process of collaboration, which is inherently participatory at its implementation stage. To enhance practice these theoretical concepts of collaborative management require a more extensive look at details like those related to these three situations.

ORDINARY AND NETTLESOME PROBLEMS

The conceptually operational concerns illustrated above, however, are getting ahead of the story. Collaboration between public entities or between public entities and NGOs is a means to facilitate activities that are designed to solve public issues. In the fast-paced world of public-sector agents, there are problems that call for rather easy solutions and there are problems that appear to be so intractable that the path(s) to resolution are unknown, complicated, or need a multiagency approach, or most frequently are some combination of all three.

The easy public problems are straightforward. A rural road floods at a certain point every time it rains, and the township government obtains county money and expertise and builds a bridge. A relatively healthy, employed, low-income person suffers an injury and goes to the emergency room at the local public hospital and receives treatment. A medium-sized suburban community wants to showcase local gardens, so the city council appoints a volunteer garden tour committee. A financially pressed school board decides not to replace the retiring French teacher, so it sends the Spanish teacher to do summer graduate work in French. A small cluster of recent Somali immigrants who do not speak English have moved to town and the local social services agency finds a volunteer bilingual translator. A city government wants to build a convention center, but it fails to obtain either philanthropic or state grant funding and so it creates a "special convention district," authorized under state law, and floats bonds to finance the project. Another city wants to begin a recycling program, so it amends its current contract with its garbage collection contractor for this new service. Many issues are very much like this.

Many other public problems, however, are considerably more complicated and require protracted efforts by several jurisdictions and organizations. Examples of these need to be explored in greater detail, such as the environmental and natural resources arena. The Elkhorn Mountain Range in Montana contains several types of ecosystems—mountain grasslands, various forest types, and agrarian zones—that involve a variety of landowners: the US Forest Service, the US Bureau of

Land Management, and private families or individuals. Additionally, the Montana Department of Fish, Wildlife, and Parks has jurisdiction over wildlife in the entire region. Before the early 1990s this mix of landownership led to conflicting management practices (even in three ranger districts)—for example, poor land use, uncoordinated timber cutting, and unmanaged wildlife habitat protecting—with little coordination and almost nonexistent communication. Agencies often worked at cross purposes, under different mandates and toward different goals. In 1997 the various parties signed a memorandum of understanding to designate the entire region as a cooperative management area, which set in motion a process and structure for achieving interagency cooperation and substantive management goals (Wondolleck and Yaffee 2000, 87–88).

Another difficult problem is that of rural development. The federal government recognized that America's rural (nonmetropolitan) and sparsely populated areas are being left behind because of small-scale, low-density populations and distance from urban centers, so it encouraged the establishment of state rural development councils, which comprise representatives from the federal government, state governments, local governments, the private sector, the nonprofit sector, and higher education. Some thirty-eight of these sister councils were ultimately organized and were supported by federal funds and the cooperative efforts of two essential agencies for rural development, the US Department of Agriculture's rural development program and state government departments of economic development. The councils engaged in a number of collaborative activities to make an impact on rural development policy, promote statutory and regulatory relief, develop management improvement and information systems, foster demonstration projects, seek new funding sources, launch cooperative ventures, and organize leadership development (Radin et al. 1996, 155). The councils came about because no one agency or level of government had been charged with the responsibility for rural development; instead, it was fragmented among three or four federal departments and programs, two to five state agencies, the federal–state extension services at land-grant universities, substate planning districts, farm cooperative services and farm associations, state or county government associations, state and municipal associations, and state and local chambers of commerce.

The events surrounding Hurricane Katrina provide another nettlesome problem. It revealed a national emergency management system that was incapable of responding to the immediate needs of communities along the Gulf Coast and was unprepared to coordinate the massive relief effort required for recovery. Public criticism pointed to the lack of leadership among the three levels of government—Federal Emergency Management Agency, State of Louisiana, and City of New Orleans—to mount a disaster response and coordinate relief. In addition to the charge of a lack of command and control, which was heard often, the critics focused on a narrow set of functions: search and rescue, emergency medical services, temporary shelter and food, and restoring lifelines. Emergency management also includes hazard mitigation to prevent or lessen the impact of a disaster, disaster preparedness (emergency planning and training), disaster response (search and rescue), and disaster recovery (restoration of lifelines and basic services). Unlike military-type analogies, emergency management, when it is effective, relies less on command and control and instead on "a more dynamic and flexible network model that facilitates multiorganizational, intergovernmental and intersectional cooperation" (Waugh and Streib 2006, 131).

Transportation planning and financing at the local level also require coordination because they now take place in two primary venues. One is within city and county governments, where minor and arterial streets and roads that primarily affect given jurisdictions are organized, engineered, and built. The other venue, for most urbanized areas and their surrounding counties, is the metropolitan planning organization (MPO). The Des Moines area MPO, for example, is made up of elected and administrative officials and transportation professionals from thirteen cities and four counties, along with state highway department and federal transportation and mass transit officials. The MPO is charged under the US Transportation Equity Act for the 21st Century to look at all transportation needs for the area, including bicycle, highway, paratransit, pedestrian, and public modes. It does this through its long-term Transportation Improvement Program, which incorporates short-term allocations of federal funds for local projects (Agranoff 2007, 75, 80).

In 1996 welfare reform included block grants to the states for Temporary Assistance for Needy Families (TANF), primarily for young, single mothers. TANF places a five-year lifetime limit on the recipient of welfare benefits and requires most welfare recipients to work at least thirty hours per week. States have considerable discretion over program eligibility and administration, typically through local government and NGOs. Most important, for a state to reach its TANF goals of removing clients, it must help local administrative agencies deliver a set of support services that are funded under different federal titles, particularly Medicaid (health care services); food stamps (nutrition); child day care (social services block grant); education and training (several federal titles and state programs); pregnancy and parenting (US Public Health Service); housing (federal and state programs); employment services (federal–state employment service); and a host of possible case management, information and referral counseling, legal, substance abuse, and other services (Riccucci 2005, 15–17). Although few TANF clients require this full array of services, many need employment, education, health care, housing, child care, and nutrition services to remain employed and stay off welfare. This requires a concerted effort at interorganizational coordination on behalf of the client, with the client's participation.

In 2001 the State of North Carolina completely revamped its mental health, substance abuse, and intellectual/developmental disabilities services by converting its county-level service delivery units into local management entities (LMEs) (initially thirty-three, with multicounty units). The LMEs do planning, provider network development, services and financial management, service monitoring, and evaluation of core services through a system of contracts for services with for-profit and nonprofit NGOs. The LMEs are also the gateways for admission to and discharge from state hospitals, because they perform screening, assessment and referral, emergency services, and consultation–prevention–education as they coordinate services (Lin 2007, 13–14). Recognizing that local public agencies are involved in both coordinated system development and the delivery of services, the state removed the LMEs' direct service delivery function under the assumption that building local networks of providers and coordinating those services is a needed and different function from that of delivery, one on which the public sector needs to place greater emphasis.

Finally, the City of Cincinnati is representative of many larger cities that must work hard to maintain their economies in the face of a loss of manufacturing and service jobs to other US regions and overseas. The city coordinates these efforts through its Department of Economic Development. Most important, it maintains an active intergovernmental presence. It has formally adopted an intergovernmental economic development policy and pursues numerous discretionary grants and actively negotiates regulatory programs every year. It has broad and deep experience in the development areas, dating back to the Model Cities and War on Poverty programs of the 1960s. The city retains lobbyists in Columbus, the state capital, and in Washington. The city manager's office is a focal point for daily communication with state offices (e.g., highways, economic development, and water finance authority), members of the state legislature, the congressional delegation, and federal offices (Department of Housing and Urban Development, Department of Commerce, and Department of Transportation). The city forges many interlocal partnerships, particularly with the area chamber of commerce; Downtown Cincinnati, Incorporated; Hamilton County, of which it is a part; and local developers and entrepreneurs (Agranoff and McGuire 2003, 10–11).

The concerns of land use management, rural development, emergency management, metropolitan transportation, welfare to work, mental disability services, and maintaining city economic infrastructures are all representative of the second category of difficult problems that are not solved by singular public action. They instead require concerted action by different levels of government and NGOs. Moreover, they require the actions of these different organized entities as they work "among themselves" to execute their own operations *and* work together or "with one another."

NEW FUTURES: A MEGACOLLABORATION

There are times when concerted action over long periods of time requires new structures that enhance combined efforts of numerous public and nongovernment agencies. Usually they approach the most "wicked" social or economic problems. Such was the case for New Futures for Dayton Area Youth in the 1990s. New Futures was a collaboration of youth-serving agencies and community leaders. Its mission was "to build permanent capacity within the community to create the conditions for youth success." New Futures was one of five such experimental projects funded by the Anne E. Casey Foundation with matching funds, designed to reform systems—schools, health, human services agencies, criminal justice, and other major actors—to produce more favorable outcomes for young people. Its intervention was specifically focused on a group of middle-school students in three target schools. New Futures was a relatively well-financed operation, with $10 million for a five-year period. The project operated with a rather extensive governance structure comprising boards, advisory councils, and focused work groups for its various targeted initiatives. New Future's coordinated services presence was manifested by a subsidiary organization, Community Connections, which performed case management, access, and advocacy services.

The goals of New Futures were focused on public–private collaboration to ensure that (1) all young people will come to school healthy and ready to learn, (2) the community and its schools are committed to the success of every child, and (3) higher education and/or career opportunities are available to all Dayton-area graduates. These original goals were then translated into three priority initiatives: (1) an integrated services model, (2) early intervention and prevention, and (3) implementing a youth employability strategy. To achieve these goals, New Futures basically engaged in three strategies: to act collaboratively (i.e., by sharing resources to improve youth outcomes), to use information strategically, and to build the legitimacy to lead reform in the various systems.

A range of youth-serving organizations made up the New Futures collaborative structure and operations. Three types of "interests" were represented in the governance and operational structure. The first were the major youth-serving agencies: the Dayton public schools, Department of Human Services (public welfare), Montgomery County Children Services (child welfare), Miami Valley Child Development Centers (Head Start), Montgomery County Juvenile Court, the Mental Health Board, and the Combined (city–county) Health District. The second were the governmental and public agencies: the City of Dayton, city manager's office; Montgomery County, Community Human Services Department, Miami Valley Hospital; University of Dayton; Sinclair Community College; United Way; Ohio Governor's Office; and Township Trustees. And the third were various community representatives from a variety of fronts, for example, business and labor, civic associations, Dayton's neighborhood priority boards, and citizen activists. These activists included some very influential people in the community, who represented various shades of the political spectrum. This was the first group of direct line youth provider and youth-serving organizations that had the most at stake and instrumental involvement in New Futures and thus carried the greatest influence over the project's course.

New Futures began by working directly with three city pilot middle schools, first by enhancing the direct schooling experience of the targeted students and later by linking these students with associated services. This was accomplished by creating a core of community associates in the schools, who initially functioned like teachers' aides. Later these associates became more like case managers, with less involvement in educational intervention. The three target school nurses were also made full time, in order to work with the students in matters relating to pregnancy prevention, substance abuse, and general health. New equipment, such as computers, was provided for the schools. An extended day program was also established to provide after-school activities. All this was financed by New Futures. The community associates were part of Community Connections, the project's subsidiary organization, although they were outstationed in the schools.

A second wave of New Futures activities was designed to expand the project's scope beyond schooling. Many initiatives were undertaken to develop integrated services among the major child- and youth-serving agencies. A series of interagency agreements was developed and implemented. Another effort in the health area led to the changing of policies of health clinics (particularly with regard to birth control) and the opening up of a new adolescent health clinic. Another planned major initiative involved agreements between the schools, employers, and local colleges to expand job opportunities, apprenticeships, and scholarships. Finally, New Futures launched other efforts to increase parental involvement, provide earlier intervention, develop site-based building instruction plans, and reduce chronic absenteeism.

^J New Futures was governed by a collaborative comprising agency directors, public agency managers, and citizen representatives. The collaborative served as the project's board of directors. It was advised by a group of young people from the county. The board of Community Connections was directly connected to the collaborative; in practice it participated in collaborative meetings but did not vote. Three of the board's eight members overlapped with the collaborative. Decision making for the collaborative was generally by consensus; issues were discussed, refined, and agreed upon in a manner that accommodated most interests. Only rarely were votes taken. Most of the detail work of New Futures was done by staff members and an executive committee, or by a host of task forces, advisory groups, or some other form of working group.

Although New Futures had many successes in meeting its goals, it was not without its challenges. The Dayton public schools began to resist cooperation with New Futures when the project moved from school-centered programs and services to non–school-based integrated services. School personnel were reported as resistant to noneducational services, particularly because they had to share needed external Casey Foundation and matching resources with other human services agencies, and had to participate in collaborative efforts that did not involve education agencies. To a certain degree, the schools also resisted the money spent on Community Connections. Moreover, they resisted the effort made to bring chronic absentees (up to 40 percent of some of the schools) back into the schools. In New Futures' fourth year, the schools began to object to the previously selected (and Casey-mandated) middle school target population, arguing that earlier intervention was necessary.

The representatives of human services agencies, conversely, were generally supportive of New Futures. However, there was some lingering resentment about the creation of Community Connections because many agency directors felt that this subsidiary of New Futures, which was primarily responsible for case management, duplicated services that they already performed. Some even took it personally— they felt that their agencies were being deemed incapable of helping this population. But generally the agency directors proved willing to support the work of New Futures and forged many new interagency working relationships. Indeed, it was the agency directors who were the most frustrated with the Dayton public schools' unwillingness to cooperate with any effort that involved school-based integrated services. The issue came to a head during New Futures' fourth year, when the school administration resisted the chronic absenteeism indentification/ intervention effort and were accused of bad faith.

On the positive side, New Futures' participants give themselves the highest marks for their ability to develop this broad-based collaborative project and maintain it over time. The Casey funding ended in the fifth year, and the project continued with local financial support. The collaboration of citizens and the major partners in youth services and the linkages and interagency agreements that have emanated from this interaction are considered to be the project's major achievement. Most Dayton people feel that long-term success lies in the effective working collaboration they developed. Other achievements included an adolescent health center, the above-mentioned schooling improvements, and the case management (community associate) system for at-risk children. Concrete outcomes—such as a reduction in dropout rates, reduced teen pregnancies, a lower incidence of substance abuse, and high school achievements—were also measured, and they moved in a positive direction. However, some participants reported that there was too much emphasis on these outcomes, and that the Casey Foundation had pushed them too hard to make "tangible impacts on the system."

NEW FUTURES' COLLABORATIVE LESSONS

The Dayton New Futures project brings out in bold relief several of the issues that are discussed in this book. Although New Futures is depicted as a megaproject, it also highlights six key normal experiences and challenges in collaborative management. First, collaboration for the most nettlesome problems almost always crosses the public and private sectors, and the latter involves nonprofits and frequently also for-profits. Often the "public" involved in collaboration is targeted toward improving public institutions and processes, in this case the Dayton public schools. Second, the aim of New Futures was to deal with difficult problems on a focused basis, such as youth problems related to health, school dropout rates, and employment preparation. Such an effort normally requires that many programs, public and private, try to work together. Third, a lead agency such as Community Connections is often tasked with coordinating the actual services while a community board comprising many interests steers overall policy for the collaborative. Lead agencies provide focal points for multiagency, multi-interest projects that are otherwise difficult to identify. Fourth, these interests seek adapted problem-solving strategies, which normally are based on some level of shared, albeit uneven, resources. At the same time, participating agencies rarely implement the entire agreed-upon course of action, which is normally shared among several agencies. Fifth, as difficult interagency problems are approached and agreements are reached, diffused power becomes real; the power that key agencies bring to the table and resources that can be delivered or withheld; and the technical power of working groups—along with the power of administrators, politicians, agency boards, granting agencies, and citizen groups—may also come into play. Sixth, and finally, collaborative projects often need broad public support and/or public legitimacy because they normally represent the facilitated sharing of power and resources from many agencies and affected persons. Thus they require extended support in lieu of various forms of ascribed legal or licensed organizational legitimacy that public organizations or NGOs possess.

The case of New Futures also underscores the seven major themes that organize this volume. First, it demonstrates the essential multiagency and intergovernmental nature of public programs, whereby several tiers of government and NGOs are involved in complex webs of interactions. Second, as a result of this complexity, public agencies and managers have had to learn to retool to work outside as well as inside their agencies. Third, though a public servant's external work was once more or less limited to the awarding, distribution, and monitoring of funds and programs through grants, loans, and cash (or cash and in-kind) payments, it now involves a range of external activities, for example, contracting, partnering, joint problem solving, and network building. Fourth, these roles in turn have led to the honing of new skills well beyond the standard "bargaining and negotiating," for example, creating interoperable processes and joint strategy making. Fifth, today's complex problems and divided responsibilities mean that both public and private administrators increasingly must learn to work within networks. Sixth, new tools of organizing, which range from nonhierarchical structures to the use of information and communication technology, are changing organizations and organizational cross-boundary transactions. Seventh, and finally, despite many barriers, with concerted effort and understanding, the process of collaboration can be made to work.

THE MIX OF COLLABORATIVE ACTIVITIES

In this complicated world of increased pressure to innovate through interorganizational cooperation (Borins 2012, 176), there are many different types of collaborative activities for which the definitional boundaries are sometimes difficult to determine. They range, as Mandell (2001, 130) suggests, from "loose linkages and coalitions to more lasting structural arrangements." Take, for example, a public agency such as a state government department of tourism or a city department of economic development. Both will have legal or statutory connected relations and nonlegal collaborative connections. Legal collaboration could be by grant arrangement; contract for service; procurement contract; formal interagency agreement with another (state) department or adjacent (city) jurisdiction; and direct agreements or contracts with NGOs, along with participation of informal networks. Indeed, today many public agency collaborative contacts are between departments within the same government or between one level of government (e.g., the US federal government) and other levels, including state and/or local governments. These are called intergovernmental contacts, and, of particular importance, they include collaborative contacts between governments and NGOs (Agranoff 2008). They range in formality from informal contacts for information and minor adjustments on program management matters to such formalized structures as working partnerships and joint services networks (Agranoff and McGuire 2003; Agranoff 2007).

Indeed, a considerable range of collaborative contacts has emerged in these highly interdependent times. Table 1.1 lists a number of them, including both specific actions and structural arrangements, although it is by no means exhaustive. Collaborative contacts are listed by four categories, or two by two, depending on the degree of engagement, minimum or maximum, and the frequency of interaction, intermittent or regular. This classification is entirely arbitrary, and though some contacts may appear to fit into more than one category, they are placed where they fit best. Most important, this fourfold classification is meant to demonstrate that not all collaborations are alike. Some are not involved and are infrequent, some are not involved but are frequent, others are less involved but require more contact, and still others require high levels of interorganizational commitment on a regular basis.

Because these are examples, the entire table does not need an extensive explanation. To simply highlight the first category, minimal engagement with intermittent interaction, it would include the many information and interpretation contacts that administrators make across organizations, sectors, and contacts about grants of various types that tend to be "front-end loaded," with much less contact over the life of the grant. The second category, minimal engagement with regular interaction, includes all types or vehicles for information exchanges, even networks and councils that frequently meet among themselves but rarely if ever have the authority to make any kind of decisions. The third category, intermittent interaction with maximum engagement, includes collaborative vehicles where there are fewer contacts (e.g., infrequent meetings or occasional transactions) but the partners are not locked in to regular types of transactions. For example, a public–private development partnership may meet quarterly, but its work is primarily to hear what the staff has been doing or to authorize the parties' infrequent transactions such as signing, payments, and audits. Finally, the fourth category of maximum engagement with regular interaction involves a host of collaborative vehicles whereby the work of one party—even if it is the mere exchange of program

TABLE 1.1 The Range of Collaborative Contacts: Actions and Structures

1. Minimal engagement, intermittent interaction
   - Contact between agencies/organizations to seek information/interpretation
   - Occasional executive liaison meetings
   - Electronic bulletin boards
   - Electronic citizen advisory referenda
   - Regulatory negotiations
   - Grant negotiations
   - Environmental/building permit acquisition
   - Referral of clients from one agency to another
   - Research-based grant
   - Grant preapplication; grant conditions met
   - Grant funds with fewer restrictions in exchange for performance

2. Minimal engagement, regular interaction
   - Distribution or listserve
   - Exchange of agency/organization newsletters
   - Counterpart exchanges of information
   - Emergency services boards
   - Intergovernmental partnerships
   - Councils of nongovernmental organizations/public agencies
   - Private industry councils (employment and training)
   - Networks that exchange information
   - Procurement of goods, basic services contracting

3. Intermittent interaction, maximum engagement
   - Government insurance
   - Government loan
   - Government loan guarantee
   - Networks that blueprint strategy, nonpolicymaking/program adjustment
   - Tax abatement district financing negotiations
   - Councils of funder partnerships
   - Public–private partnerships
   - Joint ventures
   - Research and development consortia

4. Maximum engagement, regular interaction
   - Formal information exchange networks
   - Networks that regularly enhance partner capacities
   - Standing communities of practice (different disciplines, same program area) (e.g., youth services, disabilities, literacy)
   - Community development corporations
   - Purchase of direct (client-based) services contracting
   - Technical workgroups/committees
   - Councils of public agencies—policy and program adjustments
   - Networks/networked structures that develop joint strategies, policies, financing
   - Jointly (two or more agencies) sponsored and operated indirect services operations

Source: Compiled by the author.

or policy information—is highly affected by the work of others on a regular basis. Of course, the quintessential examples of this category include policy or program councils and networks and the joint direct services operations of multiple agencies.

Table 1.1 thus reveals that there are different ways in which managers can use "synergy as a logic" to network or otherwise work together in collaborative linkages, alliances, ventures, or other types of exchange relationships. The use of the term "network" in this book follows common usage in the public management literature; to network means to undertake a variety of goal-directed collaborative activities and is not restricted to the distinctly organized chartered and noncharted networks, which are also goal directed, that have been studied by Agranoff (2007) and Koliba, Meek, and Zia (2010). Thus, in this volume network activity goes beyond serendipitous interactions to incorporate this variety of regular and purposive interorganizational contacts. Network activity is thus a variant of collaboration, which is often used to connote some form of connection between agencies and other types of organizations (Kilduff and Tsai 2003, 91).

Andrew Campbell and Michael Gould (1999, 3–4) identify six different aims for collaboration: (1) shared know-how (exchange of knowledge and competencies across portfolios); (2) shared tangible resources (benefits from economies of scale and elimination of duplicated efforts); (3) pooled negotiating power (cost or quality benefits from purchasing scale); (4) coordinated strategies (aligning strategies of two or more units or organizations); (5) vertical integration (coordinating the flow of information products or services between units/organizations); and (6) combined new unit creation (extracting activities, creating new organizations, forming alliances, or creating internal joint ventures). They conclude that managers can overcome the obstacles and achieve benefits of successful collaboration if they clearly define the targeted benefit, intervene only when there are points of resistance, account for the skills needed to collaborate, and consider both the potential effects and risks (Campbell and Gould 1999).

To meet these challenges, the agencies of government are becoming more "conductive"; that is, they are organizing themselves to match internal challenges with external expectations and opportunities, particularly those that involve collaborative relations. These activities are added on to the otherwise internal work of the public agency. This means that public agencies, like all contemporary organizations, have had to change their structures. They have had to become more "de-differentiated" (Clegg 1990) and flattened or less centralized. Organizations now look different, as they blend knowledge and people into structures that recognize the primacy of human capital. Rather than rigid hierarchies with all their departmental, line-staff, and headquarters and superstructure trappings, the more boundaryless or centerless organization is flatter, with a network of interdependent units and strategic alliances managed by groups of executives. It is less horizontal but more nonlinear, meaning that rather than everything flowing up and down, flows occur in whatever direction is most effective. Different structures are formed for different needs and challenges (Pasternack and Viscio 1998). The insides of today's public agencies thus look different. Employees are less likely to be in their offices doing routine activities (e.g., processing grants, checking compliance, and reading reports). They spend more time outside their bureaus, where they observe external services, explore and solve problems in cooperation with other government agencies and NGOs, and participate in organized bodies that involve several sectors (Agranoff and McGuire 2003; Agranoff 2011).

Collaborative activity flows through both unorganized and formal networks now that we are living in the time of the interorganizational network—the signature structure of the current information age (Castells 1996). It will be demonstrated in the chapters that follow that these networks do not replace previous group, hierarchy, and bureaucracy structures but instead are added on to the organizing complexity of managerial challenges. Networks involve people who represent different types and parts of organizations and who engage in exchange, mutual adjustment, strategic design, and/or joint production. They help meet the challenge of greater complexity, scope, speed, flexibility, and adaptability (Agranoff 2008; Alter and Hage 1993). As we further seek to unlock current bureaucratic thinking, we are just learning about these structures. For example, network or "teamnet" principles are said to include a shared commitment to goals and projects, independent but cooperative goals and organizations, voluntary linkages that involve extensive participation, crisscrossing relationships, multiple leaders, and people working at different levels within and between organizations (Lipnak and Stamps 1994).

THE BUREAUCRACY, THE CONDUCTIVE AGENCY, AND THE NETWORK

Contrary to the assertions of those who believe that with NGOs, contracts, and externalized direct services, the importance of the public agency has diminished, today it is more appropriate to argue that bureaucracies have changed (McGuire and Agranoff 2010). A very useful action-oriented manual, *The Boundaryless Organization* (Ashkenas et al. 2002, 42, 45), indicates that hierarchies are not on the verge of elimination. But they need to be made to work in a boundaryless world by restructuring them to meet the twenty-first century's success requirements—speed, flexibility, innovation, and integration. Most organizations still have hierarchies designed around the old success factors of size, role clarity, specialization, and control. Instead, the new organization must maximize and open the flow of information, recognize distributed competence throughout the organization, accept authority flowing from whatever points are appropriate, and move from position-based to accomplishment-based rewards.

This new type of organization with open boundaries can position itself for collaboration by becoming conductive. A conductive organization is one that organizes itself to work "outside" the agency as well as inside it. Saint-Onge and Armstrong (2004, 213) define a conductive organization as one "that continuously generates and renews the capabilities to achieve breakthrough performance by enhancing the quality and flow of knowledge and by calibrating its strategy, culture, structure, and systems to the needs of its customers and the marketplace." Though first intended for business organizations, this concept equally applies to public organizations (Agranoff 2011). As is the case with regard to collaborative management, Saint-Onge and Armstrong emphasize how important it is for organizations to create partnerships, build alliances and coalitions, form and reform teams across functional and organizational boundaries, and actively manage interdependencies. These collaborative activities are important because an organization creates value when individual staff members interact externally, and collaboration can serve as a platform from which human capital can increase the value created for staff members from other organizations as well as service clients. As Saint-Onge and Armstrong (2004, 38) conclude, conductive organizations' intangible assets are made up of the capabilities and relationships that are built through exchange, and these intangible assets form a system that must be managed through an integrated approach.

Agencies that engage in more collaborative behavior and the processes of open boundary management require a new paradigm for the collaborative–information–network age. Classical management theories—Taylorism (one best way), Fordism (assembly line), Weberian bureaucracy (rule-bound), and administrative management's POSDCORB (planning, organizing, staffing, directing, coordinating, reporting, and budgeting)—do not fit as well into the new structures or collaborative processes (Morgan 1993). Moreover, newer approaches such as total quality management (continuous improvement) and Six Sigma (productivity enhancement) differ from external collaboration. For example, network processes that involve multiparty activation, framing, mobilizing, and synthesizing (Agranoff and McGuire 2001) are entirely nonhierarchical undertakings. Collaborative "groupware" requires social capital, shared learning, a culture of joint problem solving, and negotiation among role-based actors. Also, the role of power in a collaborative enterprise, which is normally thought to be governed by mutual exchanges and creativity, is present but not well understood. Management theory needs to shift to these issues (Agranoff and McGuire 2001; Bardach 1998; Bingham, O'Leary, and Carlson 2008) and to provide supplements to hierarchical practices. Many electronic breakthroughs (e.g., the primary development of personal computers, the use of geographic information systems, and the ability to flexibly machine through electronic settings) came about creatively through interactive processes (Fountain 1994), whereby the old theories of management were set aside in the interest of fostering more interactive models and techniques. They have generated new ideas about management and are currently being developed as more suitable to the conductive or open boundary organization. The emergent conductive public organization is a major theme of this book and is the particular focus of chapters 3 and 8.

OVERCOMING THE BARRIERS

This book's exploration of collaborative management also includes concerns about how to overcome the forces that make it difficult. To collaborate often connotes some state of euphoria, in which nothing but "love and kisses" prevail in a sort of a soothing, hot tub atmosphere, and where collaborating agency representatives assume more or less equal partnerships, goal agreement emerges out of shared norms, and further investigation leads to some problem-oriented solution (Buchanan 2002, 201). In the real world, however, numerous collaborative successes are equaled or exceeded by stalemates or failures to launch.

There are many reasons for these failures. The most notable are investigated in this volume. They are introduced here so the reader can keep in mind the negatives along with the positives of collaboration when the positives are emphasized.

1. Unequal power among the partners, which is exerted by stronger or more powerful actors (Rhodes 1997, 9).
2. Agency protection of its turf, that is, its "domain of problems, opportunities, and actions over which an agency exercises legitimate authority" (Bardach 1998, 164).
3. Extensive time and processing effort placed in collaboration that leads to slow progress, painful experiences, a lack of achievements, and sometimes the collapse of an effort; also, various types of collaborative inertia (Huxham and Vangen 2005, 3; McGuire 2002).
4. Time and opportunity costs taken away from internal organizational management for technical work (Agranoff 2007, chap. 8).

5. Narrow scope and mission and/or agenda of the collaborative effort because of lowering sights to reach a consensus, because of an absence of power to act, or because of a public policy financial or legal barrier to action (Agranoff 1986).

6. Internal organizational forces: (1) overenthusiasm for synergy among top managers who do not see the complexity of the undertaking; (2) upper-level managers' presumption that an opportunity for collaboration will not be addressed without their help or urging of subordinates to collaborate; (3) a failure to recognize knowledge and skill gaps in relational skills or technical knowledge, wherever it may be, and a reliance on "natural champions"; and (4) a neglect of internal opposition or other downsides, such as how a project could affect other aspects of the organization (Campbell and Gould 1999, 7–17).

The strategies discussed in this book will not automatically enable one to overcome these barriers, but awareness of them is a first step. The operational suggestions that follow in subsequent chapters should also be useful for facing the challenges of collaborative management.

PLAN OF THE BOOK

This book is designed to capture some of the realities faced by the collaborating manager, as illustrated by the examples of difficult public problems presented above—the New Futures case and the variety of collaborative actions and structures that are characteristic of today's public management. Together, they demonstrate why and how collaboration has become such an important managerial activity, as the thematic orientation of this book demonstrates. They do not capture every single facet of this daunting challenge but do capture many of the experiences that public and NGO operatives have experienced and related, either to the author or through the literature. This book is neither a complete manual on how to [fill in a favorite subject] nor a complete academic study of any one of the topics brought together to explain collaboration, for example, how to contract, network, or build knowledge communities.

This book rests on six thematic overlays stimulated by experiences with collaboration. The first is the contemporary "conductive" nature of all organizations that serve the public. Externally, they are increasingly interactive. Second, the tools of interaction—grants, contracts, reciprocal services, audits, and so on—need to be understood for their basic relational natures. The DNA of collaborative management depends on more than mechanics of process, for example, negotiation or joint learning. The best of auditing, networking, contract management, and so on also includes new dimensions of transactional interaction. Third, an increasing amount of collaborative activity is being undertaken beyond the more visible formal contracts and two-party connections in various formal and informal networks. As a result, one must learn how networks and other transactions are managed, and how they are managed differently from the organizations represented in these collaboratives. Fourth, network activity and other related linkages lead to a world of shared power. How and when power is shared is important, particularly to sift myth from reality with regard to how much of government's role is given up in the new world of multiple program involvement. Fifth, because the work of the public begins with government and is shared, collaborative management is highly intergovernmental, which raises the need for intergovernmental management. These types of interconnections are both vertical (e.g., federal–state–local) and horizontal (county–city–NGO), and they also include many permutations of these two dimensions. Sixth, intergovernmentalization and collaborative management in general are changing the nature of public agencies from less rule-bound hierarchical entities to ones that work collaboratively outside themselves. This means that public agencies today are beginning to look different from the traditional hierarchical bureaucracy.

The following chapters touch on all these themes but follow a different sequence. Chapter 2 looks at how the collaborative era arrived by tracing the evolution of public programs starting in the nineteenth century, when government roles were more compartmentalized, through the growth of overlapping functions, to contracting with NGOs, and ultimately to the current era of the network. The chapter also introduces the many tools of a government and its partner agencies, along with the contemporary challenges of how to "govern by network."

Chapter 3 focuses on evolving public agencies, namely, agencies that are the result of the post–Fordist/Taylorist/bureaucratic organizing of the collaborative enterprise. In this book these agencies are referred to as "conductive" public organizations and as "collaborarchies." The chapter examines how the classic "Weberian" bureaucracy has given way to flatter structures that are more open, whereas networks display nonhierarchical reciprocal governance structures. It also looks at the extent of lateral versus vertical power, the four stages of managing within networks, and four different types of collaborative performance and accountability.

The collaborative fundamentals of grant and services contract management as they have evolved are the focus of chapter 4, which explores the fundamentals of core functions in collaborative management, including types of relationships between government and contractors, contract challenges and drawbacks, and how service markets are maintained. Contracting has become one of the most important tools to connect government to direct services. As a result the challenge is quite different and is more complex than a straightforward contract to procure goods. A systemic approach must be taken that links funders and contractors in networks of services. The chapter also looks at the process of how to reach agreements collaboratively and how to maintain them.

Chapter 5 looks at the links between conductive public agencies and their partner NGO agencies. It examines a case of co-governance between a public agency and its partners, looks at how nongovernment agencies deliver direct and support services, and describes partnership maintenance. It also explores how the tools of governance can be employed interactively, and it takes a more detailed look at interoperability, knowledge management, and how communities of practice operate in collaborative settings.

Just as the standard agency needs detailed procedures, such as the proper sequence for preparing a budget, the public agency that makes contracts and engages in other connective activity needs to focus on how to work with external entities. Thus chapter 6 looks at managing in a network, going beyond the tools of grants and contracts to explain the varieties of collaborative activities that define operating networks. It considers when to engage while networking, power structures within networks, administrative structures within networks, and communication and operation within networks. It also offers suggestions for how to operate in networks.

Chapter 7 examines the issues related to identifying and overcoming the barriers to collaboration. It considers a detailed case of collaborative breakdown in the North Carolina mental health operation and the lessons learned, as well as the use of deliberative power to overcome agency power or the power of resistance. It also discusses the seven common barriers to collaborative agreements, ranging from agency turf to policy; the practice of deliberative negotiations and intergovernmental bargaining; collaborative trust and trust building; and how to understand and overcome collaborative inertia, that is, the fatigue and blockage that often accompany extensive interagency processing.

Chapter 8 highlights what the conductive public agency of the future might well look like. It presents a case study of a highly networked public mathematics and science school that is independent of any jurisdiction; identifies emerging organizational features, that is, futuristic organizing; explores new approaches to making public agencies more conductive, for example, civic engagement and the New Public Management; and highlights the probable organizations of the future. Each of these innovations could help make the conductive organization even more interactive.

The concluding chapter 9 returns to the themes introduced earlier in the book—conductivity, tools, network management, shared power, intergovernmentalization, and conductive agencies—and examines them in the light successful findings related in twelve case vignettes. It also offers twelve useful ideas from the literature on collaboration and seeks to provide a capstone for this emergent facet of public management and thus hopefully better prepare the reader for an uncertain future.

CONCLUSION

The late management guru Peter Drucker (2001, 313) indicated that the essence of management is not so much a bundle of techniques, although like any field it has its techniques and procedures, but the quest to make knowledge productive. Management is a social function that involves understanding how science can be transformed into practice, and thus it is "truly a 'liberal art.'" Today the practice of managerial work requires intensive human capital that can be applied to particular types of data, information, and knowledge in complex situations. So it is with collaborative public management.

This examination of collaborative processes and how to achieve results does not present all the answers in this difficult area. Many are yet to be discovered. Hopefully, however, it can help practitioners perform better and it raises additional questions for academics. The field of public management has clearly entered a new era, where problems are recognized as multifaceted in both cause and solution. Because complexity is the order of the day, both practitioners and academics need to be able make the best-informed efforts to break down this complexity and make things work.

CHAPTER 2

Intergovernmentalization and Collaborative Public Management

THE LOWER PLATTE RIVER CORRIDOR ALLIANCE in Nebraska is a partnership of three local natural resource districts (NRDs), special districts that have taxing power and mitigation authority. In addition to the NRDs, this alliance comprises state government department representatives, federal officials, and a host of activists from nongovernmental and other organizations. Other than the three NRDs acting individually, the alliance has no direct authority to take any environmental action, yet it has become an important force in studying public policy, looking for mitigation technologies, and urging the NRDs and state and local governments to take action within the overlapping frameworks of the federal, state, and local regulatory web. The alliance urges the NRDs and local governments to seek federal and state grants, negotiate regulations to fit local needs, and educate local governments, landowners, and conservation organizations on proper land use and water management (appendix A). Although the alliance's work is mostly indirect and long term, its work through the NRDs is quintessentially collaborative and highly intergovernmental with respect to management.

This intergovernmental pattern is repeated in many arenas in addition to environmental management. The practices and programs of emergency management, youth services, economic development, intellectual disabilities/mental retardation, long-term employment and training, and public safety, to name a few, are also intergovernmental and collaborative. To make public programs work collaboratively, some understanding of the financing and regulatory framework of federal and state governments is needed—the rules and guidelines of local program operation—along with who the local program sponsors and services providers are and how they link with these regulatory and financing programs. These concerns were implicit in the activities within New Futures in Dayton described in chapter 1.

This chapter seeks to explain how this intergovernmental situation came about, and thus accelerated the need for collaboration. It begins with a rather brief explanation of the horizontal and vertical nature of intergovernmental programming. Then a developmental sketch of four phases of intergovernmental development is explained, ranging from more compartmentalized governments to the current era of the network. Next, an overview accounts for the multiple intergovernmental tools and partners. Finally, the challenges of collaborative managing in the current era of the network are explored with a focused look at how services for intellectually and developmentally disabled citizens have evolved. Subsequent chapters then build on this base by considering the various practical aspects of collaborative public management.

A more detailed example of this intergovernmental process in collaboration involves a large city government that wants to redevelop its core or downtown area and promote jobs. It will be heavily engaged both horizontally and vertically. Horizontally, it will no doubt form a partnership with the local chamber of commerce and the county government, and even form an economic development corporation, to build support and spread the risk. It will also seek out the local downtown business association for support, and work with it on the anticipated construction disruption. The city will contact with several large local firms about the possibility of expanding and locating in the target area, and will carefully explain which costs the businesses will need to incur and those that might be subsidized. Other issues like parking potential and traffic flow will also be at stake. Vertically, the city will apply to the US Housing and Urban Development (HUD) state office for redevelopment and job creation funds under the Community Development Block Grant program, to which it is entitled under the law, but eligibility for this project must be negotiated with HUD officials. For example, the target area must contain at least 60 percent low- and moderate-income citizens. The city will also negotiate with the state government department of economic development and attorney general's office about two programs for which it has chosen to finance the infrastructure: (1) tax increment financing, which means working with the bond market; and (2) tax abatements to attract business. Finally, it will be negotiating with state legal authorities over proper use of the land for the project and any exceptions to the state code for infrastructure development. In actuality, this is a simplified overview of the potential intergovernmental points of contact. They do not include the actual transactions that will ensue, many of which will be quite protracted.

This simplified overview of the potential collaborative points (but not the actual transactions) demonstrates the highly intergovernmental nature of many collaborative undertakings, which now includes nongovernmental organizations (NGOs).

HORIZONTAL AND VERTICAL INTERGOVERNMENTAL ACTIVITY

The New Futures human services, watershed management, and core city develop-ment illustrations offered thus far suggest that collaborative management involves multiple and numerous contacts with many different public organizations and NGOs, both nonprofit and for-profit, in a way that must take into account mul-tiple differentiated efforts to promote some core jurisdiction and other interests. Moreover, managing in an intergovernmental fashion does not merely entail some federal–state, federal–local, or state–local effort but also many governments and nongovernmental actors. In fact many public and nonpublic entities have bound-ary spanners that promote their organization's aims through various types of collaboration. Some specialists' roles are to bring together the public and private sectors to work together on projects. Intergovernmental (vertical) and interlocal intergovernmental (horizontal) activities are linked in practice, as the examples given above make clear. Vertical efforts are often triggered by interlocal collabora-tion, and by the same token a great deal of horizontal action is the result of federal and/or state programming or regulatory action.

In their study of intergovernmental collaborative activity in the city economic development arena, Agranoff and McGuire (2003, 70–71) found that the real world of collaborative activities includes both these horizontal and vertical activities. Vertical actions involve different information-related transactions or adjustments to the normal workings of grant, regulatory, or other programs. These include seeking funding information, interpretation of rules, and technical assistance, along with such adjustments as regulatory flexibility or waivers of rules, policy changes, and funding innovations. Horizontal collaborative actions involve the joint development of local policies or strategies, designing projects or seeking and/or exchanging different kinds of resources. Again, these included formal part-nerships, consolidated policy efforts, joint financial incentives, and joint project efforts.

THE DEMAND FOR COLLABORATION: THE EVOLUTION OF INTERGOVERNMENTAL PROGRAMMING

The issue that gives rise to coordination is the nonhierarchical tradition of govern-ments within the US federal system. American state and local governments inher-ited from England the idea that local administrative offices owed allegiance to the law—that is, the statutes of Parliament—rather than to an administrative superior, and that if necessary legal compliance would be secured by court litigation. However, the American system is different from England's in that American local and state officials are not appointed by the crown or some central administration but are elected at each jurisdiction level. The result, concludes Goodnow (1900, 101), "was to make impossible any state administrative supervision over the main body of officers entrusted with the execution of the law." The only controls that could lead to coordination between "expressing and executing" had to be found in the power of legislatures to regulate the duties of officers. The result, as Elazar (1984, 3) concludes, is constitutional diffusion and a sharing of powers among centers: "The model for federalism is the matrix, a network of arenas within arenas," which are larger or smaller rather than a higher and lower, and lead to interaction and sharing through bargaining or negotiated cooperation. Therefore, "a substantial share of American government has been the search for such methods to provide for the necessary collaboration among the various units in the system" (Elazar 1962, 305).

As a result of this legal and constitutional basis, from the time of the founding of the United States and its 1789 Constitution there has always been some intergovernmental activity, particularly of a vertical nature, but it has traditionally been limited. From the beginning most federal activity was through the states. Initially, the federal government assumed some of the states' Revolutionary War debts, and for those states that had paid theirs, federal land was donated for state sale. This was followed by the practice of setting aside one section of federal land in each new state's townships, to be sold to raise money for schools. The National Road, from Cumberland, Maryland, to Springfield, Illinois (originally to Saint Louis), was financed by the federal government and built by the states using private contractors. There were also other, minor forms of subsidies to the states (Elazar 1962), but the developmental intergovernmental pattern in the nineteenth century was, with few exceptions, of funded federal programs for veterans and mothers' pensions, accompanied by "waves of similar legislation across many state legislatures" (Skocpol 1995, 24). Most domestic social and educational programs were primarily at the state and local levels. As Skowronek (1982, 23) concludes, "The national government throughout the nineteenth century routinely provided promotional and support services for the state governments and left the substantive tasks of governing to these regional units. It led to a profound devolution of power accompanied by a serviceable but unassuming national government." It reflected the first of four intergovernmental eras (Agranoff 2011) that led up to accelerated collaborative activity, or the need for such activity.

The first intergovernmental era, that of law and politics, emerged with the building of the integral nation-state, primarily in the nineteenth century, where legal distinctions of governmental isolation and "jurisdiction" held true, particularly in federal countries like the United States. Generally, responsibilities were more separated and isolated. In the United States, the dual federalism doctrine held that the national government and the states each were sovereign in certain spheres and that between them exist areas of activity in which neither can enter. In this scheme of things, activities with respect to poverty and welfare, the development of local economies, the control of the environment, land use, education, and many other areas were considered to be state and/or local responsibilities. Indeed, nineteenth-century social policy quite commonly included state and local support for primary and secondary public education; benefits for the elderly, Civil War veterans, and their dependents; and support for widows and orphans. Although reasonable evidence has been presented that separate spheres never existed in practice (all but education had some federal support), these legal distinctions and intergovernmental norms held for some time, despite the fact that by the middle 1800s modern communications, which required a series of local delivery units (e.g., postal units, roads, canals, and railways) and cross-links, had pushed jurisdictional separation to its limits.

This situation evolved from the early twentieth century through roughly the 1960s, when the welfare state ushered in the second epoch. It proved to be a period of a growing interdependency that linked state-local and federal governments. In the United States nationwide social insurance and public assistance programs were launched, but inasmuch as the Social Security Act was rooted in prior state programs and/or state programs under debate at the time, in the 1930s "contradictory regional interests ensured that national standards could not be established in most programs" (Skocpol 1995, 25). Nevertheless, the welfare state was very much of a top-down effort that enhanced the fiscal and program strength of national governments in many countries (Loughlin 2001, 389). Most central social policies (welfare, social services, employment, economic development) were top-down or countrywide because central governments everywhere were suspicious of universal local commitment, so national financing and programming was linked with local execution, in the United States and abroad. Later in the era came such newer social welfare programs as those addressing drug abuse, child and family abuse, mental disabilities, and new efforts in community development, which were less suited to central organizations like the US federal government, bringing on the need for "important intergovernmental adjustments" (Ashford 1988, 18–19). The resulting impact was considerable jurisdiction overlap (Watts 1999, 38), or what one study identified as a complex of (1) central policy control/subnational administration, (2) central normative/subnational functions/control, (3) shared powers, (4) joint powers, or (5) some asymmetrical arrangement. Today these interdependencies extend well beyond social welfare into what is referred to as the broader welfare state, in areas like public security, tourism and culture, environmental policy, and public education (Argullol et al. 2004).

By the middle of the twentieth century governments like the US federal government began to recognize the gradual introduction of organized actors outside government as also involved in funded programming. In fact, many of these private organizations had been in business for more than a century but heretofore had not been operationally linked very directly with government or extensively publicly financed. As this situation changed, these NGOs began to become agents and partners of the state. Through some grants but predominately with contracts, the government linked with nonprofit service agencies and for-profit vendors of services. In the case of nonprofits, despite the fact that they had been around for decades, the boundaries of the state were now expanded to include them in direct services delivery, something like governments "for hire" (Smith and Lipsky 1993, 5). For-profits have always been part of government procurement, and certain basic services like security and road building were regularly contracted out, but such direct government services as public health care, employment and training, services for the disabled, vocational rehabilitation, mental health, substance abuse, and family violence are now contracted out, along with more extensive outsourcing of finance and accounting services and other management functions.

Just as the welfare state philosophy once expanded the role and number of interacting governments, beliefs in the primacy of market forces, reduction and importance of the public sector, deregulation of state controls, and abandonment of the principle of equality led to a prevailing political view that was one of a more "minimalist" state with less direct government intervention in the economy and society (Loughlin 2001, 390). It followed that "market superiority," which could either provide for the needs of people or a market model of government services, could lead to greater efficiencies than public operation. Among some government officials, it prevailed as an attitude. This was also the era of the New Public Management, which borrowed heavily from the private sector, with its benchmarking, performance targeting, competitive bidding, outsourcing, and the like—all of which reinforced intergovernmental activity by expanding the number of government–NGO partnerships. In the last two decades of the twentieth century, contracting out not only involved the direct purchase of services but also followed a business model and moved to new nonservice support sectors, including information management, transportation support, public marketing, and legal representation. In both the direct service and support sectors, there developed new sets of alliances between governments at all levels and a host of public and private bodies: service delivery nonprofits and private businesses, law firms, finance specialists, banks, and insurance companies. As a result, "the public administration problem . . . spread well beyond the borders of the government agency" (Salamon 1995, 2).

Although all the answers to managing within this partnership/contract era have not been developed, another new era soon emerged to compound the challenges. The fourth intergovernmental, or network, era emerged out of the previous one and became visible in the first decade of the twenty-first century. Today, because everything is linked, this world is one where everything is connected in networks (Castells 1996). Currently people connect in many ways: electronically based social networks; networks that operate for the purposes of manufacturing; the Internet, which links millions of end users by satellite-transmitted narrowcasting; and networks that link sellers and buyers in a host of ways. Public agencies and NGOs also network to exchange information, and they thus enhance one another's capabilities, to smooth services interactions, and to solve policy/program problems (Agranoff 2007).

In some ways intergovernmental networking began as a parallel activity to contracting, whereby funders and their agents began to build contractor–government networks (Brown, Potoski, and Van Slyke 2006). Why should intergovernmental collaboration be any different? In fact, networks of local governments, human services agencies, business associations, and economic development agents have worked among themselves at the community level for four or five decades. As mentioned above, these entities have had extensive links with higher-level governments in order to secure critical program supports and promote local economies (Agranoff and McGuire 2003; McGuire 2002) or other local interests. As a result, networks like these need to be treated seriously in public management. They are defined by O'Toole (1997, 45) "as structures of independence involving multiple organizations or parts thereof, where one unit is not merely the formal subordinate of the others in some larger hierarchical management." This is clearly a period in its earliest stages, where there are dozens more questions than answers (Agranoff and McGuire 2001). What is the most interesting about the emergent set of intergovernmental networks—and what makes them different—is the way officials from the federal government, state governments, local governments, public and private universities, and NGOs representing both the nonprofit and for-profit sectors sit down with one another *at the same table* to discuss, explore, negotiate, and solve issues (Radin et al. 1996). In earlier days, the most visible intergovernmental transactional interactions tended to be bilateral and focused on government–government or government–NGO transactions. The network approach is clearly multilateral and collaborative, and it thus enables actors to attack issues that transcend bilateral intergovernmental concerns.

To manage within the contemporary intergovernmental system is thus to engage both vertically and horizontally through networks and grants, contracts,
and other tools in a highly interdependent and overlapping system that remains
based in law and jurisdiction. This is clearly the situation depicted in chapter 1
with regard to the Dayton experience. Although the life of a collaborating public
manager would be easier if these four eras simply meant the replacement of one
era with another, the hard reality is that all four eras are still very much alive and
the games of collaboration thus occur within these four varying contexts. Today,
most public collaborative undertakings are somewhat framed by the intergovernmental developments that have been revealed. And the tools of collaborative
management are filtered through these foci.

Multiple Tools

With the exception of a handful of agencies like the US Postal Service, the US Social Security Administration, and state weights and measures departments, public
programs rarely involve only a single unit of government that delivers a program
by itself. Governments at the various levels nearly always collaborate with other
entities to achieve their purposes. For example, more than 70 percent of US federal
government dollars are spent by agents other than that of this funding government, through grants, contracts, loans, and other means. These vehicles have been
labeled by Lester Salamon (2002, 9) as the "*tools*, or *instruments* through which
public purposes are pursued" (emphasis in the original). They have expanded in
both number and scale during the past few decades. Most important, indicates
Salamon, is how they establish interdependencies between public agencies and
third-party actors, and thus give rise to a variety of complex exchanges that must
be understood with respect to operating across boundaries.

Eleven of these tools are introduced in table 2.1, which is designed to illustrate
the types of exchanges that might be generated by each. The examples are hypothetical but the programs are real, and the dynamic collaborative interactions are
typical of what might happen in the use of each tool. For example, under "direct
loan," cities are eligible for loans to upgrade and place into compliance their water
systems under the US Clean Drinking Water Act. Federal loans—for example,
the State of Nebraska's water loan programs—normally require a supplemental
or matching loan from a local bank or other lending institution. Normally, these
projects are paid back with a combination of higher water fees and special local
tax assessments, which results in multiple involvement from citizens, businesses,
local lending institutions, local government (or a quasi-government water authority), and state and federal governments. So it is with each of the other ten tools
illustrated here, which has its own unique web of participants.

TABLE 2.1 Collaborative Tools

Collaborative Tool	Description	Hypothetical Example	Core/Sponsor Jurisdiction	Major Partners	Other Involved Organizations
Direct government service	Good or service by public agency	Jefferson County Public Health Department operates an inoculation program	County government	F/S/L	Schools, home nurses' association, other voluntary organizations
Regulation	Standard setting/prohibition	Municipal clean drinking water standards	Federal government	F/S/L/NP/FP	Home owners, contractors, school districts, counties, other voluntary organizations
Grant	Award, cash payment	Temporary Assistance for Needy Families	Federal government block grant to states	F/S/L (in some states)	Education and training organizations, child care, food stamps, Medicaid and NGO voluntary associations
Contracting	Payment for goods or direct service delivered	Columbus refuse collection and recycling pickup and disposal	Municipal government	S/L/for-profit/county waste district programs	Citizens neighborhood organizations, businesses, institutional clients
Direct loan	Cash for a project, normally at lower than market rates	Fillmore City, Nebraska, borrows $950,000 to upgrade its water system	Federal/state government	F/S /L/private lending institution	Business and homeowners through special assessments
Loan guarantee	Interest buy-down and backup of private loan	Oskaloosa, Iowa, builds a new community center	State government/private lending institution	S/L/private lending institution	Community organizations, chamber of commerce, local economic development corporation
Insurance	Protection against unusual risk/cost	Federal/state unemployment insurance in Wisconsin	Federal/state government	F/S/employers	State chambers of commerce, statewide business associations, local offices of state employment service
Tax expenditure	Cash incentives to encourage a project or program outside of government	Chico, California, provides 15% of cost of new office complex in core of city	City/county government/ private developers	L/private sector	Contractors, building materials companies, labor unions, Downtown Chico, Inc.
Fees, charges	Payment by users of services, full or partial	Medicare Part B payments, client copayments	Federal government	F/medical and hospital industry/pharmaceutical industry	Other for-profit and nonprofit health and allied health organizations
Vouchers	Authorization for access to government goods or services	Food stamps	Federal/state/local governments (in some states)	F/S/L/food vendors	Local social welfare organizations, local case managers
Government corporations	Special government entity, normally for one purpose, quasi-public agency	Des Moines Transit Authority	Special unit of local government under state government authority	F/S/L	Paratransit contractors, area planning agency, county governments, 13 municipal governments

Note: F = federal government; S = state government; L = local government; NP = nonprofit; FP = for profit; NGO = nongovernmental organization.

Source: Prepared for this volume, based on The Tools of Government by Lester M. Salamon (2002, 21).

The tools are legally based and can and often are intergovernmentally interactive in a rather complicated and overlapping fashion. To demonstrate how the legal base can frame the collaborative undertaking, appendix B, taken from the framework for a Lower Platte River watershed regulatory study, illustrates how one often must begin with the legal framework. In this case it served as a guide for any mitigation activity on the Lower Platte River. The regulatory framework includes four federal areas, nine distinct state regulatory arenas, and numerous land use, planning, zoning, and preservation issues at the local level. The document behind these contents led to a number of proposed collaborative actions by federal, state, and natural resource districts, and by county and city officials. It became an important regulatory first-step framework in their "public policy study," which allowed them to move on to mitigation measures and land use and zoning changes designed to preserve the river. They illustrate the multiple levels of regulatory activity in search of collaborative managing.

These tools are not always the exclusive province of the sponsoring level of government given in the illustrations. All levels of government have some direct services, though local governments perhaps sponsor the most. All levels regulate and award contracts. Most offer grants and become engaged in loans, offer tax expenditures, charge fees, and establish government corporations. Some are included with insurance and vouchers. But that is not the point here, which is simply to demonstrate the multiple partnerships for sponsorship and the greater number of organizations that are involved in most programs. As we begin to look at the ins and outs of collaborative management, the implications will become clear. Salamon (2002, 13) observes that many of the diverse organizations have little experience in working with each other when the tools are initially enabled. Each organization has its own interests and frame of reference. They are interdependent, but in an asymmetrical, or independent way, and their relationships face constant change. The concerns vis-à-vis how to apply the tools that can enable actors to work toward collaboration are matters of analysis and debate in subsequent chapters.

Multiple Partners

Multiple tools lead to multiple partners. These devices bring on the need for agencies to work together. It is further maintained that these intergovernmental partners now involve more than governments—federal, state, local—in the person of NGO operatives who are tied to government through such tools as grants, loans, contracts, and others. The multiplicity of partnerships demonstrated here heightens the need for agencies to collaborate, particularly in areas where the single program, single delivery agency no longer exists.

Partnership plurality is demonstrated by examining five program arenas outlined in table 2.2. The policy and program areas encompass intellectual and developmental disabilities, community economic development, watershed protection, metropolitan transportation, and family income support. For each area the core or landmark enabling federal and state intergovernmental programs are identified. It becomes immediately apparent that multiple titles are normally involved in a single program area. Then the most relevant administering public agencies are identified. Again, basic implementation responsibility is spread over several agencies at both federal and state levels, and in some cases courts get involved in the details of administration. Most important, rarely is a "single agency" at either federal or state levels in charge of programs in a given area. The next column identifies the delivery agents, where local or regional public authorities combine with NGOs of all types, depending on the arena to make things happen. Depending on the policy or program area, the delivery agent can be a nonprofit organization, private business, special district government, a local unit affiliated with a state or federal program, state agency, higher education institution, or third-party contractors of normal government services. The last column of table 2.2 identifies the variety of organizations that are nonservice supports for the respective policy program. This group can involve state legislative leaders, interest groups or associations, clients of programs or their advocates, regional planning agencies, quasi-governmental bodies, special boards and committees, supply vendors, and support services firms. Clearly, the game is very involved and requires certain connections among the major players within each arena.

The nature of involvement can be demonstrated by selecting one area, community economic development, from the list given in table 2.2. This is an area where the author and Michael McGuire once did considerable empirical collaborative investigation. Community economic development is one of those areas where a lot of the development action is "bottom up" and the bulk of the intergovernmental contact is local–state government (Agranoff and McGuire 2003). In a city government, for example, working with potential expanding or locating businesses, city officials will work with their local economic development corporation (city, county, chamber of commerce) to get the support of affected neighborhood organizations, city council citizen committees, the workforce investment board, and the local community college on issues of worker preparation and land acquisition and preparation, along with any type of possible tax or regulation adjustments. When a local program is outlined and approved by the city council, it will begin

TABLE 2.2 Multiple Partners and Agents in Selected Policy and Program Areas

Policy/Program	Keystone Programs	Public Agencies	Delivery Agents	Supporting Organizations
Intellectual Disabilities/ Developmental Disabilities (ID/DD)	Medicaid–Intermediate Care Facilities/MR (ICFMR) Medicaid Home and Community Services Waiver (1115 and 1915e) Supplemental Security Income State Medicaid matches State-funded services programs Grants to the states Rehabilitation services programs (13) Individuals with Disabilities Act (10) Special education funding	Federal agencies of US Department of Health and Human Services (HHS) State Medicaid agencies State ID/DD agencies State vocational rehabilitation agencies State departments of education State income support agencies Federal and state court rulings	Local public ID/DD authorities Local school districts Local welfare/rehabilitation agencies Nonprofits and for-profits providing residential care, supported living, managed care, forensic, state institutions, group homes, ICFMRs, day services, transportation, medical clinic, family support, pre- and after school	State legislature leaders and commissions Provider industry associations (e.g., state rehabilitation facilities associations) Advocate associations (e.g. Arc) Families/guardians/advocates Provider agencies ID/DD services workforce organizations, public employee unions
Community Economic Development	Federal and state administered Community Development Bloc Grants US grants, Small Business Administration, state-sponsored development loans and grants State-authorized development instruments (e.g., tax abatement, tax increment financing, incentives tax credits) Modification of regulations Promotional activities Provision of services (water, sewer, parking, recreation)	US Department of Housing and Urban Development State departments of economic development State public works and water commissions City government County government Special district (water, transportation, school) Public utility companies	Chambers of commerce Local economic development corporations Special rehabilitation districts Contractors Expanding and locating private businesses	Neighborhood organizations Community and technical colleges Realtors associations City council citizen committees Downtown merchants' association Workforce investment boards Regional planning agency Community action programs

Watershed Protection	US Historic Rivers US Clean Water Act US Urban Rivers Program State water protection and construction programs	US Environmental Protection Agency (EPA) State environmental agencies Local government: cities, counties, townships, natural resource districts State parks and games departments US Fish and Wildlife Federal Services/state court rulings	US Department of Agriculture, Soil and Water Conservation Services City and county governments Local landowners Businesses	Sewer districts State EPA research entities Local growth control agencies Planning districts Environmental organizations (e.g., Nature Conservancy, land trusts) Citizen organizations
Metropolitan Transit/ Transportation	US Transportation Equity Act for the 21st Century Urban Mass Transit Act Clean Air Act State infrastructure funding programs	Federal Highway Administration, US Department of Transportation (DOT) US EPA State departments of transportation Metropolitan planning organizations County governments City governments Transit districts Airport districts	City governments County governments Transit and airport districts Regional planning agencies Transportation and paratransit for-profit and nonprofits Private construction contractors	Alternative transport committees and associations (e.g., bicycle and pedestrian) Handicapped organizations Business roundtables (e.g., freights, access roads) Neighborhood associations Chambers of commerce
Family Income Support	Temporary Assistance for Needy Families (TANF) Childcare and Development Bloc Grant Food stamps Medicaid Job Training Partnership Act (US Department of Labor)	HHS; TANF; child care; Medicaid US Department of Agriculture (food stamps) State welfare/social services agencies State labor/workforce development agencies	Local/regional workforce development agencies and boards Local/regional welfare departments Contractors of services (e.g., IBM, Electronic Data Systems) Nonprofit organizations (e.g., eligibility employment) Religious organizations Private employers Transportation providers Child care providers	Counseling and testing firms Job placement firms Community and technical colleges External advisory groups State legislative leaders and specialists Client associations

contacting the state government about potential funds (loans or grants) and about the legal aspects of its tax adjustment and long-term borrowing program. It will also seek out the HUD office in the state for possible federal funds. It will coordinate with the county government to seek help with any local matching funds needed for grants. It will discuss loan matches with local lending institutions. Finally, numerous meetings will be held with local utility companies about new service hookups, with the transit district about improvements and rights-of-way, and with the affected school district about the potential for rapidly expanding enrollments and any possible property tax effects. This scenario, though somewhat simplified, demonstrates the breadth and depth of partners needed to serve policy and program needs.

In reality, fewer public efforts today are the kind of "single shot" contacts with government where a problem is raised, a single contact is made, and it is over with. Perhaps an example would be if a consumer feels aggrieved by a local merchant who advertised a special price and failed to mention that only two were available and contacted the city consumer affairs office. The city employee could call the merchant and say this was a violation of the city consumer code. The merchant agrees to desist and to order another item for the consumer at the special price. But the public sector today is also involved in considerably more intractable issues, for example, integrating persons with mental disabilities in their communities, upgrading local economies, protecting degraded watersheds, providing coordinated multimodal transportation, supporting geographic information systems among government users, and mitigating income poverty. These concerns require multiple intergovernmental programs, multiple public agencies, many delivery agents, and a variety of supporting organizations.

Multiple Agency-to-Agency Vehicles

Given the multiple partners and multiple tools that have resulted from the rise of intergovernmentalization, it should be no surprise that a number of formal mechanisms exist to facilitate coordination. Concern about these issues of adaptation through collaboration first arose as metropolitan problems became a national concern in the 1960s. State governments at the time were considered unresponsive to problems of central city decline, rapid suburbanization, and the issues and concerns that cut across fragmented jurisdictions. Roscoe Martin (1965, 172–74) argued that metropolitan problems were an important concern for the whole country because they were national in scope, required federal government revenues, would establish a floor on program quality, would upgrade management in urban governments, could achieve specified national goals, and would result in a marked growth in the practice of cooperative federalism. As a result of this challenge, Martin (1963) and others (ACIR 1962) began to look at existing forms of cooperation in metropolitan areas. They were identified as procedural and structural mechanisms for solving the problems produced by governmental fragmentation in metropolitan areas.

Obviously a great deal of change has occurred in the intergovernmental system since the mid-1960s. Programs, tools, governments and special units of government, and NGO involvement have accelerated. State governments are now more involved in federal programs that go from the federal governments to communities and they are more active in local government affairs. As a result, the original Martin list has been updated in figure 2.1. It contains twenty-seven different types of possibilities and includes modes of connecting NGOs as well as governmental units. They are presented from the standpoint of three categories: informal practices, governance tools, and formal arrangements. The range of activities is considerable, from informal or nonbinding exchanges between two organizations to complete consolidation or integration, that is, a merger of the operations and programs of two or more agencies.

Although the three-category list given in figure 2.1 is no doubt an incomplete representation of the universe, it makes clear why the use of the term "network" or "networking" used in chapter 1 can often be confusing. Notice that organizing a formal network is identified as number twenty-six of twenty-seven items, meaning that at least twenty-six additional possibilities exist for connecting public and nonpublic entities. They, of course, include the more familiar contracting, service exchanges, interagency agreements, shared staff, federated councils, and service partnerships, along with less familiar parallel actions, the use of open sources, joint ventures, integrated services partnerships, and limited powers intergovernmental public–private organizations. Thus, whereas "network" has become a buzzword, "the network" or "to network" often actually refers to actions related to one or more of the connecting modes listed here.

Why have so many means of collaboration involving public and public-serving organizations arisen? The answer should be clear from the earlier sections of this chapter. Federalism has been redefined into intergovernmental relations that involve the expansion of governments at all levels—more governments, more laws and regulations, more government agents or partners, more programs, and more managerial concerns. In the United States we are in an era where the law and jurisdictional boundaries are maintained, where the welfare state reaches deeper into the world between governments, where government works with nongovernment partners, and where the quest to connect and network is necessary. Clearly, a variety of vehicles has emerged to meet such challenges.

Informal Practices and Links

- *Informal discussions/sharing of information:* Nonbinding exchanges by personnel of two or more agencies* focused on some program purpose.

- *Informal cooperation:* A nonbinding connection (required by law, contract, written exchange) between two agencies to improve programming.

- *Parallel action:* An agreement, usually formally adopted, between two or more agencies/operations to pursue a common course of action. The decisions are agreed upon jointly, but their implementation requires individual action by the agencies/organizations involved.

- *Continuous public open source facility use:* One organization makes sustained noncontractual use of another public facility, e.g. schools and public libraries and museums, small city governments and county planning agencies, community organizations and public buildings, small town leaders and agricultural extension service, chambers of commerce, and small business development centers in colleges.

- *Conference approach:* Bringing together, at regular intervals, representatives of given agencies/organizations within an area to discuss common problems, exchange information, and develop agreements on issues of mutual interest.

- *Shared staff:* Specialists and professionals perform tasks or services on loan for a cooperating agency but remain on the sending agency's payroll.

- *Outreach/liaison staff:* Employees of one organization assigned to work primarily or exclusively with another agency, e.g. police in schools, social workers in mental health centers, occupational health and safety specialists in shipyards, ambulance crews in fire stations, etc.

Government Tools

- *Dedicated task forces:* Multisector, ad hoc, bodies charged to look at a particular problem; and to study, research, and propose tentative solutions to public problems that cut across multiple populations, jurisdictions, communities, etc.

- *Grants:* Payments from a donor government agency to a recipient, public or NGO, normally for the provision of service by the grantee.

- *Regulation:* Legally enforceable rules that govern expected behaviors or outcomes that require administrative arrangements by the regulator and regulated.

- *Government loans/loan guarantees:* For a loan, state or US Treasury funds are loaned to other governments or private-sector borrowers; for a guarantee, government enters into an agreement with a private lender to make full payment if the borrower defaults on the loan.

- *Vouchers:* Government provision of a subsidy, normally transmitted intergovernmentally and through NGOs that grants limited purchasing power to individual clients to choose among designated goods or services.

- *Contract for services:* A written, binding (and legal) agreement by one agency or organization to supply direct services for another agency.

- *Interagency agreements:* Written collaboration supports between two or more code departments or agencies within the same government, e.g., social services and parks and recreation departments, economic development and tourism.

FIGURE 2.1   Public-to-Public and NGO Agency Connecting Modes

- *Joint venture:* Two or more agencies seek to invest in and launch an auxiliary operation—e.g., a business or spin-off café or service station—as part of their respective programs while maintaining the rest of their operations independently. Based on shared risk capital, with shared liability.
- *Joint stock venture:* Engagement similar to a joint venture, but the participating agencies raise capital by selling stock in the operation. Liability is limited to the joint venture.
- *Joint commissions:* Private multiorganization bodies that evaluate standards of operation, entry and exit to a field, and sometimes outcomes that are licensed or "franchised" under public auspices, e.g., accreditation of hospitals, rehabilitation facilities, geographic information systems specialists, and social workers.
- *Limited powers/intergovernmental public–private organizations:* Area-based multigovernment or super municipal/county representative bodies that have no formal or have limited powers over aspects of planning or programming, e.g., transportation metropolitan planning organizations, area agencies on aging, workforce development boards, regional planning boards, rural development councils, museum or zoo authorities.

Formal Public–NGO Arrangements

- *Advisory boards:* Citizens, community leaders, service clients, students and parents representing different organized and nonorganized interests meet with public officials, provide advice, respond to proposals and/or actively participate in plans and proposals.
- *Councils/federations of agencies:* Information sharing, information creation and sometimes pooled fundraising, with no or few decisional controls over an agency's operations.
- *Compact:* Two or more agencies/organizations undertake mutual obligations, for example, to serve clients from neighboring communities where no services are organized.
- *Transfer of functions:* Shifting of an agency's particular service, e.g., nursing, intake, case management, to another agency more adequate in knowledge, experience and/or resources.
- *Limited partnership:* Two or more agencies/organizations formally agree to work together and integrate certain functions while remaining separate in their core operations, e.g., fund-raising, public relations, financial management, and supportive health services.
- *Formal agreements with a philanthropic body:* Written compact to work with a philanthropic entity for research, funding, and public relations.
- *Integrated services/partnerships:* Two or more agencies/organizations contractually or legally agree to unify one or more of their services into one operation while operating separately on other functions. Normally involves intake/assessment, case management, evaluation and assessment, support or management services.
- *Formal networking:* Multiparty agency involvement in regularized, organized multiagency/multiorganization bodies that exchange information, build mutual capabilities, build collaborative services strategies, and solve programming/policy problems at points of service.
- *Agency merger:* Two or more agencies/operations form a new, blended agency that combines the mission and efforts of the dissolved units, a complete and final integration move. Over time, program design, operation, evaluation, and management functions are unified.

*"Agencies" in this figure refers to both NGO organizations and government agencies.
Source: Author's adaptation and expansion of the modes given in *Metropolis in Transition* by Roscoe C. Martin (1963).

FIGURE 2.1   *Continued*

THE CASE OF INTERGOVERNMENTALIZING SERVICES FOR INTELLECTUALLY AND DEVELOPMENTALLY DISABLED PEOPLE

As is the case with any of the policy and program areas illustrated in table 2.2, the many players, public agencies, delivery agents, and supporting organizations today strive toward a form of cogoverning cooperation by various approaches to collaborative management. The quest for collaborative management through intergovernmentally generated networks of programs and services will be illustrated in the area of intellectual and developmental disabilities (ID/DD) (mental retardation, cerebral palsy, autism, and related disorders), where programs have become highly interactive. A summary of the six major intergovernmental forces that have led to this intergovernmentalized and externalized system is given in box 2.1. Though ID/DD is increasingly federal and national in how systems of services are defined, it remains oriented toward state government—that is, the lead of state government in the broad organization of systems of services—whereas funding is increasingly federal, along with all the rules related to funding. It is also demonstrated that the smallest nonprofit or for-profit service delivery unit is tied

Box 2.1 The Intergovernmental Context of Servicing Intellectual and Developmental Disabilities in the Network Era

1. Multiple programs and funding sources at all levels: federal, state, local, nongovernmental organizations, and private families.

2. Influence of the federal and state courts on all forms of services based on client rights, which has led to the details of state-level programming and administration.

3. Research/clinically based national movement in service content to establish more normalized environments and experiences, leading to federal advocacy for the creation of more integrated services programming at the state level.

4. Integration, in turn, has led to both clinical professional and federal and state government encouragement in supportive core services: personal assistance, public accommodations, employment, housing, and technology access.

5. Federal and state Medicaid home and community-based waivers lead to core guidelines and outcome expectations linked to goals in all the above clinical and services movements.

6. Subsequent actions also lead to the quest for building integration/normalization networks of all types, ranging from those that provide timely supports to comprehensive systems.

Source: Compiled by the author.

to state and federal funding rules and standards, whereas the drive for integrating ID/DD persons pushes programming into collaborative models that entail system building.

Programs and State Systems

The federal funding connection is primary, because most programs are blended with state funds and operated through state agencies. Figure 2.2 lists these various sources and makes clear how the intergovernmental connection begins with federal programs matched with those of the states. It includes an involved list of federal programs, some formula sharing and project grants, and state matches and state programming that complement federal funds. The largest single program here is clearly Medicaid, a federal–state program of some $300 billion per year. Most important is growing spending for community services under Home and Community-Based Services (HCBS) waivers, which have doubled during the past decade. One estimate places total HCBS waivers for ID/DD recipients at about $40 billion in 2004 (Thompson and Burke 2008). Other Medicaid spending for ID/DD in 2002 is reported at $13.8 billion (Braddock, Hemp, and Rizzolo 2004, 358). Also included in this figure are important federal operational grants to the states for promoting state ID/DD programs, special education and rehabilitation, some thirty programs identified here.

State programs to develop ID/DD services outside institutions have been operational since the mid–twentieth century. Each state has moved through periods of grants and later contracts to support its own programs, designed according to its traditions and political considerations, buttressed by federal funding. Each state varies as to the completeness with which it builds such systems and the vigor with which it integrates them at the community level. Some states still rely quite heavily on congregate care in larger residential facilities (from 50 to 60 percent of all clients in some states) for those whose services are virtually all outside larger facilities in foster care, supported living in group homes, and in a family home (90 to 95 percent). State service levels also vary from a low of 103.23 persons per 100,000 population in Virginia to a high of 989.05 persons in Idaho (Prouty et al. 2008, 83–84).

Using the cafeteria of federal funding programs, particularly Medicaid and its HCBS waiver, states are shifting programs from institutions into financing and the purchase of services models that are in search of collaborated or networked systems. However, states are not doing this with equanimity. Texas, New York, and Illinois, to name a few, have community programs but substantially cling to their

Institutional services funds for 16+ persons

State Funds
ICF*/ID Medicaid match
- General funds (not including state ICF/ID match)
- Other state funds (not including state ICF/ID match)
- Local funds in excess of rematch

Federal Funds
- Federal ICF/ID
- Title XX/Social Services Block Grants
- Supplemental Security Income

Private 16+ institutional services funds

State Funds
- ICF*/ID Medicaid match
- General funds (not including state ICF/ID match)
- Other state funds (not including state ICF/ID match)
- Local funds in excess of rematch

Federal Funds
- Federal ICF*/ID
- Other federal funds

Community services funds for 15 or fewer persons

State Funds
- ICF*/ID Medicaid match
- General funds (not including state ICF/ID match)
- Other state funds (not including state ICF/ID match), e.g., state services programs
- Local/county funds in excess of match
- SSI state supplement funds

Federal Funds
- ICF*/ID Medicaid match
- Small public ICF/ID (<16)
- Small private ICF/ID (<16)
- HCBS** Waiver (1115 and 1915e of Social Security Act)
- Other Medicaid services Title XX/Social Services Block Grants
- SSI Adults Disabled in Childhood (HCBS Waiver Participants)

Federal-state general ID/DD programs/nondirect services (selected)

Federal Funds
- Basic state grants
- Basic state grants: protection and advocacy
- Projects of national significance in developmental disabilities
- University centers for excellence in DD
- Workforce Investment Act, vocational programs
- Individuals with Disabilities Education Act (10 programs)
- Rehabilitation services programs (13 programs)
- Special education funding
- Office of Disability Employment Policy

*ICF = intermediate care facilities for the mentally retarded.
**HCBS = home and community-based services (Medicaid) waiver.
Source: Agranoff (2009).

FIGURE 2.2   Federal and Nonfederal Funding and Program Sources for Intellectual and Developmental Disabilities (ID/DD)

state hospital beds. At the other end of the spectrum, Vermont, New Hampshire, and Oregon have completely deinstitutionalized. Others—like Indiana, New Mexico, and Maryland—have almost totally deinstitutionalized. A federalism feature that thus persists is that despite federal funding, federal regulations, and court rulings, states do differentially organize their ID/DD systems to achieve roughly similar aims and utilize similar intergovernmental programs (Prouty et al. 2008, 83–84).

Intergovernmentalization has nevertheless moved ID/DD services into a new era of noninstitutional services in search of more interactive or coordinated systems that are both managerial and services oriented. As Castellani (2000, 452) observes: "Supported living, managed care, long-term care, forensics, and the current institutional and community-based service system are distinct approaches to providing developmental services. There is not a new paradigm in developmental services which forms an overarching framework for delivering and managing developmental services. Instead, the earlier state institutional framework which was supplemented by the group home-community program model has evolved into a plurality of approaches, each with a distinct clientele, its own approach to services, separate types of financing, and distinct types of service providers. This has important, and largely unacknowledged, ramifications for administration of developmental services." It is an array in search of systems of coordinated services.

Olmstead and Intergovernmental Management

A US Supreme Court ruling, *Olmstead v. L.C. and E.W.* (1999), ruled that states could not institutionalize persons if they were clinically ready for community-based services and the individual chose these options. To maintain such persons in institutions is in violation of the 1991 amendments to the Americans with Disabilities Act, which states: "A public entity shall administer services, programs, and activities in the most integrated setting appropriate to the needs of qualified individuals with disabilities." *Olmstead* requires states to make "reasonable modifications" to their programs yet not "fundamentally alter" these programs and services (Rosenbaum and Teitelbaum 2004).

This case has moved many state programs considerably faster in the direction of building interactive services (NCSL 2003) and has triggered many lower court suits that interpret "reasonable progress" and "fundamental alteration." It has two important collaborative implications for ID/DD. First, many *Olmstead* follow-on suits have put the federal courts into the details of federal–state program administration. Judgments have primarily been with regard to Medicaid and HCBS Medicaid waivers over such issues as funding evening services, refusal of home care after minor income standards adjustments, limits on prescription drug benefits to five per month, changes in eligibility criteria, states' waiting list sizes, length of time clients are on waiting lists, funding levels for waiver services and numbers of waiver slots allocated, types of "optional" community services, and administrative time taken to process applicants (Agranoff and McGuire 2005; Rosenbaum, Stewart, and Teitelbaum 2002; Human Services Research Institute 2005). This puts the federal government right in the teeth of state ID/DD programming, more or less using Medicaid "carrots" to create "sticks" to build systems of services.

A second *Olmstead* influence is the moves the states are taking themselves toward compliance actions designed to integrate services. With some small federal grant incentives under Executive Order 13217 in 2001, at least thirty-nine states developed *Olmstead* plans that not only included direct services but also housing, transportation, data collection on persons with developmental disabilities, waiting list reduction plans and actions, education programs regarding services options, and assuring quality care (NCSL 2003). These programs have been supported by Real Choice Systems Change Grants, at about $100 million per year. These efforts are not designed to replace state systems but to encourage the pace of state progress within the parameters of existing state design.

Building Integrated Systems

States are challenged to wrap integration-related services around core rehabilitative and health ID/DD services funded by Medicaid, HCBS waiver programs, and state-funded programs. Integration as a concept in ID/DD derived from a number of treatment philosophies that encourage the "normalization" of living for all persons (Wolfensberger 1972) and by the long-standing movement to organize fragmented human services around clients (Agranoff 1991; Agranoff and Pattakos 1979). Integration is designed to be consistent with the definition given in the Americans with Disabilities Act: "when consistent with his or her unique attributes and strengths, an individual enjoys the opportunity to participate fully in all aspects of life" (quoted by Stewart et al. 2003, 8). This emphasizes equality of opportunity, full participation, independent living, and economic self-sufficiency. Stewart and others (2003, 2–4) identify supportive services as consisting of the following groups:

1. Personal assistance, including medical and nonmedical supports, often accessed by working age adults who have the ability to function on their own.
2. Public accommodations, including public transportation, assistive supports in lodging, appropriate customization of buildings, and access to health care.

3. Employment, by reducing economic, physical, and social barriers to work, along with support for employers to assist them in making reasonable accommodations, such as hiring incentives.
4. Housing, particularly for transition for institutional living, balancing services and supports, placing a premium on interagency communication, and coordination for the development of supportive housing.
5. Technology, by reducing persons' limited access due to financial, educational, and information barriers, along with access to assistive technology, opportunities for training, and information sharing regarding various technologies.

Some have added to this mix education, including literacy training and adapted classes, from schools and public adult learning programs, along with monetary assistance (food stamps, general assistance) (INARF 2005).

Medicaid Standards and Core Delivery Agencies

Another potent intergovernmental force on states and service delivery agents are the HCBS waiver program guidelines for quality management, which were promulgated by the Centers for Medicare and Medicaid Services in 2000. They include consumer protection; ensuring the health, safety, and general welfare of participants; planning for comprehensive, individualized support services; protection of the rights of all persons who apply or enroll in public ID/DD services; provider oversight, ensuring that all providers of community services and supports meet qualifications and standards; on-site monitoring of the overall performance of the service delivery system; financial integrity, that is, the capacity to ensure that payment claims and audits are managed in an accountable manner; monitoring of the health standards of persons receiving services; monitoring of consumer satisfaction and outcomes; and quality enhancement, that is, assessing and improving weaknesses in the service system (Gettings 2003, 227–32). Until the middle decade of the 2000s, literally hundreds of detailed provisions and expectations were listed under each of these categories in the Centers for Medicare and Medicaid Services *State Operations Manual*, a set of regulation-oriented guidelines of "compliance principles" and "facility practice statements" (Hayes, Joyce, and Couchoud 2003, 206). They have given way to sets of performance measures in the same guideline areas as before. They are geared toward a new set of policy outcomes developed by persons at the leading edge of the field (Shogren et al. 2009). Within these managerial and policy guidelines, state-level management design features remain varied from state to state within common capabilities, regardless of how states might configure them (see Gettings 2003, 227).

These federally driven services guidelines establish sets of parameters for potential systems of services delivered by NGO agencies. They are now at the core of ID/DD guidelines for NGO agencies and programs. In effect, they are evolving to form a code of performance. The guidelines sit alongside the governance provided by NGO boards and in many ways control what agencies do in serving clients. Some support network building and some do not. The Medicaid guidelines clearly intergovernmentalize the system. In most states these agencies are, as mentioned, publicly funded and range from the small agency providing one or a small number of services to large and complex multiservice agencies with hundreds of employers and budgets in the several millions. Castellani (2000, 454) describes the core array in search of a system as:

> In some states, multiprogram agencies provide individuals with an all-encompassing array of residential, day, recreation, transportation, clinic, and other services. Many of these large agencies are also vertically integrated, with children entering early intervention and preschool programs, school programs, after-school programs, family support programs, and other services leading to the multiprogram adult services and involve the person with the disability and family virtually from birth to death within the same agency. In other states, horizontal integration of day, residential, and ancillary services as well as vertical integration by age is discouraged. The organizational mix in locales and across states presents myriad problems for state administrators. The experience of the past thirty years has been one of managing highly regulated networks: certifying providers, shoring up fiscally fragile agencies (large and small), attempting to ensure some equity in availability of services within and among locales, and managing access of individuals into provider organizations.

This growth and variety of provider agencies, ranging from small supported living agencies to large multistate developmental services corporations, "presents an exponential increase in complexity for state administration in budgeting, rate setting, contract administration, quality assurance, constituency relations, and policy making" (Castellani 2000, 454). Medicaid waiver standards present tremendous system building challenges if services are to be integrated beyond the boundaries of the agencies.

Building Networks

There is recognition that integrating persons with ID/DD must go beyond issues of regulation, certification, waiting lists, or dealing with problematic agencies. Managing the access of individuals to providers requires a more accelerated type of collaboration, which perhaps includes many aspects of networking. The network challenge actually involves two groups of individuals. The first is one rapidly expanding group, a Type I mostly living at home or recently in programs outside institutions that have entered the adult service system and possess an ongoing network of family, friends, and peers who support and advocate for them. Primarily due to special education and childhood-related programs, this generation has grown up in their communities, and adult services can be built on existing personal networks with timely government and agency support, building on personal bonds that normally have been maintained over a lifetime. It is estimated that by mid-2006, a total of 224,264 persons with ID/DD on HCBS were living with their families, almost double the number as of 1999 (Lakin, Prouty, and Coucouvanis 2007).

A Type II situation involves persons who have lived in an institution or a large or small residential facility for some time, have fewer personal network supports, and who are trying to adjust to community settings. These individuals find themselves without personal allies or supportive networks that typically assist young adults, and who lack the benefit of personal vigilance or advocacy. Evidence indicates that this group is considerably disadvantaged with regard to the ability to make everyday living and support service choices (Lakin et al. 2008, 339): "The challenge for government and support agencies is to create a network of support and safeguards for each individual from scratch, to build durable community connections, and to maintain this new network" (Sundram 2003, xx).

Although federal and state government programs can stimulate network building, direct action is required locally within substate or county-level planning and service areas. At least four options for network building appear to be on the table. First, case-by-case linkages can be built around each person's needs, accessing those noncore services that round out integration but are not currently employed. For example, transportation to a client's supported employment service could be arranged by tapping in to an existing handicapped transportation program, or dental care could be arranged through the network by dental offices that serve the developmentally disabled. This type of networking could be of the most direct relevance for Type I persons identified above.

A second level involves creating collaborative task forces to plan for and attempt to solve generic and long-standing accessibility problems on a singular basis—for example, access to private medical providers, dental services, physical therapy, and related health services for an ID/DD population in a local area. Such a network could examine the extent of such problems, gauge the depth of need in each subarea, identify funding sources, provide information and referrals, and develop interorganizational and interagency policies and procedures. The agencies could work toward the coordinated delivery of services, particularly the exchange of resources. The group might even work on operating policy, developing continua of preventive, corrective, and/or ameliorative services (Agranoff 1991). This approach would appear to serve both Type I and Type II persons.

A third approach would be to create area-based functional or services-processing networks among providers within an area. This type of network is what Alter and Hage (1993) call a joint production network or what Agranoff (2007) has identified as an action network. For example, all of the advocates and providers of day services or transportation or behavioral supports, or personal assistance services or some combination would work together to provide a seamless system of assessment, referral, intake, service, quality control and reporting across the various public and nonpublic agencies. The aim would be to build an interactive, problem-oriented system that blueprinted strategies and operated elements of a system. This approach would appear to primarily benefit Type II persons, although it could also be useful for Type I.

The fourth network approach would be for area-based ID/DD advocates and providers to work with local governments and providers of human services to create comprehensive systems. Schorr (1988, 6) calls these "interventions that work," that is, that form a broad spectrum of services, crossing traditional and bureaucratic boundaries, flexible programs, viewing clients in family and community contexts, coherent services, and a willingness of professionals to redefine their roles to respond to severe but unarticulated needs. It would involve agencies and programs far beyond traditional service providers and would entail developing models that include *functions* (client management, client rights, protection, and advocacy), *services* (health, residential, social, and recreational), *support* (transportation and legal), *settings* (high levels of supervision and functionally independent living), *organizations and agencies* (lead agency, consortium, and core and support agencies), and *options* (grants, contracts for the purchase of services, in-kind services, an exchange of resources, the contribution of resources and/or services, and an interagency agreement) (Agranoff 1991, 537). In many ways this comprehensive approach could incorporate the three case-by-case linkages identified above, a singular problem plan, and functionally based networks into broader scope networks that approach the issues of integration from planning to operating to evaluation arrangements. This appears to be the most essential approach to Type II persons with ID/DD identified above.

The collaborative challenge for ID/DD is not only to build collaborating networks but also to build different kinds of networks. Although, on the surface, it appears that local leaders in ID/DD might start with building linkages or problem planning and then move on up the line to partial or total systems, the real world suggests that the kind of "wicked problems" with their first- and second-order effects makes this problematic (O'Toole 1997). The challenges of coordinating services and moving communities to support persons ranging from those in institutions to those in large residential facilities or group homes without support suggests that a full frontal assault on all four categories of network building is necessary. Without a multipronged network-building attack, life for many of these persons who are not at home in a family remains institutional, so only the bed location has changed to a smaller facility. Indeed, multinetworking appears to be the very nature of working with highly intergovernmentalized programs.

Finally, this "walkthrough" of how to manage intergovernmental ID/DD programs in the network intergovernmental era is not exclusive to this functional arena. When one thinks of emergency management, for example, a similar specter of building linkages, problem-focused planning, and partial and fully functional systems also arises. First responders are a disparate group, and emergencies require developing the channels for each to be able to participate in a flood, fire, hurricane, or the like. Before an emergency the coordinator looks for gaps and potential partners and tries to enlist uncovered services into the system. Concerns like communication, evacuation, food distribution, medical services, and volunteer coordination must be organized and potentially operationalized. The various elements of the emergency management "system" must be functionally put together into an interacting system. Emergency network management building and maintenance require activation, framing, mobilizing, and synthesizing (McGuire and Silvia 2008). Similar intergovernmentally induced collaborative network building is required in relation to economic development (Agranoff and McGuire 2003), environmental management (Thomas 2003; Wondolleck and Yaffee 2000), hazardous chemicals (Koppenjan and Klijn 2004), community development (Bryson and Crosby 2008; Gazley 2008), and social services (Page 2008), to name a few. Network building is the signature intergovernmental collaborative management activity of the first decades of the twenty-first century.

CONCLUSION

The rather long case example for ID/DD programming given in this chapter brings out in bold relief how the US intergovernmental system of separate jurisdictions and independent NGOs has become an intricate part of the US federal system. This case also demonstrates that the four eras—law and politics, welfare state interdependence, government partners, and network management—are all alive in the quest to integrate persons with disabilities. These intergovernmental issues provide important starting points for anyone who is involved in one or more of the connecting modes illustrated in figure 2.1. The actions of collaborative interactions begin with a basic understanding of how the system is framed. This framework, no matter how tedious and daunting it may appear, is basic to starting any activity in collaborative management. Most everything—regulation, tools, programs, agents—flows from the intergovernmental framework. This kind of understanding enhances the management of collaborative activity.

Collaborative management thus begins with a basic understanding of the structures and interdependencies in the system. Programs and delivery organizations exist in a complex array of opportunities that, if combined and/or connected, can work at solving some of society's most intractable problems. This complexity necessarily means that to manage collaboratively is a work in progress that begins with understanding the terrain as well as the potential offered by variegated practices. No matter what public endeavor one is attempting to collaboratively manage, the overlapping powers, resources, and responsibilities of governments, and how they are carried out, are important places to start. Questions such as "What programs address particular problems?" "How do they work?" and "Who is responsible for delivering and supporting them?" obviously become paramount. Mapping out the programs, tools, primary agents, delivery partners, and supporting organizations therefore constitutes an important initial step.

The discussion of the new roles of NGOs does not necessarily indicate that government has phased out all aspects of primary operation in its current situation or that all intergovernmental programs are totally uncoordinated. With regard to the latter, Seidman (1986, 225) once concluded that all the talk about the need to coordinate creates the false impression that most efforts are not coordinated: "Without informal or so-called lateral coordination, which takes place at almost every stage in the development and execution of national programs at every level within the federal structure, the government probably would grind to a halt. . . . Managers who are motivated by a desire to get something done find ways of bridging the jurisdictional gaps."

Nor is government rendered either passive or powerless in the so-called hollow state, when externalization is a common practice (McGuire and Agranoff 2010). In a profound and far-reaching conclusion, Wondolleck and Yaffee (2000, 244) found that government agencies continue to play both authoritative and participatory roles in the collaborative environmental efforts they studied:

> Government agencies and institutions have a unique role and responsibility in these processes. While they should be capitalizing on opportunities to collaborate, they must recognize that they—and only they—are the final decisions makers. Some argue that the role of agency participants in collaborative processes is solely

as a facilitator of other participants' interactions. However, based on our review of successful collaborative processes, it is clear that where a group succeeded and was held in high regard by the broader community, the agency did not step back into a purely facilitative role. Rather, it provided essential leadership that guided the group while simultaneously representing its own interests within the process. It ensured that the sideboards provided by existing law and regulation were in place and understood, and that those individuals present recognized that implementation of decisions could occur only through established administrative processes, including procedures for public review and comment. It took on the responsibility of ensuring the accountability of the process while still promoting collaborative interaction among multiple participants.

As subsequent chapters indicate, public collaborative management means that the government agency's representatives are actively involved in exercising leadership while retaining their responsibilities to maintain the public's interests.

CHAPTER 3

Conductive Public Agencies

IN THE 1990S THE AUTHOR had a most interesting eye-opening experience for a professor of public administration. It was in Des Moines, near the Iowa state capitol, while studying an intergovernmental council that happened to be housed in the Iowa Department of Economic Development (DED). It was not located in any of several large bureaucratic edifices up the hill at the capitol office buildings complex but near the central business district in a leased suite of offices that housed businesses and state associations. Upon entering the DED offices, one encountered forty or so open desk areas, very few of which were presently occupied, and the place was laced with about fifteen small conference rooms. Other than the secretaries and a few DED staff members who had appointments, almost everyone was not at their desk but out of the office. Upon my discussions about the council, it was revealed that DED actually had a professional staff of about thirty-five. Most of their work was with individuals, groups, committees, task forces, partnerships, and networks outside state government. Although DED did do some intersecting work with other state departments and federal officials, its staff worked more with local governments, private businesses, university and community colleges, regional planning agencies, state associations, and other entities involved in the major productive sectors of business, manufacturing, and agriculture. And though DED administered a handful of federal and state programs, its main thrust was outside promotion and partnership in the state's economic and community development effort, most of which substantially un-folded outside the state government complex.

This chapter looks at how public agencies at the federal, state, and local levels have become externally oriented like the Iowa DED. After an introduction to the new public agency, an in-depth case example of the Iowa DED's emergent structure is presented. Then the chapter attempts to configure how new emergent collabora-tive public organizations function internally and externally. What then follows is a series of diagrams that demonstrate what these public agencies look like. Then elements of collaborative management within the public agency are identified.

It will become clear at this point that in addition to the standard hierarchical downward "tree branch" depiction of organization, one must now diagram the overlapping circles and connections that characterize today's agencies. Finally, the chapter identifies a set of emergent managerial practices to enable the conductive agency to manage clientele relationships.

THE NEW PUBLIC AGENCY

There was a time when the typical bureaucrat was stereotyped as a faceless and inflexible rule-enforcing person who followed the strict hierarchical principles of classical public administration. Protecting the "boundaries" of the organization was one expected function. Standard practices such as planning, organizing, staffing, directing, coordinating, reporting, and budgeting (POSDCORB) became the core of management. Over time, these rigid principles and practices gave way to greater measures of flexibility, but in some quarters they no doubt persist nevertheless. These basics—for example, rules—persist, however, in changing and modifying bureaucratic form because they do "protect as well as restrict," "coordinate as well as block," "channel effort as well as limit it," "permit universalism as well as provide sanctuary for the inept," "maintain stability as well as retard change," and "permit diversity as well as restrict it" (Perrow 1986, 26). Yet a new overlay has been placed on the standard bureaucracy; it is not only more flexible but also more open to work with external agents, with outside agencies in one's own government, with other governmental jurisdictions, and with the nongovernmental sector.

No one seriously suggests that bureaucracy should be done away with completely. But it needs to become adaptive. More than half a century ago, Charles Hyneman (1950, 3) reminded us that "bureaucracy is an unavoidable consequence of modern government. The things that government does today cannot be accomplished by laws alone. Men and women have to be employed in great numbers to put the policies of government into effect. And men and women, brought together to work in large organizations, constitute bureaucracy." Bureaucracy is a long-standing form of organizing, and bureaucrats "have become an increasingly significant part of the governing apparatus of virtually every country in the world" (Peters 1996, 1). Within organized structures, only a few modern configurations drive effective organizations like bureaucracies—capturing the division of labor in distinct tasks and efforts to coordinate tasks—on the basis of direct supervision, standardization of work processes, standardization of outputs, standardization of skills, and/or mutual adjustment (Mintzberg 1983, 7). Now these processes also reach across the boundaries of organizations, particularly with mutual adjustment, skills, and work processes—in systems of governance. Governance speaks to the shifting rather than the shrinking role of the state, "a mix of all kinds of governing efforts by all manner of social-political actors, public as well as private, occurring between them at all levels, in different governance modes and orders" (Kooiman 2003, 3). As such, contemporary issues are not just public or private but shared.

Today's public agencies at all levels consequently look less like the hierarchical, rule-bound, and routine operation organizations found in the days of the emerging bureaucratic organization, which was referred to in chapter 1 as Weberian, Taylorist, or Fordist; nor can they be organized according to the simple principles of earlier times (Olsen 2006, 16). Within, organizational structures have become more flexible and permeable during the twentieth and early twenty-first centuries (Clegg 1990, 181). This has two important implications for collaborative public management. The first is that those public administrators and program specialists who work in public agencies are now more attuned to internal organizational experiences that are less rigid, cross the divisional boundaries of their own structures, reach out to other agencies of their government, and involve an increasing number of cross-sector and intergovernmental experiences. Chapter 2 makes this point clearly for those who work within intellectual and developmental disabilities state agencies. Second, this exposure and experience with a changing hierarchical paradigm have brought on a host of cross-boundary transactions, which are identified in chapter 2 as tools of governing. Boundary-spanning approaches—grants, contracts, regulatory interaction, cooperative agreements, joint ventures, networks, and the like—are familiar and now are regular administrative transactions beyond the walls of the agency. As a result of these two forces, public administrators today are more attuned to processes that engage and co-create with an array of agencies and organizations, cutting across organizational silos and connecting with other participants that add ecosystem value (Tapscott and Williams 2006, 247). Consequently, collaborations like New Futures in Dayton (see chapter 1) and networks like that on the Lower Platte River (chapter 2) would in no way be a surprise to today's government bureaucrat.

The emergent public organization increasingly faces the challenge of regularly collaborating externally. Any of the management books published in the past decade or so stress this theme, particularly how collaboration is changing the operation of the traditional organization (e.g., Campbell and Gould 1999; Drucker 2001; Pasternack and Viscio 1998). Among the most comprehensive of this genre is *The Conductive Organization*, by Hubert Saint-Onge and Charles Armstrong (2004, 213), in which they define the conductive organization as "an organization that continuously generates and renews the capabilities to achieve breakthrough performance by enhancing the quality and flow of knowledge and by calibrating its strategy, culture, structure and systems to the needs of its customers and the marketplace." Writing primarily to business organizations, they address emergent organizational processes, including the importance of creating partnerships through internal–external interaction, building alliances and coalitions, forming and reforming teams across functions and organization boundaries, and collaborating to actively manage interdependencies (Saint-Onge and Armstrong 2004, 191): "The capability to effectively manage complex partnerships is growing in importance as organizations are reconfigured. Organizations are becoming more and more involved in complex value-creation networks, where the boundaries between one organization and another become blurred and functions become integrated. It's becoming a critical organizational and leadership capability to be able to create and leverage participation in network-designed and -delivered solutions."

Today's public administrators particularly experience collaborative management in dealing with the operations and practices of nonprofit and for-profit organizations external to their structure. As has been indicated above, this represents the phenomenon of an expanding network of alliances between governments and a host of public and private bodies—other levels of government, private business, banks, insurance companies, and, increasingly nonprofit agencies (Salamon, 1995, 2). These nongovernmental organizations (NGOs) are engaged in using the tools of government and are part of the core of the "third sector" among governments and businesses that constitute structured organizations located outside government.

IOWA'S DED: A COLLABORATING PUBLIC AGENCY

DED was formed in 1986 as part of a state agency consolidation effort that brought together programs in business development, community development, employment and training, and tourism. DED's portfolio is quite comprehensive, and it thus administers a number of notable programs—Community Development Block Grants, federal housing programs, the state Jobs Training Partnership Act, youth employment and training programs, and other workforce development programs—plus its own state programs, including the Agricultural Enterprise Fund, Rural Enterprise Fund, and Rural Community Leadership Program.

DED sees its role as providing assistance and "empowering communities" to make the right choices. Thus community leadership efforts are important to DED. Industrial recruitment is clearly another part of the DED's strategy, but unlike the functions of agencies in many other states, it is not an exclusive focus. It shares emphasis with business expansion, increased agriculture production, and human resource development.

Sixteen councils of governments (COGs) serve as direct DED substate planning and delivery arms. These COGs are charged with directly assisting communities with planning and development. The state once funded COGs to promote DED programs to assist communities, but in the mid-1990s DED staff began to work on a more direct basis with local development groups. DED also has strong links to the state cooperative extension service at Iowa State University, where cooperation on training programs and special grants has been strong. There is some contact with other public and private colleges that are involved in economic development, and strong links are being developed with area vocational schools. Private-sector representatives from banking, health care, agribusiness, telecommunications, farm producers, and manufacturing are regularly involved with DED in developing rural policy and programs.

Generally speaking, when the state moves into a policy arena, it creates a task force of public and private actors. The task force typically studies the issue and then makes a proposal. Thus, public–private cooperation is a very common feature of the Iowa style. Because Iowa's approach involves substantial networking, private-sector actors are seen as integral components of the policy leadership. Indeed, Iowa is as likely to use its government resources to spin off a new program to the private and nonprofit sector as it is to operate its own program. Thus, though the state agency is important, these new partnerships are just as critical to understand as are those of this form of governmental structure.[1]

CORE AND LATERAL RELATIONS IN THE CONDUCTIVE AGENCY

To grasp the entirety of how the public agency now works collaboratively with other entities, one can see that there is now a range of possibilities. Figure 3.1 is a diagram of a more or less typical or hypothetical public organization. It can exist at the federal, state, or local level. This figure attempts to explain the work of the agency in both its internal and external relations. It is designed to depict the potential variety in collaborative management. The agency's hierarchical or core operations include its legal authority and hierarchical operations, POSDCORB or standard operations, its mission-pursuit operations, its resource inputs/outputs, and so on. Connected to this operating core are both legally and statutorily connected relations and nonlegal collaborative relations, for example, signed inter-agency agreements. Among the former, represented by solid squares or rectangles

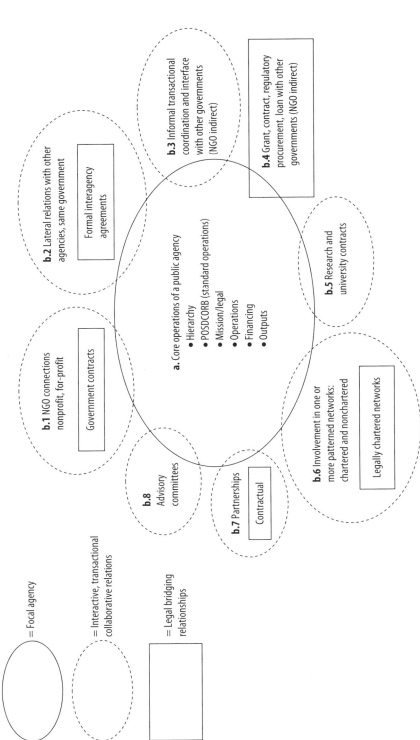

KEY

= Focal agency

= Interactive, transactional collaborative relations

= Legal bridging relationships

a. Core operations of a public agency
- Hierarchy
- POSDCORB (standard operations)
- Mission/legal
- Operations
- Financing
- Outputs

b.1 NGO connections nonprofit, for-profit

Government contracts

b.2 Lateral relations with other agencies, same government

Formal interagency agreements

b.3 Informal transactional coordination and interface with other governments (NGO indirect)

b.4 Grant, contract, regulatory procurement, loan with other governments (NGO indirect)

b.5 Research and university contracts

b.6 Involvement in one or more patterned networks: chartered and nonchartered

Legally chartered networks

b.7 Partnerships

Contractual

b.8 Advisory committees

FIGURE 3.1   Core and Lateral Connections in a Hypothetical Conductive Public Agency

in the figure, are grants, procurements, contracts, loans, and other legal ties to other governments and NGOs; formal interagency agreements with lateral agencies; direct agreement and contacts with NGOs; legally chartered networks; formal partnerships; university contracts; and advisory bodies. The dotted circles that overlap the core agencies represent less formal but real collaborative activity, including lateral relations with other agencies at one's level of government, connections with NGOs, informal transactional coordination efforts with other governments, and involvement in one or more patterned networks that are either chartered (some of which have legal standing) or nonchartered. Clearly all these noncore activities make this hypothetical agency highly conductive.

In figure 3.1 panel "a" shows the hypothetical agency in core or traditional bureaucratic form, whereas panels "b.1" through "b.8" describe the larger context of different types of collaborative relations and juxtaposes them with the agency's core operations. In the real world most collaborative transactions almost always cut to the core of the agency's operations, a sort of "ab" or "ba" rather than "a" or "b." Nevertheless, one must bear in mind that a substantial number of the operations of the public agency remain "a" only because of the fact that, except for completely externalized agencies, conductive relations add to but do not replace portions of the core work of the government organization. It is sometimes convenient to refer to all these relationships as network connections, but in reality chapter 2 demonstrated that network relations represent just one of several bureaucratic connections, the others being direct NGO connections (b.1), lateral contacts with other agencies of the same department (b.2), informal transactional coordination with other governments (b.3), grant/regulatory/procurement/loan connections with other governments (b.4), research and university connections (b.5), partnerships with other governments and NGOs (b.7), and partnerships with various advisory committees (b.8). Again, the potential for agency collaboration goes far beyond networking and network involvements.

FEDERAL, STATE, AND LOCAL CONDUCTIVE AGENCIES

The conductive potential of actual public agencies is now explored. First, a close examination is taken with a federal agency that seemingly looks insulated. The US Department of Agriculture's rural development unit (USDA/RD) has operations in each state, and a look is taken at a typical state in figure 3.2, constructed hypothetically as a model federal conductive unit. The core functions include twenty grant and loan programs. In a medium-sized rural state—for example, Nebraska—this involved $105 million in fiscal year 2004, a professional staff of ninety-five, and

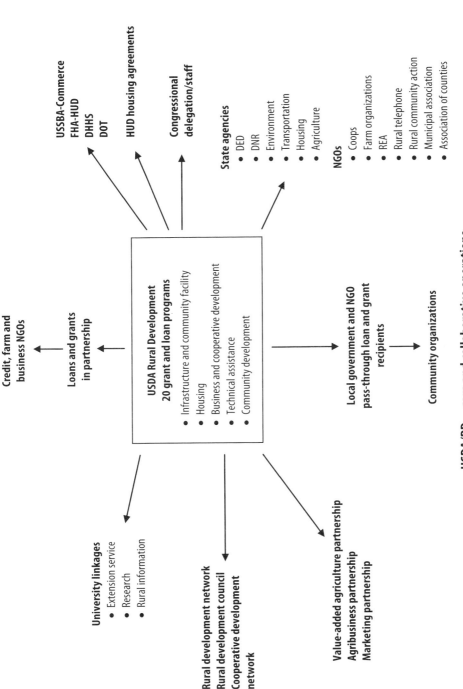

USDA/RD—core and collaborative operations

FIGURE 3.2 A Typical US Department of Agriculture Rural Development (USDA/RD) State Office as a Conductive Public Organization

The following text appears within the figure:

Credit, farm and business NGOs

Loans and grants in partnership

USSBA-Commerce
FHA-HUD
DHHS
DOT

HUD housing agreements

Congressional delegation/staff

State agencies
• DED
• DNR
• Environment
• Transportation
• Housing
• Agriculture

NGOs
• Coops
• Farm organizations
• REA
• Rural telephone
• Rural community action
• Municipal association
• Association of counties

USDA Rural Development 20 grant and loan programs
• Infrastructure and community facility
• Housing
• Business and cooperative development
• Technical assistance
• Community development

Local government and NGO pass-through loan and grant recipients

Community organizations

University linkages
• Extension service
• Research
• Rural information

Rural development network
Rural development council
Cooperative development network

Value-added agriculture partnership
Agribusiness partnership
Marketing partnership

eight offices around the state. As the core indicates, this money is for various local infrastructure projects, housing, business, and cooperative development; community development projects; and technical assistance in these areas.

As the diagram indicates, this work is done almost entirely with external agents. Moving clockwise, much of its lending activity is in loan sharing with banks and other lending institutions and NGOs as matches of different ratios with partners are negotiated. USDA/RD works with other federal agencies (e.g., the Small Business Administration, Federal Housing Administration in the Department of Housing and Urban Development [HUD]; Department of Transportation; and Department of Health and Human Services). It has a number of housing agreements with HUD, inasmuch as USDA's 10,000-population legal mandate limit means that some communities switch in eligibility over the life of some loans. There is constant interaction with staff of the state's delegation in Congress, with both the Senate and House over information and projects, and with congressional staff members often involved in negotiations with potential project partners.

State agency contacts are also frequent, particularly with the state's economic development department over potential matches or alternative funding, but also with each state's environment, natural resource (if separate), transportation, housing, and sometimes agriculture agency, if the latter's mission goes beyond weights and measures. State NGO contacts, mostly over potential projects and their negotiations, include a series of service and advocacy organizations that have aspects of rural development as part of their mission, for example, agricultural cooperatives of different types and local government associations. USDA/RD also works directly with small local governments and indirectly on loans and grants with NGOs that receive the benefit of these funds, along with those community organizations that often carry out these projects in small communities.

Each state's USDA/RD can be involved in various partnerships with universities, community organizations, state agencies, and statewide associations. Three of the more frequent are identified in figure 3.2: value-added agriculture, agribusiness, and the marketing of state rural products. The state program can also be a formal member of one or more rural development networks—in this case one of the states' regional planning and development agencies, the USDA-inspired state Rural Development Council, which emphasizes intergovernmental issues—and a network that promotes the development of cooperatives.

Finally, USDA/RD is likely to have one or more connections with higher education institutions, particularly the state's land grant university. This normally involves a direct linkage (and shared funding) for community development and leadership projects executed by the federal–state extension service, located at land grant schools or with rural development centers at other universities and colleges.

Although USDA/RD does not fund research, the agency is interested in the latest in technology and the various economic and social indicators in the rural sector, and thus it is in regular contact with research organizations. These conductive activities clearly make this federal agency more than its core functions, given that its activities are as external as internal in operations, and its staff are heavily involved outside the "box" in figure 3.2 (Agranoff 2007, chap. 9).

The typical state economic/community development department (ECED) is considerably more conductive than the standard public agency, as suggested by the Iowa DED case. Figure 3.3 demonstrates in a nonexhaustive but extensive fashion the range of connections of an ECED. It does not include the employment and training and/or unemployment functions that Iowa DED contains. The core agency is small, depending on the size and scope of its mission, with as few as twenty professional staff members, who administer a limited number of state development programs: loans, grants, leadership development, information, planning, and promotion.

The core work is even more outside than the federal USDA/RD agency. Working clockwise again, one starts with other state agency contacts, particularly transportation and environment. There are also numerous federal government contacts, such as, with USDA/RD, the Department of Commerce (Small Business Administration, Economic Development Administration) and HUD, but also the state-administered Small Cities Community Development Block Grant, housing, and such special programs as Main Street.

Next come the ECED's contacts with city and county governments over state and federal pass-through programs, and interactively over various economic development tools, for example, tax credits or loans. The same types of contacts would be made with local economic development bodies. Further contacts are made with substate planning and development agencies and/or councils of government on matters of planning and program development, aging, transportation, land use, and zoning for small communities.

Because development involves leadership and skilled workforces, higher education interaction is regular about leadership training and curricular issues. Some departments are also in contact with higher education for basic research, for example, projects that might be commercialized and/or with some technology applications. The next set of key contacts is with representatives of the state's productive sector: banking and financial institutions, chambers of commerce, rural cooperatives, venture capitalists, and manufacturing associations.

Most state agencies also have involvement in a series of networks in various areas, ranging from an export council to affordable housing. Along with networks are a series of partnerships, normally formal agreements for business promotion

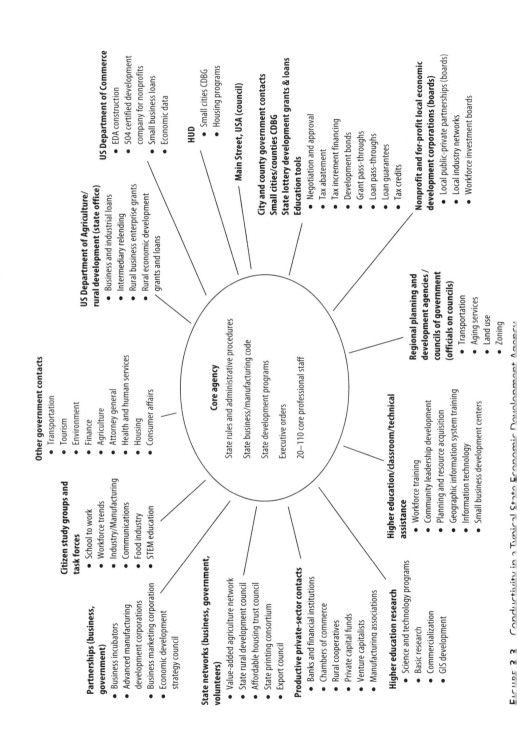

Core agency

State rules and administrative procedures

State business/manufacturing code

State development programs

Executive orders

20–110 core professional staff

Partnerships (business, government)
- Business incubators
- Advanced manufacturing development corporations
- Business marketing corporation
- Economic development strategy council

Citizen study groups and task forces
- School to work
- Workforce trends
- Industry/Manufacturing
- Communications
- Food industry
- STEM education

Other government contacts
- Transportation
- Tourism
- Environment
- Finance
- Agriculture
- Attorney general
- Health and human services
- Housing
- Consumer affairs

US Department of Agriculture/ rural development (state office)
- Business and industrial loans
- Intermediary relending
- Rural business enterprise grants
- Rural economic development grants and loans

US Department of Commerce
- EDA construction
- 504 certified development company for nonprofits
- Small business loans
- Economic data

HUD
- Small cities CDBG
- Housing programs

Main Street, USA (council)

City and county government contacts

Small cities/counties CDBG

State lottery development grants & loans

Education tools
- Negotiation and approval
- Tax abatement
- Tax increment financing
- Development bonds
- Grant pass-throughs
- Loan pass-throughs
- Loan guarantees
- Tax credits

Nonprofit and for-profit local economic development corporations (boards)
- Local public–private partnerships (boards)
- Local industry networks
- Workforce investment boards

Regional planning and development agencies / councils of government (officials on councils)
- Transportation
- Aging services
- Land use
- Zoning

Higher education/classroom/technical assistance
- Workforce training
- Community leadership development
- Planning and resource acquisition
- Geographic information system training
- Information technology
- Small business development centers

Higher education research
- Science and technology programs
- Basic research
- Commercialization
- GIS development

Productive private-sector contacts
- Banks and financial institutions
- Chambers of commerce
- Rural cooperatives
- Private capital funds
- Venture capitalists
- Manufacturing associations

State networks (business, government, volunteers)
- Value-added agriculture network
- State rural development council
- Affordable housing trust council
- State printing consortium
- Export council

FIGURE 2.3 Conductivity in a Typical State Economic Development Agency

and industrial development. Finally, many departments have citizen boards or study groups that examine intractable policy problems, for example, school to work, and/or science/technology/mathematics/engineering education, and make recommendations through the agency.

There are no doubt many more such contacts not illustrated in this highly external ECED. Unlike USDA/RD, the typical state ECED has a few small programs of its own, but most of its work is mobilizing and engaging the work of others through information, leveraging, and small seed fund programs (Agranoff and McGuire 2000).

The development approach can be illustrated at the local level by looking at a large metropolitan core city's economic and community development collaborative connections. Figure 3.4 extrapolates these functions from the rest of city government for demonstration purposes. In this hypothetical city government, the planning and community development department is the lead development agency, but finance, public works, social services, and neighborhoods also play key conductive roles of a facilitative and operational nature.

Looking at the figure clockwise again, the council has instituted a number of important engagement-oriented committees (nine are illustrated), ranging from communications technology to the more standard library board. Next are citywide mixed citizen/association/council member task forces devoted to planning, promoting, and orchestrating important community/economic development programs such as downtown and civic events.

Federal contacts are minimal inasmuch as most programs go through the states, but the city is a direct recipient of Community Development Block Grant funds and is also in regular contact with HUD about housing and with the Department of Transportation about mass transportation programs. There are also state government (and infrequently federal) grant and loan contacts, which often include bodies like a state public works or water development commission.

The neighborhoods department works with city's nine ward/neighborhood planning associations and citizen councils. Meanwhile, social services works with the independent park and school districts as well as with social and health associations. Public works is in regular contact with the water and sewer district and private utility companies, whereas the legal department engages in numerous state regulatory and some federal inquiries and negotiations.

The city's chief executive and one council member sit on the metropolitan planning organization's transportation policy committee (a network), and several planning department staff are regularly involved with the organization's technical committee. The most regular and extended contacts are made with the city's

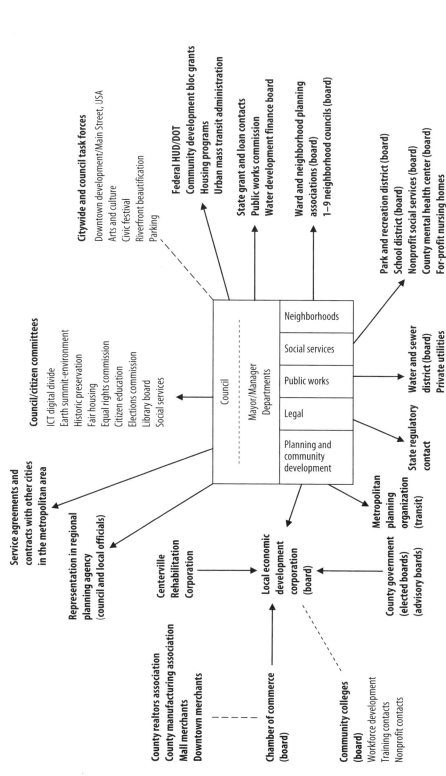

FIGURE 3.4 Conductivity in Local Government Economic and Community Development

economic development corporation, a partnership with the county government, the chamber of commerce, and other important entities. This body carries the economic development load for the city government through the planning department linkage. There are some contacts with the substate regional development agency, mostly through city council representation, for occasional assistance. Finally, as with most core metropolitan cities, there are numerous mutual service agreements (e.g., fire services) and contracts with other cities (e.g., library branches in the suburbs).

When one looks at the economic and community development function, this illustrative city is not only connective through its boards, task forces, and intergovernmental contacts but also operates its economic development operation through a joint venture or public–private partnership. Although not every city would form a partnership through such a development corporation, virtually all local government community development functions form partnerships in some fashion and are similarly conductive (Agranoff and McGuire 2003).

Through these reflections on the reality of public organizations today, we have gained a very different picture of a "bureaucracy" unlike the former stereotypical rigid hierarchies and rule-bound structures, and thus instead see one that needs to be more flexible because it is reaching across boundaries so much more than it did in the past. Added to the agency's internal operations are the tools of government identified in the previous chapter applied to intergovernmental and intragovernmental processes (Salamon 2002). In dealing across boundaries, the conductive agency neither completely controls the entities with which it deals nor are they controlled by these external agencies. Each party to conductive relations has its legally or contractually chartered mission, roles, and rules. The joint efforts, that is collaborative management, complement rather than supplement the core operations of each party, although now both parties must be willing to work together to smooth the flow toward broader program and policy aims. In this sense they also become mutually dependent.

This interdependence is fostered by interactive engagement in a world where exchange opens the door to success through myriad linkages. USDA/RD cannot advance the cause of improving the lives of rural citizens without local leaders, community organizations, and lending institutions reaching out and successfully working with them through winning projects. An ECED cannot successfully advance its state economy and expand employment to contemporary expectations without engaging the business, financial, educational, and local civic association communities. No city's leaders can attract new businesses or make their community a better place to live without lots of citizen involvement, organized partners, and joint ventures. These entities thus are highly conductive in the sense that all leverage their public investments by working with other organizations. That is why the conductivity burden is constant, regular, and so heavy. As Saint-Onge and Armstrong (2004, 34) conclude, "High-performing organizations know how to build and maintain the relationships that are conduits for knowledge flow, leveraging capabilities, and strategy-making processes."

A LOOK AT CONDUCTIVE MANAGEMENT

At this early stage in the identification and operation of conductive public organizations, it is difficult to tell which new techniques of management are growing alongside the older ones. Because most public agencies retain some degree of their core missions, one assumes that newer techniques sit alongside older ones and some of the older ones are being modified. A preliminary look at this phenomenon is taken up here, and more detail is added in subsequent chapters. It has already been demonstrated that networks are not replacing hierarchies in the public sector, but exist alongside them with a host of other lateral relationships. Earlier in the decade Agranoff and McGuire (2001) raised the question of whether a network (or collaborative) POSDCORB is replacing the old techniques. Our subsequent research as part of a larger project on network formation (Hunter et al. 2008) revealed that a process of sorts seems to unfold: *activation*, or enlisting partners and gathering information; *framing*, or visioning and creating guidelines and principles; *synthesizing*, or reaching an agreement and organizing operations; and *mobilization*, or reaching an agreement and taking action. This sequence does indeed take place, and in somewhat overlapping fashion. It is suggested as a management approach for a large number of conductive actions.

Another way to look at the evolution of management is to examine how the standard management functions—POSDCORB—are modified by collaborative activity. Figure 3.5 provides a snapshot of how these functions are moving toward the same kind of flexibility, shared authority, and mutual adjustment that are at the core of collaboration. These processes are distinctly nonhierarchical. Take budgeting, for example, with which in a conductive agency external partners have some involvement, however uneven they may be in resource contribution. Moreover, some amounts or parts of several budgets are interactively "adapted" and include hard money commitments, such quasi-fungible agreements as in-kind or an exchange of personnel, and other contributions, for example, volunteer efforts or donated space. This makes budgeting a much looser and adjustable management process, than that of agency appropriation.

PLANNING is vision based, adaptable, and nonlinear, where cause may not be known or even linked to proposed effects.

ORGANIZING is very late in the game, almost after the fact, lateral, or open to external partners rather than hierarchical, designed to promote discussion, learning, and reaching agreement.

STAFFING is based on knowledge rather than rank, ability to mobilize needed resources and be open to external input and participation, and the ability to mutually solve problems with external organizational representatives.

DIRECTING is based more on self-direction and facilitating the knowledge and resources needed by staff to collaborate.

COORDINATING is more simultaneous than sequential, as parties mutually go through various processes of activation, framing, synthesizing, and mobilization.

REPORTING is based on parties mutually exchanging problems, progress, and results.

BUDGETING is ad hoc; in a collaborative enterprise there is rarely one budget, but a collection of adapted and adjusted resources, quasi-fungible commitments, and other contributions by the parties, normally on an uneven basis.

FIGURE 3.5   POSDCORB Modifications for the Conductive Functions of a Public Agency

Another key dimension of the collaborative enterprise is the importance of knowledge seeking. As the public organization works with its interlocutors, it needs new kinds of cross-program data and information that can help point to solutions. This involves much mutual learning through exchanges of information, joint interpretation, and adaptation to real-world situations. In some cases, people come together from different disciplines (e.g., geologists, chemists, ecologists, toxicologists, and other environmental scientists) but share similar outlooks.

Recognition must be paid to the fact that collaboration faces many obstacles, such as knowledge gaps, legal barriers, resource scarcity, exercise of agency negative power, and political opposition. It is often necessary for a collaborative undertaking to "move a mountain" of obstruction toward some purpose. The state rural development councils, for example, found that it was virtually impossible for them to engage in rural policy development because their governors' offices and state economic development departments, along with their state legislators, consider policy to be their turf, which they were reluctant to yield (Radin et al. 1996). In most cases rural policy development fell off the table for the councils.

Once a collaboration undertaking that includes a conductive agency has reached agreement, it has partially mobilized. Then it needs to carry out the program. To implement across boundaries is more than mere bargaining and negotiation over who does what. It entails articulation of the details of programs of their boundaries by the two or more parties that seek to collaborate. Here is where lots of the technical details (e.g., a multipronged land use and mitigation strategy that includes strict zoning, chemical bans, fertilizer reduction programs, and tree planning) are worked out. Shared or multiple implementation means at best semicontrol or some form of remote control by the public agency, inasmuch as many different parties are normally involved in carrying out an agreement. A state environmental management agency may have taken the lead in forging some mitigation agreement, but the city governments must zone, businesses and agencies need to cease the chemical use, the landowners must cut back on fertilizers, and the USDA's county soil and water conservation service offices are needed to plant the trees. All this comes at some postarticulation time, often over years.

Finally, many collaborative activities undertaken by the conductive public agency are regularized. They can be a one-time effort, for example, a USDA/RD small grant to the state municipal league for small-town leadership training. More often, however, these connections are regular, for example, with respect to an effort to jointly promote a value-added agriculture campaign, improve the technical skills of a state's workforce, develop a new section of a city's industrial park, or expand another city's civic performing arts center. These longer-lasting or longer-run activities will require a structure or body where there can be discussion, negotiation, and learning, and an agreement and monitoring can be reached.

Whether long-term or project committee based, here mutually interactive nonhierarchical bodies, both formal and informal, advise and exchange. These bodies are neither hierarchical bureaucracies nor voluntary boards of nonprofit organizations that elect their officers. Rather, leadership *emerges* through processes and decisions by a form of learning-based processed consensus building. Elsewhere (Agranoff 2007, chap. 6) I have called these "collaborarchies." Such conductive collaborarchies rarely vote formally or even use *Robert's Rules of Order*, which leads to potential division or at least is counter to the spirit of learning and agreeing together. Indeed, majority rule is not in order in these collaborative structures because (1) some nonagreeing parties may be outside the mutual structure, and (2) a near consensus or complete agreement among major parties is the norm.

Collaborative accommodation through these mutual structures can also lead to new or modified policy decisions. For example, in environmental management the next step beyond command-and-control regulatory activity is to explore how to harness the incentives that regulation by command and control cannot reach. In the endangered species arena it may include removal of subsidies for converting land for agriculture, differential tax rates by land use practices, an offer of conservation subsidies, establishing individual transferable land use quotas, and recognizing community property rights. Of course these practices will not just happen, but they will take the best collaborative efforts of state environmental agencies, local governments, landowners, conservation and environmental associations, and scientific researchers working together to establish common knowledge bases, which will enhance the various organizations' ability to scan the environment, understand alternative practices, and adopt multipronged strategies around commonly identified property that accept these nonregulatory practices (Thomas 2003). The public-sector conductive agency increasingly will be expected to take the lead on these collaborative issues, or at a minimum be deeply involved as a partner, as it works outside with a myriad of other agencies, jurisdictions, and organizations.

RULES OF ENGAGEMENT FOR BUILDING CAPACITY TO MANAGE THE PUBLIC CONDUCTIVE ORGANIZATION

Public administrators experience elevated connectivity in dealing with the operations and practices of nonprofit and for-profit organizations external to their structure. As mentioned above, during the past half century we have witnessed the phenomenon of an expanding network of alliances between governments and a host of public and private bodies—other levels of government, private business, banks, insurance companies, and, increasingly, nonprofit agencies. These NGOs are part of the core of the "third sector" among government and nongovernment business that constitute structured organizations located outside government. Some of these public contractor, vendor, or otherwise agent organizations are not designed to distribute profits to their owners/investors, are self-governing, and involve substantial voluntary effort, whereas others are public serving but strictly for-profit. As a result, to the manager in a conductive public agency, a new and different set of "clientele relationships" would appear to be important. The agency's external publics are now not only potential service recipients, rule followers, or recipient organizations but also potential partners in some type of joint or collaborative effort. This brings on an emergent set of external rules. Here I identify nine of the more significant ones.

First, an element of cogoverning is introduced: There is an incredible variety of interest associations, nonprofit organizations, substate planning agencies, public–private ventures, statewide networks, government-to-government linkages, intergovernmental contacts, and many others, along with elected and appointed advisory boards. Examine, for example, the myriad partnerships, study groups, advisory bodies, and other links undertaken by the state economic development agency, as depicted in figure 3.3. Many parties become involved in the policy/implementation process. Administrators must see that many of these vehicles go beyond the traditional advice giving to involve the type of "co-governing partner-ships" (Fung 2006, 69), for example, the four illustrated in figure 3.3. In this type of process more than consultation is involved, as what were once thought of as advocates become partners in many ways. The public administrator operates in a broad field of potential deliberative mechanisms in response to myriad "external agents."

Second, the public conductive agency administrator is directly involved in the process. Deliberative work under these circumstances involves a different kind of process than monitoring, consultation, or reacting to proposals. It involves grow-ing and learning together. In deliberative work actors integrate the worlds of "is" and "ought" as well as "science" and "ethics" as they learn how to get something done and what ought to be done to address new and unique situations (Forester 1999, 62). For example, this would include the work of city officials portrayed in figure 3.4 with their counterparts in the local economic development corporation. The administrator in the conductive agency cannot sit back and react but must become a part of this process of looking for and helping respond to concern and need by forging the new and possible. Partner creators rather than bureaucratic responders are needed.

Third, the home public agency will increasingly become open to structure a variety of lateral processes. It will be called upon to calibrate the organization to be able to work with external groups, needs, and interests. This goes well beyond the normal tenets of organizational design, including the standard building of teams. The key is not divisional realignment or designing more tasks but to be open to linking these functions to the organized agency clientele through constant processes that inform the agency's thinking, actions, and relationships through constant knowledge flow, that is, an intimate understanding of its external working interlocutors. This is clearly one challenge for USDA/RD as shown in figure 3.2, as it works with credit, farm, and business NGOs to advance its loan programs and business development projects. It can invoke a number of mutual actions, such as continuing work with stakeholders, codeveloped solutions, accepting input on shaping rules, cross-functional integration (e.g., joint production), integration with external organization operating systems, developing solutions based on externally perceived value, and strategic partnerships (Saint-Onge and Armstrong 2004, 57). In effect these practices have become part of the new organizational design, a set of lateral overlays on the enduring hierarchical structure.

Fourth, the new public organization is challenged to recognize the information-based nature of its conductive agency. Deliberation works better when the parties engaged in joint undertakings are better informed. For example, one of the most essential tasks that state rural agency administrators can perform is to gather information about communities and to assess the capacities of their institutions and people. This would be a major function of the councils and networks listed under "state networks" in figure 3.3. Through their community assessments, often conducted locally by citizen groups with state agency or university assistance, the uncertainty felt by small or rural communities can be reduced and can raise the level of policy/program possibility, fitting the array of programs with the community (Agranoff and McGuire 2000, 394). These types of information strategies definitely make the quality of network deliberation easier, and that is why conductive administrators invest increasing resources in technical assistance, planning and skill building, community leadership, needs analysis, action planning, education and training, and impact studies.

Fifth, the conductive organization needs a knowledge-oriented administrator base. Knowledge employees are wanted. As information is converted into knowledge that is transacted and modified through deliberation, the agency needs to capture those invisible assets that reside largely in the minds of humans, requiring less strict supervision and with "worker" and manager working side by side. This typically is the case of project-oriented staff members who work for state agencies like the one illustrated in figure 3.3. Most are on a "loose" nonhierarchical leash to go out and work with those who can make things happen. The rules of supervision for such knowledge workers are different. According to Davenport (2005, 92–101), they entail (1) participation by managers in the work instead of overseeing work, (2) from organizing hierarchies to organizing communities, (3) retaining workers rather than hiring and firing them, (4) building knowledge skills rather than manual skills, (5) assessing invisible knowledge achievements instead of evaluating visible job performance, (6) building knowledge-friendly cultures instead of ignoring culture, (7) fending off bureaucracy rather than supporting it, and (8) relying on a variety of human resources, wherever they may be located, instead of relying on internal personnel. These principles of human resource management clearly apply to those public agency employees who are working outside the organization with others on the joint resolution of issues and problems.

Sixth, building high-quality relationships through communities of linked professionals and practitioners both inside and outside government is another essential human resource challenge. It is a common practice for conductive agencies to deliberate through the building of communities of practice and to take advantage of epistemic communities. For example, as exemplified in figure 3.4, local officials, the business community, local planning officials, and employers have worked together for a long time on many projects, and they have sifted through the same data and information and therefore have come to many understandings over the years. Many of the joint ventures, networks, consultative bodies, partnerships, and the like operate as communities of practice, that is, as self-organizing systems that share the capacity to create and use knowledge through informal learning and mutual engagement (Wenger 2000). Most such self-organized communities bring in new knowledge bearers when needed, from wherever they can be found. In addition to operational leadership, participant commitment, and top executive support, the maintenance of communities of practice requires effort to keep different types of knowledge bearers involved, by challenging busy people with solving important public problems and by calling on their experience and know-how in an interdisciplinary manner. Through shared commitment to a domain of knowledge that members care about, a community of practice generates "social capital" that enables new levels of collaboration and coordination—to build and share collective knowledge and to develop members' skills (Snyder, Wenger, and Briggs 2003, 20).

Community can be facilitated by mobilizing a multiagency group of professionals from different disciplines who share common outlooks and similar solution orientations. Epistemic communities can be important knowledge sustainers, as they can have a disproportionate effect on organized learning and behavior, and even though epistemic community members may not constitute the most powerful decision makers, they "are well situated to provide a driving logic for cooperation" (Thomas 2003, 41). Bringing together these communities for enhanced deliberation is among the new tasks of the collaborative administrator.

Seventh, an agency knowledge strategy enhances conductivity. It has been suggested that the conductive organization enhances value by interacting with its organized external clientele in collaboration, particularly through communities. A conductive organization can then capture intangible assets through the exchange of knowledge. This is why the state development agency illustrated in figure 3.3 has such close linkages with higher education and with its productive sectors. They possess a great deal of data and information that provide raw material for the knowledge bases the agency and its partners need to develop and manage in order to create value-added knowledge. This value creation involves the managed interaction between (1) the human capital of the agency, (2) the structural or organizational capabilities, and (3) interacting external agents and partners. All three need to be developed in a knowledge strategy on an integrated basis. Many activities are involved in the process of knowledge management (Davenport and Prusak 2000), a process that entails identification, extraction, and capturing fluid mixes of framed experiences, values, contextual information, and expert insights that constitute the assets of any organized undertaking. In the case of public conductive organizations, knowledge is derived on a highly interactive basis and is geared toward adding forms of public value (Agranoff 2007, chaps. 7, 8).

Eighth, critical supports build conductivity through electronic communication. It will come as no surprise that knowledge activities are now supported by the use of different types of information and communications technology (ICT): e-mail, teleconferencing, Web-based geographic information systems, decision-support software, and the like. These are essential tools because partners are situated in disparate organizational locations. Thus USDA/RD, as shown in figure 3.2, uses ICT heavily to link its dispersed internal staff but also to interact with its many potential and actual collaborators: small town banks, regional planning agencies, rural NGOs, state associations, and the like. However, because of the collaborative nature of agency tasks, ICT is not a substitute for face-to-face contact but only a parallel mode of collaborative work. In the same way that organizations seek structured predictability, organized collaborative actions require the use of open-ended processes to coordinate the activities of purposeful individuals so they can best apply their unique skills and experiences to the particular problems that confront the collaborative undertaking at hand. They are part of the distributed knowledge systems that are created across boundaries, which possess somewhat fewer constraints or rule-bounded actions. Often, at the center of such relationships, the conductive agency needs to foster ICT links along with the more direct community-building efforts mentioned above.

Ninth, and finally, it is also useful to calibrate, assess, and account for the collaborative values added. Agency managers should not be impressed by the idea of collaboration per se, but only if it produces better organizational performance or lower costs than its alternatives (Bardach 1998, 17). The rationale for investment in collaboration normally entails more than collective public purpose, vaguely understood, and thus also includes those advantages that collaboration can bring to each partner's mission and operations and to the specialists and managers as professionals (Radin 2006). Thus the city government depicted in figure 3.4 must have a clear sense of where its joint development strategies are going, and whether its investments are paying off in jobs or added local income. The value added can be accounted for from the perspective of the (1) administrator/specialist, (2) participating organization, (3) network process, and (4) network outcomes. This added value helps to bridge the gap of difficult-to-measure outcomes by shifting the ground to intermediate ones.

These nine elements of building conductive capacity can be built as public agencies, and their working contacts operate through collaborarchies. Most important with regard to the conductive public agency, the processes of joint engagement can provide the potential value in both process and tangible ways. From a process standpoint, collective—rather than authority-based—organizing, decision making, and programming prevail but follow group dynamics similar to those of single organizations. Managing a collaborative enterprise involves formal or informal benchmarking of joint steering of interaction processes that sequence several processes: activation, guided mediation, finding a strategic consensus, joint problem solving, and the activities of maintenance–implementation–adjustment (Kickert and Koppenjan 1997, 47–51; McGuire 2002). These actions contribute to productive collaborative products. Tangible outcomes vary considerably by joint undertaking, but specific products can include websites, service agreements, mutual referrals, joint investment projects, incidents of business assistance, loans arranged, grants facilitated, and investments leveraged. Another set of tangible results includes end states of collaborative processes: adapted policies, joint or collaborative databases, exchanged resources, new program interfaces, mutually adapted technologies, and enhanced interagency knowledge infrastructures (Agranoff and McGuire 2001; Kopenjan and Klijn 2004; O'Toole 1997).

CONCLUSION

Recognition of the high degrees of conductivity in twenty-first-century public agencies is relatively recent. One survey of local government officials (Agranoff and McGuire 2003) estimated that they spend about 20 percent of their time on the type of conductive activities identified in this chapter, with the remaining 80 percent on internal operational matters. Of course others—like most of the staff members identified in figures 3.2, 3.3, and 3.4—devote considerably more time to these functions. Other boundary spanners spend virtually all their time working across the lines of their agency. This means that even though the traditional hierarchical management is not eliminated, the lateral or conductive activities in which public managers engage are substantial. Given increasing intergovernmentalization, the proliferation of the tools of governance, and the broadening number of NGO governmental agents, the conductivity of public organizations is no doubt expected to increase. And this means that the public service and NGO administrators and specialists of both the present and future must come to grips with such external work.

All the management and organization questions and answers to operating conductively are not addressed in this chapter. It has attempted to explore the variety of lateral relations, network and otherwise, to illustrate how conductive some agencies have become at federal, state, and local levels, and it has attempted to introduce how public management appears to be changing as a result of expanding agency openness. Many of the managerial observations shared here are really only first cuts at explaining how planning, human resources, or organizing is changing. More solid ground in these and other areas needs to be explored by today's public management researchers. Yet other findings are already solid, for example, the importance of knowledge and knowledge management or the mutual learning and problem-solving nature of collaborative agreement making. As a result, these issues will now be explored in greater detail, for we already know that collaborating managers both inside and outside governments must broker knowledge and form the communities of practice that are the hallmark of mutual learning and deciding.

NOTE

1. This is adapted from Robert Agranoff (1995).

CHAPTER 4

Forging External Agreements

THE BROWARD COUNTY, FLORIDA, Areawide Council on Aging—the area's designated agency on aging (AAA)—is a public consortium consisting of the City of Fort Lauderdale, Broward County government, and twenty-eight smaller communities within the county. Like hundreds of other Aaas it is responsible for planning, advocacy, and services access under Title III of the federal Older Americans Act. It is focused on the estimated 345,064 Broward year-round residents sixty years of age or older. Title III programs are based on grants to the states, in this case the Florida Department of Elder Affairs, and in Broward County its lead service agency is the Aging and Disability Center of Broward County, a tax-exempt nonprofit under Section 501(c)(3) of the federal tax code, which operates a series of multipurpose senior satellite centers and day activity centers under contract from the AAA. Broward satellite centers not only rely on Title III funds, with county and local government matches, but also Florida's Community Care for the Elderly and Home Care for the Elderly acts, Alzheimer's Disease Initiative for Legislation, Medicaid, and Emergency Home Assistance for the Elderly (www. arcbroward.org).

As is the case with regard to more than three hundred other AAAs, Broward's core services are initially authorized by the federal Older Americans Act and administered by the Office on Aging of the US Department of Health and Human Services, through a grant program to each state's unit on aging within state governments, which in turn work with the AAAs within each state. Some AAAs are organized as a public consortia like Broward, whereas others are units of city or county governments, housed in substate regional planning agencies, or operate as nonprofit agencies. Virtually all AAA funded or accessed services are delivered by nongovernmental organization (NGO) vendors under contracts that are guided by federal and state regulations.

The Broward case demonstrates that a grant or contract in the public sector is often more complicated than a two-party exchange; they engender collaborative network activity. Each year since the Older Americans Act of 1965 was passed, its

Title III services for senior citizens opens up a series of transactions connecting small armies of public and NGO managers, staff, and providers. It begins with changes in the law and accompanying regulations and ends with AAA-arranged transportation and meals, along with access and advocacy for supportive health and social services for clients at the delivery level. The process involves not only federal officials but also state agencies, AAA regional bodies that plan and arrange for services, and literally thousands of nonprofit and for-profit contractors that deliver services. Following these program transactions is a fiscal auditing trail that begins with the paperwork filled out by service providers and compiled by the provider agencies, submitted to AAAs, and then to state auditors, to be followed some years later by federal auditors. In this chain, Broward County AAA audits its vendors, the State of Florida audits all its AAAs, and the federal government audits the states. Over a period of years program relationships among agencies, particularly at the state government and regional levels, have moved from rather routine grantor–grantee contacts toward emerging networks involving clients, NGO contractors, regional staffs, and government, because the parties involved have recognized the interdependent nature of their transactions. These Title III program and audit chains are mirrored by hundreds of other programs that mix grant, contract, and other federally funded programs. Title III is just one of some six-hundred-plus federal grant programs.

This chapter looks at the grant/contract collaborative process, that is, how government basically connects with NGOs. It begins with a basic look at grants and contracts. Then it gives an overview of the collaborative aspects of grants management, with particular emphasis on that process, along with an overview of the type of contact points that are made in the process. Then the contract process is taken up, ranging from its legal managerial components to the kind of interactive contract behaviors that can ultimately lead to long-term collaboration and networking. The next major section looks at the processes of reaching multiparty agreements, reaching typical multiparty decisions and actions, and their implementation. A look at the importance of emergent collaborative management behaviors required by public-sector administrators concludes the chapter.

THE GRANTS AND CONTRACTS

There was a time—during the high point of the grants era—when managing collaboratively was relatively easy, particularly at the program implementation stage. In some situations cities reported that it was a matter of searching through the catalogue of assistance for opportunities, filling out a brief application, spending the money, and sending in a report. To implement meant administering federal and, to a lesser extent, state grant funds, including a set of straightforward interactions and accommodations around the program under designation. Grants remain easy to some degree; however, over the years more detailed program implementation has been introduced, as regulatory approaches and crosscutting rules have been added, particularly in such arenas as environmental protection and health and safety. Then the other tools identified in chapter 2—such as loans, loan guarantees, and partnerships—joined grants in the workings of governance. The most notable tool or vehicle of implementation since at least the 1980s has been the services contract, which has built on earlier procurement transactions. Today, contracts are not only the most prevalent tools of program delivery, but many of the large grant programs—for example, Older Americans Act services—have really become contracts at the "distribution" end, that is, at the last stage between funding and service delivery.

By fiscal year 2002, grants to state and local governments totaled $443 billion (Beam and Conlan 2002). The largest of the group include Medicaid and its waiver programs, along with dozens of smaller ones—Head Start, Section 8 Housing Certificates, Community Development Block Grants, Older Americans Act Services, Social Services Block Grants, Highway Planning and Construction, and many more. Generally, these are grants to the states or cities in their end stages (but are often in written contract form). When services are delivered they almost always, as mentioned, end up in some contractual relationship between government funders and vendor recipients. For example, a person with developmental disabilities who is being maintained in supported living by the Medicaid Home and Community-Based Services waiver is no doubt serviced by a community day service, or a rehabilitation NGO that has a contract with the state agency for intellectual and developmental disabilities from state Medicaid office fund transfers. This primary contract for supported living could well include several subcontracts for physical therapy, day activity/training, speech therapy, and a few others. In this example, it is clear that a grant program has become a set of contracts, raising a whole series of issues that are very real for the players involved. Unfortunately, they are rarely at the forefront of managing publicly. In many cases like this, grants and contracts are joined at the hip, so to speak, with important implications for collaborative management.

These program end stages are important for the work of collaborating managers. It is relevant and important, as Radin and Posner (2010, 448–49) indicate, "to differentiate between intergovernmental behaviors at both the policy making and implementation stages." With regard to the latter (and primary focus here), it is part of the problem-solving process with similar intent to that of policymaking, to make programs work and add value through effective implementation. The process uses different tools and behaviors from those used at the policy stage that are equally important to adding public value. It is therefore important to look with some depth at the primary tools of grants and contracts in their most practical or operational phases, along with their related behaviors. They are indeed continuing to emerge in forms of collaborative management, through formal and informal connections among involved administrators down the line.

GRANTS BY MANAGERS

Grants are payments from a donor government to a recipient organization (public or NGO) or to persons. Their aim is to stimulate or support a service or activity for the recipient. This is the major device through which a government agency (the grantor) participates in the program while leaving task performance to another agency (the grantee) (Beam and Conlan 2002, 341).

In the early days of grant expansion in the 1960s, the prime management concern was thought to be how to meet the grantor's or donors' objectives. Measurement by the monitoring agent was based on meeting obligations to the donor. It went something like this: plan submission and review, application submission, detailed reporting, plan review and approval, application approval, monitoring, evaluation, auditing, and resubmission (Shapek 1981, 186). Until scholars began to study the implementation process and the practice of bargaining and negotiation was revealed, it appeared that it was mostly a "checking off the boxes" compliance game.

A lot has been written about the game of grants management, most on the process of bargaining and negotiation. Jeffrey Pressman (1975, 106–7) initially captured grants management in his study of federal aid to cities. He reminded us that "donor and recipient need each other, but neither has the ability to control fully the actions of the other. Thus, the aid process takes the form of bargaining between partly cooperative, partly antagonistic, and mutually dependent sets of actors." Helen Ingram's (1977) study of environmental programs similarly concluded that programs are not necessarily instruments of federal control but, rather, opportunities to bargain. Liebschutz (1991) also depicts an intergovernmental fiscal system in New York as one defined by bargaining and negotiation. Whereas federal officials would like to bind state and local program managers to federal policy, subnational governments seek the maximum possible leeway to pursue their own separate goals and objectives with federal help. In social services programs, as Richard Elmore (1985, 36) concludes, "this give and take has become a managerial strategy in the implementation process. [The] bargain is a two-way affair, inherently different from hierarchical control. A contract is not an instrument of coercion."

Bargaining and negotiation opened up the idea that grants management was more than a matter of checking off boxes and looking over the shoulders of recipients. The idea that it was more of a managerial game that, according to Walter Williams's implementation study of manpower and community development, "requires . . . subtle skill and much knowledge about the roles, the players, and available strategies in the federal-local bargaining situation" (Williams 1980, 197). In an early nod to the importance of bargaining and more of a process or game of grants management, Morton Grodzins (1966, 323) concluded that "the grant-in-aid technique does not tell the whole story; but it tells a good part of it. It is a story of growing expertise; growing professionalization, growing complexities; it is a story most of all, of an ever-increasing measure of contact between officials of the several levels of government within the federal system. Contact points bring some disagreements and produce misunderstanding and some enmity. But most of all, they have produced cooperation, collaboration, and effectiveness in programming and steering the multiple programs of modern government."

It is an interactive process that "nominates an item of federal interest for local political attention. Grants can stimulate healthy local debate about goals and the right balance among competing priorities" (Metzenbaum 2008, 225). It also creates a local game that can involve mustering support and competition for resources, and that initiates a local administrative process that is potentially collaborative with a host of actors.

The Grants-Based Collaborative Chain Challenge

To explain the entire range of transactional opportunities—supervisory, bargaining, collaborative—this subsection takes a closer look at the grant program that opened this chapter. The Older Americans Act of 1965, a relatively small grant program, illustrates the overlapping nature of collaborative opportunity. Figure 4.1 traces Title III of the Older Americans Act of 1965 in greater detail. As stated it provides various types of services to senior citizens in need through a network of regional AAAs and their service contractors. The act is on a five-year renewable cycle, and it is subject to intense congressional lobbying by advocates and elder social welfare and medical professionals. Each part of Title III is subject to multiple pages of program regulations and subsequent guidelines that fill many booklets. These suggestions and instructions are being continually updated. The federal government's Administration on Aging in the US Department of Health and Human Services must approve and later monitor each of fifty-six (states and

Level	Administration on Aging regulations[a]	Guidelines	Review, approval, and interpretation by national and regional offices	Federal Fiscal auditors (postaudit)	Program audit	Federal contract standards
Federal —Congress 　—Statute 　—As amended Other federal statutes (crossover provisions) OMB circulars Federal agency regulations	Draft Comment Final	(what is an acceptable senior center setup, adequate transportation program)	Negotiable over acceptable plan/interpretation Program oversight			Federal contract standards
State State unit on aging State plan for program operation (1) Meet national regulations (2) Deal with substate AAAs, state human services agency/governor's office AAA review/approval oversight supervision negotiation	Legislative acceptance appropriation[b] Oversight State statutes	Substate supervision	State, agency administration (1) statewide operations, advocacy, work with other departments, planning (2) program diversity of substate AAAs (3) federal reporting 　—program 　—fiscal (4) AAA contracts	State administrative regulations guidelines	State Fiscal and monitoring State Audit and contract monitors	Grants and contracts to AAAs
Substate/service AAA Plan/fund application Contracts for service	Board approval		AAA administration (1) areawide functions: Advocacy Pull down other funding, coordination/networking Direct services Purchase/contract for services (2) planning (3) evaluation (4) state reporting 　—program 　—fiscal			
				4. Contractors (profits and nonprofits) 　—home nursing 　—nutrition 　—visitors-day activity 　—others 　—contracts 　—reporting 　—audit	Client services	

[a] US Department of Health and Human Services, administrating unit.

[b] Legislative approvals are a practice in some, but not all, states.

Note: AAA = area agency on aging.

FIGURE 4.1 Older Americans Act Title III Transaction Points

territories) "state plans," which are actually contracts for the federal money. There are many additional requirements to the program requirements (e.g., nondiscrimination, protected-category business "set-asides"), for how federal programs must be organized, and categories of expenditures. The states, in turn, add their own legislative and administrative procedures (e.g., service priorities, purchasing, travel/reimbursement) to the process, as they prepare plans and negotiate over renewal and, when approved, contract with the AAAs.

These nonprofits or units of local government and regional AAA bodies in turn make plans and arrangements to deliver transportation, home nursing, nutritional, day activity, home helps, visitor, and other services to seniors in need. The primary mode is by contract for services with providers (e.g., the Visiting Nurses Association, paratransit companies, food vendors, and home cleaning businesses). In some instances it may be contracts with one vendor for several types of activities and nutrition, for example, with a nonprofit community senior center, such as those in Broward County.

At each stage of the process, both fiscal and program paperwork is compiled and sent from the contractor to the AAA to the states, because the state is subject to a dual (program/fiscal) audit two years after the close of the fiscal year in which services are delivered. The paperwork and audit trail begins with the client service and can take from twelve to fifteen minutes of the billable hour of service, and then moves up the line. As mentioned, AAAs are auditable by the states, and the states by the federal government. In such a process there are many interactions and transactions, most of which require cooperation, but not without some measures of conflict. As will become clearer, when the contract management process is examined in this chapter, these interactions are regular, and in the months and years when administrators work together, despite somewhat differing interests representing their agencies and jurisdictions, they all work toward delivering various types of senior services, which gives rise to many interactive opportunities.

To compound the collaborative challenge, Title III is a very small program charged with promoting coordinated services in a sea of other—many large—programs for senior citizens. For example, Title III is overshadowed in scope and dollar amount by Social Security, Medicare, Medicaid, various disability payments, employment, and housing programs, not to speak of state programs in home care, disability assistance, and education. Nevertheless, the AAAs under Title III are charged with assessing, advocating, and arranging for these services, which are external to the Title III services to which seniors are entitled but currently do not receive. The reason for this is that nearly twenty federal departments have grant programs of some types for seniors, not to speak of dozens of other programs that potentially have some senior relevance. This presents the challenge of coordinating diverse programs at two levels: at the program and community level and with respect to the needs of a particular client.

This is an exceptional challenge, which usually requires leadership and focus. For example, the City of Dayton AAA has employed a coordination strategy that includes promoting employment opportunities; accessible high-quality health services for seniors; socialization opportunities; mobilization and transportation access; protective services and reduced neglect, abuse, and exploitation; and recognizing and utilizing the elderly as a community resource. Dozens of coordinative approaches follow these strategies, for example, expanding job opportunities and access to health services so as to avoid long-term care institutionalization, developing paratransit, and linking with protective services (Dayton City Manager's Office 1983). At the client level it is the responsibility of the case manager to link seniors to these services and programs. The coordination challenge thus includes but reaches far beyond the Title III services for which the AAA is directly responsible.

Components of Collaborative Management

What kinds of activities do managers engage in when they are transacting at these junctures? The standard answers normally are "writing letters," "making phone calls," "attending meetings," "preparing applications," "writing reports," "filling out paperwork for monitors," and the like. Agranoff and McGuire (2003, chap. 4) once set out to inquire what 237 cities were actually doing in grants (and regulation) management as they worked collaboratively with state and local governments, on some twenty activities in all. The collaboratively active cities regularly engaged in virtually all these activities over a period of time. A look at the twenty activities provides an important introduction to the ins and outs of collaboration in grants management.

Figures 4.2 and 4.3 offer identifying labels and examples taken from the case studies conducted for the study, divided by vertical (state and federal) and horizontal (other cities, counties, chambers of commerce, NGOs) activities at the interlocal level. They are divided this way for illustrative purposes only, inasmuch as each can be part of a local effort to leverage state–federal action or the reverse, state–federal effort to leverage local and/or interlocal action. Note that they are broken into categories (e.g., information and discretion-seeking vertical activities). The information activities range from broadly seeking information to inquiring regarding new funds, along with standard and rule interpretation or guidance and assistance. Discretion seeking (close to bargaining and negotiation) involves attempting to make actual changes in rules or policies, and attempting new or trading off monitoring for performance. Horizontally, the activities include

Type of Activity	Example
Information Seeking	
General program information	Salem, Indiana, inquires at the Department of Commerce regarding the scope of activities allowed under the CDBG-funded Community Focus Fund Program.
New funding of programs and projects	Garfield Heights submits a grant application to the Ohio Department of Transportation to access ISTEA funds to construct noise walls alongside its freeways.
Interpretation of standards and rules	Beloit checks with the Wisconsin Housing and Economic Development Authority regarding the eligibility of a potential participant in its Revenue Bond Program.
General program guidance	Woodstock discusses with the Illinois Department of Transportation how it might deal with problems of traffic control access to its business districts through possible rerouting or four-laning of a state highway.
Technical assistance	Ithaca asks representatives of the Michigan Small Business Development Center to visit and explain to prospective entrepreneurs what it takes to successfully start a business, deal with the extensive paperwork and compliance requirements, and become eligible for SBA assistance.
Adjustment Seeking	
Regulatory relief, flexibility, or waiver	Cincinnati asks the EPA for a waiver to cease testing for certain contaminates that are highly unlikely to be in its drinking water system.
Statutory relief or flexibility	Garfield Heights, through its Department of Development, asks the Ohio attorney general's office for a zoning law exception to accommodate a new low-density development that overlaps with the city of Cleveland.
Change in policy	Cincinnati requests a review by the Ohio Environmental Protection Agency of several of its operating practices said to be prohibited by regulation in its water treatment program.
Funding innovation for program	The Ithaca LDC, Greater Gratiot Development Incorporated, seeks discretionary CDBG funding from the Michigan Jobs Commission and HUD to promote small business networks in its multicity cluster of organizations.
Model program involvement	Beloit seeks special designation in the US Department of Transportation's Urban Rivers Program to develop a new type of recreation-civic-commercial center as a part of Beloit 2000.
Performance-based discretion	Woodstock proposes to the EPA a measured results-based cleanup of a contaminated landfill as a substitute for the agency-prescribed method, which would involve extensive monitoring and reporting.

Note: CDBG = Community Development Block Grants; ISTEA = Intermodal Surface Transportation Efficiency Act; SBA = US Small Business Administration; EPA = US Environmental Protection Agency; LDC = local development corporation; HUD = US Department of Housing and Urban Development.
Source: Agranoff and McGuire (2003, 70).

FIGURE 4.2   Vertical Collaborative Activities

Type of Activity	Example
Policymaking and Strategy Making	
Gain policymaking assistance	Garfield Heights regularly uses the planning and zoning expertise of the Cuyahoga County Planning Commission to update its master plan and revise its zoning codes, and for major site preparation issues.
Engage in formal partnership	LDCs are one of the most frequent forms of partnerships; an example is the Washington County Economic Growth Partnership, a nonprofit arrangement among the city of Salem, Washington County, the chamber of commerce, and the industrial community.
Engage in joint policymaking	Beloit city officials regularly meet with the chamber of commerce, local manufacturers, local developers, Beloit 2000 leaders, and BEDCOR officials in "strategic retreats" to formulate strategic economic development plans.
Consolidate policy effort	Ithaca regularly works with the Gratiot County government and neighboring cities through GGDI, its LDC, to formulate countywide economic development strategies. The combined group has written policies in business retention, business expansion, new business recruitment, and counseling and case supports for small business start-ups.
Resource Exchange	
Seek financial resources	Salem has financed several redevelopment projects by successfully tapping into Washington County's Economic Development Income Tax (EDIT). The city has been able to use EDIT to provide matching funds for numerous federal grants, for a downtown redevelopment project, and for a number of airport improvements.
Employ joint financial incentives	In a creative example of joint financing, Cincinnati initiated a three-way property exchange among the city, school district, and Hamilton County, enabling the school district to work out a stormwater utility debt of $1.7 million to the city. As a result, land in the Downtown–Over the Rhine historic district was made available for a regional shopping complex anchored by a large supermarket.
Contracted planning and implementation	Woodstock contracts with the McHenry County Planning Department for planning and zoning assistance, data gathering, and geographic information systems. It relies on the county health department to implement health inspection permits for septic tanks and wells.
Project-Based Work	
Partnership for a particular project	Beloit 2000 is a major public-private partnership that plans and raises funds and also acquires property necessary to conduct this riverfront revitalization project. The city of Beloit allocates staff time to a Beloit technical steering committee for project operations.
Seek technical resources	Salem relies on a variety of sources for technical support beyond that which is provided locally by its LDC staff member: staff of its regional planning agency, its multicity grants and representation development corporation, and staff and advisers from various Indiana agencies.

Note: LDC = local development corporation; BEDCOR = Beloit Economic Development Corporation; GGDI = Greater Gratiot Development Incorporated.
Source: Agranoff and McGuire (2003, 71).

FIGURE 4.3   Horizontal Collaborative Activities

working together on local policies or forming partnerships with other entities, exchanging or seeking financing from others at the community level, and working on specific projects.

In these examples the practices identified are based on what cities are engaging in collaboratively to advance their economies. Although the core of these collaborative moves falls primarily around grants and financing, it also includes regulations and actions related to contracts. The specifics, however, are less important than identifying key activities that break down collaborative management. Collaborative management begins and builds links and often more regular networked relationships through transactions that seek information and interpretation; deal with purpose-inhibiting rules, standards, and regulations; bring in other entities to form partnerships or adapt local policy; and pool funding.

Leveraging Grants: First-Order Collaboration in Development

Grants (and perhaps loans, revenue bonds, tax exemptions, and other financing mechanisms) from national and intermediate-level (state and regional) governments are increasingly less conditional and/or negotiable (Eisinger 1988). For example, in local economic development they almost always require that the local development unit (e.g., a city government) arrange for some form of local financial participation in the project. As Ross and Friedman (1991, 133) maintain, contemporary governance utilizes leverage and engagement techniques to attract private nonprofit and for-profit resources to blend with public resources. This moves intermediate-level and national government agencies "toward abandoning their direct supplier role in favor of approaches that encourage other organizations to commit their resources to supply the good or service in demand."

Leveraging opportunities often require that local officials and managers be creative in reading, understanding, and using discretion when dealing with grants. For example, the US Community Development Block Grant (CDBG) was amended in the 1970s to allow flexible fund access. Cities may "draw down" or receive their annual allotment in a single lump sum, with which they can establish a revolving loan fund in a private financial institution. These funds can be loaned at below-market interest rates as a way of providing start-up funding. The City of Seattle used its entire allotment for one private developer and gained nearly $1 million in interest for its community development budget. The City of Dayton convinced the US Department of Housing and Urban Development to agree to let it draw three years of advance funding for its Urban Development Action Grant (UDAG) (now eliminated) as a grant program, which was put in a fund for interest buy-downs, guaranteeing developers an interest rate lower than the market's, thus reducing the cost of downtown development. Dayton is one of the few cities that continues to use its long-standing UDAG fund. CDBG also now allows local governments to issue guarantee notes or other obligations that may amount to three times the sum of the recipient's grant allotment. The revenues from these notes may be used to finance property acquisition for redevelopment. These are among hundreds of examples of how local development units can work together with other financing agents to use creative intergovernmental grant opportunities to move projects forward collaboratively.

To successfully leverage such development resources as grants, one must first have a broad knowledge of the various financing opportunities and arrangements. Once the strategic opportunities chosen are matched with the potential funding source, clarification may be required by contacting the granting agency official to ensure that the manager is on the right track. Next, interlocal collaboration will need to be undertaken, perhaps with the local development corporation, community development corporation, private entrepreneur, or nonprofit organization. These contacts may lead to local private lending institutions. At this point, the grant will need to be combined with local leverage partners. Next, contacts with state government officials will need to be made to move the project to the next step, authorization and approval. Leveraging along these lines has become a very central collaborative activity.

PUBLIC CONTRACTING

For a public agency to contract means that it enters into a business arrangement with an NGO or private entity whereby, in exchange for money, certain products or services are delivered to and/or for the public agency (Keleman 2002, 282). As is explored here, this is a fiduciary arrangement but it has considerable collaborative potential, particularly contracts for the purchase of services. Such contracts involve agreements under which "a government agency enlists a private organization to deliver a service to an eligible group of 'clients' in exchange for money" (DeHoog 2002, 320). A great deal of attention has been given to government contracts, which are seen by many as a panacea for the ills of bureaucratic service delivery and for cost reduction. Although not the focus of this discussion, Johnston and Romzek (2010, 397) make clear that there is a gap between the market theories that drive contracting costs and the realities on the ground. Implementing contracts calls into question aspects of the contracting panacea: "Thus, American governments have overreached, relying excessively on contracts in general, extending contracting to new unsuitable service areas, and undermining contract oversight capacity within the public bureaucracy." Contract management therefore has become an important public management issue; however, their relational dimensions are of major concern here.

Contracting for the purchase of services is of considerable interest today because of its extensive use in health services for the poor, social services, migrant worker services, mental health, mental illness and developmental disabilities, employment and training, counseling, and many other program areas. As demonstrated, contracting for services is often the arrangement of choice at the end stage of client contact for many grant programs, for example, Medicaid and senior citizens' services. As a result, such "outsourcing" is therefore of great current interest (Goldsmith and Eggers 2004, 21; see also Cohen and Eimicke 2008; Van Slyke 2007; DeHoog 2002; Brown and Potoski 2004). The detailed hows and whats of different types of contracting will be left to these important contributions. It is important to note that the latest trend in the purchase of services is contingency fee contracts, whereby an outside firm is hired to increase different forms of revenue enhancement: recovered tax dollars, increased federal reimbursements, recapturing Medicaid overpayments, launching litigation, and finding energy reductions. Generally, the firms that hunt for such dollars work for a fee of from 10 to 20 percent of collections or savings (Barrett and Greene 2010, 47).

Many questions can be raised about these relationships. Here I identify a thoughtful set of issues raised by DeHoog (2002, 328), which are given in box 4.1, on the question of whether to contract. Such concerns related to competent providers, government oversight capacity, and legality are among the more important "decisional questions" from both parties' perspectives that can help us understand the interactive nature of contracting.

The contract itself is at the heart of forging the relationship. Goldsmith and Eggers (2004, 185) conclude that the process of effectively integrating partners needs to become a core competency of government when most work is delivered through these contractors. Some years ago, a venerable set of contract principles was articulated by Wedel (1983, 190):

1. The legal base—it will be necessary for the service contract to conform to the various federal, state, and local laws and regulations.
2. The client management responsibilities—the role of management and administrators for the two partners and the contractual agreement must be made clear. This includes the role of the contractor for responsibility in assigning, reviewing, and terminating each individual client's services.
3. It is equally important to clarify the role of the sponsoring agency in terms of administrative review and monitoring of the program involved and the contracting procedure.

4. The service to be provided—to the extent possible, services should be defined in terms of intended client outcomes.

5. Contracts in which performance standards are expected will require additional specification of quality standards and the means for determining whether these standards have actually been met.

6. The unit of service cost structure—units of service and costing for the units should be spelled out in detail and specified in the contract.

7. Program and fiscal audit—procedures and criteria for the monitoring process should be as detailed as possible, clearly delineating who actually does the monitoring and auditing and under what certification requirements.

8. A special area of concern is deciding whether service delivery conforms to agreed-on plans. Both the sponsoring and contracting organizations share in this concern: the public sponsor in assuring constituents that the terms of the contract are being carried out, and the contractor in guaranteeing a continued capacity to engage the service delivery market.

Wedel's list of concerns underscores the basic framework of the contracting relationship from legal to shared management obligations (also see Padovani and Young 2012, chap. 8).

Contracts need to be managed as a process that goes beyond the formal drafting and signing of a document. Cohen and Eimicke (2008, chap. 7) identify twenty problems that can emerge in the process of operating by contract. They not only include problems related to the letting of contracts, but also communication problems, contractor internal management issues, government management issues, and political challenges surrounding government–contractor interactions. It is quite clear from their list that to contract involves constant lines of communication, direction and interaction, staffing and training, and issues of politics and conflicts

Box 4.1   Contracting Considerations

- Whether competition and choice among agencies are present in the service environment
- Whether reputable agencies are available with specialized expertise, good administrative staff, and trusting relationships with clients and/or community
- Whether the government has enough information/expertise to understand the service, agencies, and client populations
- Whether the government and contract agencies have sufficient resources to operate the contracting process effectively
- Whether any legal or administrative prohibitions about this tool exist

Source: Summarized by permission from "Purchase-of-Service Contracting," by Ruth Hoogland De-Hoog (2002, 327).

of interest. Appendix C documents the elements that Romzek and Johnston (2002) identify as the most important challenges in contracting for services. They raise new and important issues about the *relationship* aspect, such as the availability of competition, contractor capacities, funder assessment ability, shifting risks to contractors, and political considerations. In addition they raise questions concerning the advisability of contracting out services and the theoretical rationale for contracting. Most important are issues of the need for cooperation within complex sets of relationships (Fernandez 2009).

RELATIONSHIPS IN CONTRACTING

In the political discussions over contracting relationships, public agency managers are warned by some scholars to treat contractors as "treacherous thieves" and by others to treat them as "trusted partners." Academics normally call for some form of "relational contracting," which is grounded in both firmness of expectations and specificity along with trust and reciprocity between the government and its partner. The problem, argue Brown, Potoski, and Van Slyke (2008), is that this type of advice is not only contradictory but also misses the mark. The missing element is often the need to make a distinction between simple or product-oriented contracting and complex or service-oriented contracting. The former can be easily and carefully spelled out, whereas others that involve publicly sponsored services are hard to spell out and difficult to verify. With regard to complex contracts, they conclude that

> complex products are challenging targets for contracting. Markets for complex products tend to be "thin" (there are few buyers and few sellers), which means the market provides little information about the product and its price, quality and quantity tradeoffs. It is consequently difficult (and expensive) to define precise terms of exchange and ambiguous contract terms are often left to be negotiated as the product is produced and delivered. . . . The result can be a risky combination of a government under-informed about the product it is buying who is contracting with a vendor unconstrained by competitive market pressures and able to exploit contract loopholes and ambiguities for its own advantage. (Brown, Potoski, and Van Slyke 2008, 5)

In this process they conclude that the fruits of trust and cooperation in contracting are highest for complex products—and so, too, are the downside risks when trust breaks down and contracts fail.

The two most basic conceptual approaches to the contracting relationship are called (1) agency theory, based on the general idea that the government funder is the "principal" and the contractor is their "agent"; and (2) stewardship theory, based on the idea of mutual goals and high levels of trust. It is important for the collaborating manager to understand these ideas. Figure 4.4, summarized from an empirical study of the two approaches in social services contracting (Van Slyke 2007), highlights each. Agency theory is clearly control oriented, premised on the assumption that there is goal divergence between principal and agent, and tight controls and monitoring need to be imposed to eliminate situations of contractors pursuing opportunistic behavior. Stewardship assumes more of a joint goal-orientation approach, with greater mutual trust, and it places lesser emphasis on strict provisions and monitoring, and assumes more or less mutual agreement on process and goals.

AGENCY THEORY	STEWARDSHIP THEORY
Main Theme	**Main Theme**
Goal incongruence: Assumes goal divergence based on self-interested rational actors. Initial disposition is to distrust. Control-oriented management philosophy. Theoretical assumptions are from economics.	Goal alignment: Mutual goals and objectives achieved through initial trust disposition. Involvement-oriented management philosophy. Theoretical assumptions derived from organizational behavior, psychology, and sociology.
Tenets	**Tenets**
Use of incentives and sanctions to foster goal alignment: • Assign risk to the agent to ensure goal compliance • Monitoring • Reward systems • Use of bonding threat to contractor's reputation	Empowers contractor's workers through: • Responsibility • Autonomy • Shared culture and norms • Personal power and trust • Other governance mechanisms
Applications √ Eliminate opportunistic behavior √ Provide the level of incentives and sanctions which reduce the threat of information asymmetry √ Correct, through specific contract requirements, for asset specificity and moral hazard √ Uses reputation as an incentive and sanction √ Ensure goal alignment	**Applications** √ Goal alignment based on shared goals and trust √ Reward workers through nonpecuniary mechanisms √ Reduces the threat of opportunistic behavior through responsibility and autonomy √ Reduces the threat to the organization of information asymmetries, moral hazards, and asset specificity √ Reduces dependence on legal contracts to enforce behavior √ Uses reputation as an incentive and sanction

Source: Summarized by permission from "Agents or Stewards: Government Nonprofit Social Service Contracting Relationship," by David Van Slyke (2007, 167).

FIGURE 4.4   Theoretical Tenets and Applications of Agency and Stewardship Theories

Van Slyke's (2007, 182–83) study of social services contracting reveals the presence of both models in the real world, and he calls for a better understanding of relational contracting, perhaps for some sort of principal–steward relations in contracting. First, public managers in contract relationships initially act consistently vis-à-vis agency theory. The initial disposition and desire of nonprofit executive directors in contract relationships are consistent with stewardship theory. It turns out that a lack of financial incentives and an inconsistent use of monitoring are incongruous with agency theory. The use of trust and reputation is clearly consistent with the tenets of stewardship but may also be consistent with an evolved principal–agent relationship. In practice the two theories used in concert are complementary. Stewardship theory captures the state of what actually emerged and aligned what principal–agent contract management practices might look like between government and nonprofit organizations.

Van Slyke concludes that the contextual characteristics that color much of the application of public management contract practices are not well accounted for in either theory. The theories only explain part of the government–nonprofit relationship: "More work is needed on the evolved principal-agent relationships and on the development of principal–steward relations. The variables that constitute the set of contextual conditions are a very important set of factors to be considered and controlled for if these theories are used to explain how government manages its social services contracting relationships with nonprofits. In this respect, the line between an evolved principal–agent and principal–steward relationship is less precise than desired" (Van Slyke 2007, 183). In this research, the contract relationships examined suggest the importance of working toward an evolved principal–agent relationship. The empirical work of Fernandez on nearly a thousand city–contractor relationships, particularly on the importance of trust, adds credence to this conclusion. It is clear that contracting is a relational interactive process that has elements of looking out for gaming or thievery along with elements of trusted partnerships. In this respect, both the mechanics of contract management and network-oriented integrated service markets are collaborative management goals.

TOWARD NETWORKED THIRD-PARTY CONTRACTS

The evolution and frequency of complex contracting for the purchase of services means that whichever way a contracting model leans, whether agency or steward, there is a situation of joint production among many actors for the provision of government services that may be inadequately specified and for clientele groups that may have varying levels of service receiving motivation and acceptance for service intervention. For example, many recipients of substance abuse or mental health services do not want to admit that they have problems and are reluctant service clients. Some intellectual and developmental disabilities families are reluctant to deinstitutionalize their family member, for fear that their needs may not be met in the community or that it will place a greater personal burden on them to support their disabled family member. Some welfare (i.e., Temporary Assistance for Needy Families) clients resist education and training that will move them off income support, for fear of losing health benefits, child care, or even their housing support. Thus, in addition to difficulties in specifying contract provisions and contractors that game the system, reluctant clients need to be factored into any process that compounds the relational contracting process.

Despite the myriad obstacles, managers on all sides of contracts are pressured to work together to build the kind of "relational" contract models that have been identified, which fall somewhere between the agency and stewardship approaches. Relational models involve agencies and contractor providers in long-term negotiated relationships that involve trust, discretion, joint problem solving, and information exchange, and that thus contribute to mutual goal alignment and reduce measurement difficulties and intractability in service provision. Trust is built through extensive interaction and involvement focused on communicating one another's goals and approaches to service intervention, which entails investing in front-end transaction costs that build alignment.

The most important front-end collaborative investment process costs involve emergent types of human resource management. Managers who work in networked contracting require training on contract design, solicitation, and management, through which they learn to understand the trade-offs among service, client, and agent characteristics, along with market competitiveness. Training is also needed on how and when to involve contractors in several joint activities:

- formulation of goals
- agreeing on objectives
- quality standards
- reporting mechanisms understood by and agreed to by all parties
- modes of oversight that meet substantive and legal aims
- evaluation that can indicate service effectiveness, accountability, and program success.

Each of these appears to be open to joint development by the funder and contractor, and entails formulating a set of potential training goals.

The process brings out the call for new skills, that is, persons who can advance both public purpose and relational implementation. At a minimum, contract management requires new and different, some would say nontechnical, skills. They include:

- bargaining and negotiation ability
- ability at communicating policy and program goals
- working with aligning contractor goals with agency goals
- conducting oversight activities that include contract and program details
- providing technical assistance, on the contract and on the service, and
- evaluating program and client outcomes (Brown and Potoski 2004; Cohen and Eimicke 2008; Van Slyke 2007).

These are all obviously various forms of collaboration-based skills.

With regard to implementation, Goldsmith and Eggers (2004, 171) conclude that those who work in this area require a broad knowledge of processes and organizations and a deep appreciation of the importance of open information for a continuously learning organization (the focus of chapter 8 of this volume). Virtually all the skills that contract overseers need are closely related to contemporary management in the conductive agency. Cohen and Eimicke (2008, 213) capture the overall picture cogently:

> Effective contract management requires skill at the use of all the tools of standard and innovative management: Managers must understand human resource, financial, organizational, information, performance, strategic, political and media management. They also need experience with quality management, benchmarking, reengineering, and team management. But the effective contract manager must do more. In addition to deploying those tools in problem solving, today's effective public manager must learn how to elicit contract bids that result in appropriate and well-priced services and goods. They must learn to monitor contractor performance and write contracts that allow them to develop informal networks that reach deep into contractor organizations, just as they have done within their own organizations.

With respect to the development of networks and monitoring, Goldsmith and Eggers (2004, 119) point to the need for integrators to establish communication channels, coordinate activities between network participants, share knowledge, align values and incentives, build trust, and overcome cultural differences. Thus, they are on target in that contracting includes but goes well beyond the mechanics of agreements between principals and agents discussed above to illustrate the interactive process between agency and contractor.

NONCONTRACTUAL COLLABORATIVE OUTCOMES: REACHING MULTIPARTY AGREEMENTS

To the extent that multiparty collaboration leads to a positive result—added public value—it normally is preceded by some form of multilateral agreement. The multiorganizational parties at some point need to reach understandings that signify joint activity. It has been demonstrated in chapter 2 that not all collaborative agreements lead to the formation of networks, as is often assumed in the literature. Within the broad range identified above in figure 2.4, it is clear that at some point all interacting parties will seek to reach some form(s) of agreement by decision through many different mechanisms.

While examining decision making in networks, Klijn and Koppenjan (2007, 177–78) identify three types of decisions: *network compositions*, which focus on changing or influencing the composition of the network; *network outcomes*, which try to influence the incentive structure so that actors will behave differently; and, *network interactions*, which influence the rules and processes that facilitate the ongoing collaboration. Agreement does not exclude any of these three types, but the second of the three outcomes is most central to the analysis of how to reach collaborative decisions.

A long-standing body of literature on community planning and development lays out templates for reaching collaborative agreement (Bacow 1995; Brody 1982; Bryson and Crosby 1992; Bryson, Crosby, and Stone 2006; Chrislip and Larson 1994). Among the more important challenges in reaching agreements are the competing organizational logics that are brought into the collaborative venture. Thus Bryson and Crosby (2008, 69) suggest that "logics compete because actions, processes, norms, and structures that are seen as legitimate from the vantage point of one in situational logic may be seen as less legitimate or even illegitimate from the perspective of another logic." These competing logics can be overcome with thought given to several elements of collaborative processes that should be present at the outset. Chrislip and Larson (1994, 52–54) identified ten such elements, distilled from fifty-two projects of the National Civic League Collaborative:

1. Timely initiation and the readiness of some stakeholders to act.
2. The stakeholder groups involved were broadly represented, and actors could speak for their groups.
3. The involvement of many participants from several sectors.
4. A process seen as credible and open, where many groups felt free to participate.

5. Commitments and/or involvement of high-level/visible leaders.
6. Support from public agency decision makers, and leading community organization leaders.
7. Attempts to overcome mistrust and skepticism.
8. Strong process leadership was evident.
9. Interim successes sustained momentum and credibility.
10. There was a shift to broader concerns over time.

These lessons of experience help frame decision-making processes as the serious work of the collaborative enterprise takes place. In addition, Vandeventer and Mandell (2007, 62) indicate the importance of setting preconditions for increasing the stakes and risks over time; of investing time in the process; of developing new habits of thinking; and of confronting the unavoidable and ultimately beneficial importance of raising, confronting, and working through difficult political, cultural, and style differences between partners.

Some useful steps toward reaching effective outcomes in collaborative environmental management are found in the cases studied by Wondolleck and Yaffee (2000, chap. 6). They incorporated the following process elements: (1) involving the public early and often throughout the decision-making process; (2) deep or nontoken involvement of diverse interests in decision making, looking for partner buy-in; (3) consensus-based decision making, in many cases requiring approval by all representatives; (4) inclusiveness, including initially hostile interests; (5) leadership that is effective in facilitating group dynamics; (6) meetings that are managed so that they are as productive and efficient as possible; (7) institutionalizing agreements by creating structures, appointing people, or fostering ongoing opportunities for interaction that build on earlier outcomes; (8) ensuring that the involved parties view the collaborative outcomes as important; (9) ensuring that the process is self-sustaining; and (10) recognizing that in many cases public agencies cannot delegate their statutory authority to collaborative groups and that the decision making that affects public resources must be subjected to broader public involvement. In addition any resistance, as Brody (1982, 128) maintains, will need to be overcome by various forms of negotiation.

Barbara Gray's (1989) groundbreaking work on collaboration lays out a practical sequence for negotiation. Her steps include a clear delineation between the three phases of problem setting, direction setting, and implementation. The process that is outlined emphasizes "touching all stakeholders bases"; incorporating a broad range of views; the importance of leadership, research, and fact-finding; negotiated processes; and multiple agreement points. Unlike other attempts to focus on process, Gray includes the implementation process, a function that is subsequently emphasized here but is often taken for granted. She suggests that agreements can fall apart after they are reached unless deliberate attention is given to carrying out the function (Gray 1989, 86). Overall, process is key—"bond-faith efforts to undertake collaboration are often derailed because the parties are not skilled in the process and because insufficient attention is given to designing and managing a constructive process" (Gray 1989, 93).

The agreement processes suggested can be understood as well by looking at decision processes in fourteen collaborative networks from the perspective of the participants in the process.[1] Typical collaborative decisions are brokered, as Bardach (1998) concludes, as the partners work at achieving forms of consensus through joint exploration and discussion until agreement is at hand. Then another issue is brought to the table. One state official in the network study described the process this way: "Proposals are made by participating agencies; the staff there researches the proposal and does a market feasibility study; the report is distributed electronically before the meeting; at the meeting, discussion is held and questions are asked; if there are too many questions we table the issue until more research can be undertaken; in between meetings, phone calls, and one-to-one discussions ensue; the issue is brought back to the table; and if there are a lot of head nods in the yes direction, we consider it to be approved." A decision process like this, with lots of brokering, is followed in most of the networks, although normally "staff" research tends to be by the actual partners—that is, by the agency administrators themselves, who go back to their own programs and work with their home agency colleagues and later bring the agency-derived research results to the network.

One partner described the network decision process as similar to "a rural community meeting." "You get the people out, connect them, let them identify the issues, and let them come up with a solution over time." Another said that beyond setting priorities on work, and allowing the staff to do some studies, "we let consensus rise to the top." Another said, "We have Robert's Rules in our by-laws, but only use them after we have reached agreement." Another network chair said: "Parliamentary procedure rules won't work—as a last resort when we are near consensus we may resort to informal *Robert's Rules* to move things along."

The learning process is very clearly and directly a parallel component of collaborative decisions: "Once we agree that a problem is an issue we care to look into, we study it and discuss the results before any action is taken." "We try to get on the same technical page if we possibly can. That means someone or a work group has to study a problem, then we discuss it." "Our Technology Transfer Committee is charged with finding feasible small town water solutions used elsewhere; they then become the basis of Steering Committee discussions." "The Transportation Technical Committee is charged not only with looking at the feasibility of projects,

BOX 4.2   Six Predecision Learning Modes

1. Group discussion, following a loose format, where legal, technical, and financial information is converted into decision knowledge.
2. Political negotiations, utilizing government decision makers within and beyond the collaborative body process.
3. Application of technology or preestablished formats that can be converted to decision rules, e.g., market projections, utility rate paybacks, loan payback rates.
4. Use of preestablished formulaic processes to prepare partners for decisions, e.g., rotating awards, decision rules.
5. Utilization of data-driven means of producing decision-making techniques, e.g., transportation/traffic models, sewage treatment capacity.
6. Collaborative decision work laboratory, with electronic decision support software.

Source: Agranoff (2007, 146–47).

but to advance state-of-the-art [transportation] programming to the Policy Committee agenda." These quotations from the discussants highlight the centrality of making the network a learning entity in the sense of Senge's (1990) learning organization. Box 4.2 identifies six different predecision learning modes employed in the network study.

The typical collaborative decision process involves joint learning that leads to a brokered consensus. Because the effort to reach a joint agreement is self-organizing and nonhierarchical, the parties approach interactive decision processes carefully, whether to adopt an agenda or to take some form of action. Why the trepidation over parliamentary procedure or even in making hard and just decisions? Several reasons are apparent. First, these entities are not always decision-making bodies. They more frequently exist to *exchange* information and explore knowledge and become aware of potential adjustments that the participating actors can make in their own organizations (Alter and Hage 1993). Second, most partners come to the table on a *voluntary* basis, and the nature of this participation implies some form of shared participation in decisions. Third, the partners come together from very *different organizational cultures*, and the risk of clashing styles is great if not managed. Fourth, in collaborative structures decisions come as a result of these *shared learning* experiences, in which the *product is the creative solution* that emanates from the discussion (Agranoff and McGuire 2001). Fifth, decisions that create winners and losers, such as most zero-sum situations, discourage involvement and *contribution*. These concerns make clear why so few of the networks highlighted in this section engaged in the type of parliamentary decisions that membership organizations normally utilize. They clearly do not experience someone up the hierarchy to make the type of decisions that settle disputes in bureaucratic organizations.

The results of decisions and/or agreements—that is, collaborative outcomes—are sometimes written up as formal documents, or they are at least reworded as meeting resolutions or in meeting minutes: "Variously referred to as memoranda of understanding, compacts, charters, relational contracts or, simply, agreements, these documents reflect the decisions made on the range of matters discussed" (Vandeventer and Mandell 2007, 46). They can include the reasons for such agreements and outcomes; priorities; roles, responsibilities, and partner commitments; basic operational structure; role of the staff; funding and other resource commitments; and modes of assessment and accountability. To document agreements, until revised, is to create a continuing reference point for network or collaborative undertakings, enhance the collaborative body's legitimacy, and otherwise presents the effort to external publics. They are clear important precursors to any operational collaboration.

THE IMPLEMENTATION IMPERATIVE

Too often collaborative projects excel at convening stakeholders and in arriving at agreements but fall short at the implementation stage. Just as grants and contracts require successful implementation, network and/or collaborative decisions need to focus on carrying out reached agreements. A study by Bryson and colleagues (2009, 8, 23) of a Minnesota cross-sector collaboration on reducing traffic congestion reveals the importance of, among other success factors, developing effective processes, structures, and governance mechanisms at all stages, including at implementation. Here are three important insights from their conclusions:

- In contrast to the project formulation stage, more hierarchical processes and structures are likely to be necessary to implement agreed-on projects. Existing hierarchies and accountability structures can make implementation flow smoothly, although an interorganizational coordination mechanism will still be needed.
- Managing the planning and implementation phases of a cross-sector collaboration may call for spatial and temporal organizational ambidexterity. For example, sometimes fluidity and sometimes stability are required of the same organizations; sometimes informality and sometimes formality are required; and so on. To do both requires a kind of ambidexterity, mean-

ing doing different things in different places or at different times. A more fluid process was used in the Urban Partnership Agreement for planning Phase I, whereas a more hierarchical and ordered process was used in the implementation phases. This is temporal separation. Organizations like the Minnesota Department of Transportation and the Minnesota Metropolitan Council tried to keep stable as much as they could, while being more open to doing things differently in other parts of their work. This is spatial separation.

- When leaders seek to foster cross-sector collaboration within a complex intergovernmental system with various concentrations of power (e.g., US Department of Transportation, the governor, Minnesota Department of Transportation, Minnesota Metropolitan Council), tight timelines can foster innovation by forcing them to go around or bend existing rules and normal procedures, but can also ruffle feathers and require attention to go through channels, work out missing details, and repair relationships when normality returns.

Once the course of action was agreed upon, the project steering group became more formalized, roles and responsibilities were allocated, and operational and technical teams from all affected units met regularly. One participant related that although "coordination has to start at the top [but] to deliver something that's really truly coordinated, it needs to make it down to the technical level where you have champions" (Bryson et al. 2009, 22). The tone of meetings, and the report from the authors, shifted from information exchanges to operational issues like tracking construction projects and usage patterns, data gathering, inputs and expenditures, legal questions and barriers, program assessments, and the like. These issues are the main concerns of implementation of collaborative agreements.

One of the venerable manuals on services coordination (Weiner 1990, chap. 16) suggests that integrated program administration involves three overlapping joint program functions—design, operation, and evaluation. Design functions can begin with a systems analysis, which describes the logic of how the program will operate, and sets out individual agency and agency staff responsibilities as well as an action plan for achieving goals. Under operations, organization representatives must work out procedures to manage program activities, budgetary needs, and technical assistance requirements by reemploying a lead agency, a joint planning body, or a combination. In some cases such integrated programs share management responsibilities by hiring a coordinator to handle day-to-day activities who is not an employee of any one agency, while different agencies assume primary responsibilities for their aspect of the shared program, together forming a management team. Joint budgeting may or may not be possible, but most often creative approaches to budgeting responsibilities, given resource limitations and potentially restrictive funding rules, including local in-kind contributions, volunteer support, and donations of human resources and money. Finally, evaluation functions can focus on the aims in the systems analysis, particularly those items that best serve the interorganizational steering body as they oversee the program, some of which will come from existing (in-agency) data and some from new data generated (see also Rossi, Gilmartin, and Dayton 1982, chap. 5, esp. 456). Of course, any techniques and mechanisms that change over time are energized when they are joined to meet a situation-based problem or need, which is identified by Weiner as *dynamic contingency*.

CONCLUSION

Clearly there is much more to say about how to obtain and manage grants and contracts, how they can be used to advance a jurisdiction's purposes, and the thicket of interactive politics, both interlocally and intergovernmentally. The politics and management, and the place of contracts in governmental programming or the ability to use contracts to achieve program aims, are a significant part of the larger discussion on the use of these important governance tools. By the same token, collaborated multiparty agreements have filled volumes and many manuals. My purpose here is to place these important collaborative devices along a continuum of processed collaboration along with network-building arrangements.

The focus in this chapter thus has been on the collaborative or joint process elements of grants, contracts, and multiparty agreements. They are tools that by their very nature imply important interactive dimensions. In the previous chapter I identified core and cross-organization work, particularly with regard to conductive agencies. Most of the work of grantor or funder agencies is within their core activities: to secure funding, establish program parameters, make awards, transact accounting and auditing funds, establish agency mission and goals, and be accountable to the political leadership. But an increasing amount of grant work is outside the agency and across boundaries: to negotiate awards, interpret and inform about aims and rules, offer technical assistance on partnerships, find leverage funds, and build networks. The same would be true with regard to the core work of contracting agencies, where similar core activities plus contract negotiation and approval are included.

Meanwhile, grant recipients and contractors are at both ends of boundary-spanning activity, where they negotiate awards and contracts, interpret standards and rules, deal with audits, conduct inquiries, engage in forming partnerships, receive technical assistance, participate in networks, and so on. Although not always clearly understood, a great deal of "total program time" is consumed between the sponsoring agency and the delivery agents, inasmuch as these processes have significant collaborative management dimensions.

To reach multiparty agreements in situations across the boundaries of organizations is different from hierarchical organization "divisional adjustment" through hierarchical decision making and parliamentary procedural styles of decision making. The former can involve much interaction and discussion, but ultimately someone high up in the hierarchy must make or approve the decision. Of course, voting on the basis of one person, one vote is the parliamentary style in both government and nongovernmental voluntary organizations. Collaborative agreements are more based on broad participation, exchange and learning, mutual discovery, and most important general agreements among multiple parties. Working in the public and NGO sector now requires heavy doses of multiparty agreement making. Familiarity with its process elements is essential.

NOTE

1. This section is based on Agranoff (2007, 43–48, 111–18), where all the quotations in the section originally appeared.

CHAPTER 5

Managing Agency Connections

THE CITY GOVERNMENT OF Beloit, Wisconsin, was heavily involved in improving its rundown riverfront commercial and industrial area in the early 1990s. This initiative involved a number of multipartner real estate development projects that were bundled into Beloit 2000, a comprehensive riverfront revitalization effort. Among other financing tools, the city chose to access state-authorized tax increment financing (TIF), which meant that it then had to manage many interactive transactions, at least more than twenty, with other governments and with NGOs. TIF allows a city to designate all the anticipated increased property tax revenue that will result from a development project in a designated geographical area to secure tax increment bonds that in turn finance the project's supportive components—land acquisition, property rehabilitation, road improvements, building construction, sewerage expansion, and related capital improvements. Cities can create TIF districts in blighted areas and, after a baseline assessment, hold the valuation constant and use the incremental increase in value to retire bonds, usually over a twenty-year period. A TIF district thus assures private investors that their property taxes will be used to pay for project infrastructure needs and allows municipalities to circumvent tax limitations and sometimes voter approval of capital expenditures (Man 2001).

The City of Beloit engaged in this protracted TIF effort in cooperation with its local development entity, the Beloit Economic Development Corporation (BEDCOR), a joint effort of the city government; the Township of Beloit; the border city of South Beloit, Illinois; and private organizations, particularly the Beloit Area Chamber of Commerce. The project's principal players included staff members from the City of Beloit city manager's office and the city's community development authority (CDA), and BEDCOR's industrial recruiter.

Beloit's engagement imperative for the Beloit 2000 project featured managerial contacts that included private developers, a newly created "development authority" in the blighted area, state government agencies, other local jurisdictions, a tax valuation contractor, a financial consultant, various site improvement contractors, and the TIF redevelopment district's bondholders. The project process began with various site development consultations with the target area's existing and prospective businesses and one large manufacturer, which particularly included an explanation of the TIF process. Then the city's CDA drafted a redevelopment plan that included boundaries and planned site improvements. At this point the city's development team began to engage in discussions regarding approval with the pertinent state agency, the Wisconsin Economic Development Administration. This led the city council to approve the district boundaries, which legally created the tax increment district and established a district that was quasi-independent of the City of Beloit (i.e., it was a separate taxing jurisdiction). In the next step the CDA, in consultation with property developers and the city attorney, wrote an eligibility study to meet all requirements under Wisconsin law. Then this study was sent to the state attorney general's office for legal approval, including certification that the riverfront project would not be feasible without the TIF incentives. The state then designated the project area as a twenty-year TIF district. At this point the BEDCOR recruiter held meetings and discussions with existing and prospective businesses and one manufacturer on the final parameters of the TIF district and the kinds of infrastructure assistance they could expect.

The most difficult aspect followed, when the city manager's office, the CDA, and BEDCOR representatives held a series of meetings with Rock County (in which the city is located), the Beloit School District, and the community college district to review the process whereby their property tax receivables would be frozen for the TIF area, along with that of the city. About the same time, a financial estimate contractor was engaged to determine the "freeze" level of taxes for the city, county, school district, and the other jurisdictions, that is, the baseline valuation. At this point the City of Beloit was able to direct the tax increase payments to finance the project. The city government did this by authorizing the newly created re-development authority to issue tax increment bonds in lieu of general obligation bonds, in consultation with project financial advisers, who in turn conveyed the valuation data to a private bond firm in New York, which entered the municipal bond market.

Then there were hundreds of engaged interactions between the CDA and the contractors that performed the improvements, which were "front-funded" by the bond revenues and will be paid back during the TIF's twenty years with the property tax increases. Finally, the CDA and the city manager's office continues to engage in periodic consultations with state officials regarding allowable improvements in the project area and one expansion, and, most important, periodic consultations with Beloit's overlapping county, school district, township, and college jurisdictions regarding the fiscal impact of the freeze and the possibility of pro rata sharing of the tax increments during the TIF effort's second decade (Agranoff and McGuire 2003; www.ci.beloit.wi.us).

Whereas this process appears to be a uniquely involved and multistep one, it is in fact typical of agency–partner connections. The City of Beloit opted for a single economic development effort that required sequences and overlapping transactional moves that in turn triggered the need for cooperation by multiple entities on many fronts. TIF is only one of sixty-plus collaborative development approaches of its type (Agranoff and McGuire 2003, chap. 6). It demonstrates how a conductive agency like the Beloit CDA today needs to form a partnership with an organization like BEDCOR to manage numerous interactions. As the Beloit case illustrates, a city government must engage in a series of transactions inside the governmental community and with a series of NGOs, and beyond TIF for other projects and development approaches.

In other policy and program areas, when the nongovernmental sector is not directly involved, a series of government-to-government transactions may still be required. In transportation planning, for example, the nation's 381 metropolitan planning organizations (MPOs) involve layers of federal, state, and local government officials who must develop areawide perspectives on the use of area federal funds and address the long-range needs of the broader community (GAO 2009). This process involves layers of political and technical representatives, along with rather sophisticated travel demand models and consultations with area communities. Ultimately, it involves a host of partners in metropolitan areas' local governments and, at some point beyond project authorization, the contractors they hire that plan, engineer, and build.

The other face of the conductive public agency outlined in chapter 3, of course, involves its interlocutors. Without counterpart public agencies and NGOs, there is nothing to conduct. A country's most nettlesome problems cannot be solved without some aspect of complementary behavior on behalf of implementing governments and NGOs. For instance homeland security does not begin with the federal Department of Homeland Security but with a series of first responders—police, fire, ambulance companies, health providers, clinics, hospitals, local government emergency coordinators, and state officials. All these agents work before emergencies and disasters happen in preparation planning and training, then later during crises in services, and of course afterward in mitigation. Likewise foreign intelligence is spread over about twenty federal agencies—the State Department, Defense Department, Central Intelligence Agency, Treasury Department, Federal Bureau of Investigation, to name a few. In many situations the various intelligence entities need to coordinate their work, along with investigative work by state and local police forces, not to speak of private sources, to fully understand a particular case or impending crisis. Rural development is almost never situated in any one agency in a state government but is spread over economic development, agriculture, university-based extension services, small business development centers at colleges, and state housing agencies, not to speak of several federal development and conservation program offices located in the state. These government agencies work with a host of external commodity associations, town associations, rural electric and telecommunications agencies, agribusiness, and many venture capitalists and investors. Home-based services and supported living for the mentally disabled are almost always publicly funded by federal and state governments, but the delivery system involves services (rehabilitation, housing, medical educational, social services, and income support) that are supplied by a host of mostly nonprofit NGOs and some for-profit providers that must work with government. In this case government is the funder, regulator, and auditor, but day-to-day operations and services are usually provided by these NGOs. In other words, one or more *conductor* agencies facilitate most of government's linkages to other *conductee* organizations, some along the intergovernmental chain (e.g., state and local governments) and many more to NGOs, nonprofits, and for-profits.

The focus of this chapter is this interaction between the conductive agency and the organizations with which it works in both the nonprofit and public agency sectors. How does one manage, if that is the right term, the external programs of the public agency that relies so heavily on other governments and NGOs? It is perhaps not a situation of one agency that manages in any top-down or downward directional sense but instead one of helping to organize a set of self-organizing and co-managing relationships. The first section of the chapter illustrates ordinary collaborative processes between public entities and NGOs by looking at connections in transportation planning as an example of ongoing collaboration and an example of protracted interaction through rather routine negotiations of the TIF process. Then a case study is provided of how such comanaging emerged between 1997 and 2005 as a unit of the Indiana government met with its NGO partners to create community alternatives for institutionalized intellectually disabled citizens. That is followed by an examination of how the tools of government (grants, contracts, loans) can be used for conductive relationships. Next, we explore interoperability, or collaboration carried one step deeper into a set of steps that involve reciprocal operations. Then we look at how knowledge management can be used to help a set of interacting organizations work together. This is followed by a look at how conductive organizations and their partners can move toward communities of practice. The chapter concludes with a profile of how "collaborarchies" can be used to bridge the work of the conductive agency and its interlocutors.

ROUTINES OF COLLABORATIVE ACTION

The discussion of intergovernmentalization in chapter 2 suggests that it has brought on literally thousands and thousands of potential and actual routines for transacting collaboratively. The Beloit TIF process described above and the protracted processing of Older Americans Act services illustrated in chapter 4 are prime examples. The need for non-project-based regular collaborative interaction is illustrated by looking at the funding of area-based transportation via MPOs. Under the Intermodal Surface Transportation Efficiency Act (ISTEA) of 1991 and its successor, MPOs are charged with developing long-range (twenty-year) transportation plans, short-range (four-year) transportation improvement programs, annual work programs, and public participation plans. An MPO—which comprises local elected officials (policy committees), local planning and engineering staff (technical support committees), and advisory bodies—must develop these plans in cooperation with its state transportation department, local mass transit and airport operators, land use entities, and the state environmental agency. Its planning and funding processes also require constant interaction with two entities within the US Department of Transportation, the Federal Highway Administration and the Federal Transit Authority (GAO 2009, 5–7).

The MPO process involves multiple levels and layers of officials charged with the task of somehow forging a coordinated metropolitan perspective. Figure 5.1 identifies these disparate actors for the Louisville-based, two-state Kentuckiana MPO. The MPO process can be illustrated with two excerpts from an article by Edner and McDowell (2002, 15, 19):

> The institutional integrity of the MPO is a major factor in the effectiveness of this federally defined decision-making process. There is a common perception that MPOs are independent entities with institutional autonomy and clout comparable to cities and counties when they deal with the states. Practically speaking, however, this is seldom true. The MPOs were created largely as a condition of federal aid, and they have only the powers granted to them under state statutes or other sources of their charters. The metropolitan planning process requirement was created in the early 1960s but was predominantly the responsibility of the states with participation from local officials. Designation of MPOs was required for the first time in the early 1970s. The MPO was to serve as a "forum," charged with developing a metropolitan consensus on transportation investments. Prior to ISTEA, however, transportation plans were not fiscally constrained. They could include (and usually did) many projects for which funding and implementation might never be achieved. Consequently, pre-ISTEA MPOs did not have to make tough decisions to prioritize and exclude projects. . . .

- *Transportation Policy Committee: chief elected officials of area local governments and council members:* Approve transportation improvements and long-range plans
- *Community Transportation Advisory Committees: bicycle, footpath, pedestrian, paratransit, pollution:* Provide advice on community concerns impacted by transportation planning
- *Transportation Technical Coordinating Committee: planning, engineering, legal, financial staff from local and state governments, transportation staff:* Exchange data, technical reviews, coordination and assistance; and serves as predecision body
- *Federal, regional, and state transportation and environment officials, including local transit authority, airport authority, air pollution attainment district:* Serve in technical, consultation, and advisory roles through the process for the US Transportation Equity Act for the 21st Century
- *Kentuckiana staff—support for all other bodies:* Support long-range plan and transportation improvement process with data analysis, traffic counting, model application, and amalgamation of plans from the various jurisdictions

Source: Compiled by the author.

FIGURE 5.1   Layers of Collaborating Officials and Staff in the Kentuckiana Metropolitan Planning Organization

This matter of reallocation points out another dimension to the limits of MPO authority. Given that the MPO does not control construction directly, it may not be able to ensure implementation of projects. If a project sponsor (e.g., state, DOT [Department of Transportation], city, county, transit agency, or others) does not expeditiously implement an STP-funded project, the MPO's priority determination may be undermined. Indeed, the MPO may find its priorities dependent on whether the sponsor chooses to move a project quickly or is exposed to delaying factors beyond its control (such as discovery of an unanticipated archaeological site). Indeed, the lack of familiarity with federal requirements can be a two-edged sword. Sponsors can secure MPO priority only to lose momentum because of inadequate project management. In the end, the MPO is dependent on its ability to partner with others and their enthusiasm and skills to make its priorities mean something.

This description of MPOs demonstrates their interdependence. As bodies made up of local elected officials and chief executive administrators, they work almost exclusively on federal programs but are organized under state law. They plan and review federal transportation funds but their state transportation agencies also have this responsibility. Moreover, their scope does not include local projects that are not federally funded. The quotation above also illustrates how little influence MPOs have over implementation, even when they secure high priority for a given project, because someone else carries it out. What does this suggest? It connotes high levels of regular contact by MPO staff members and officers with state and federal officials on virtually every project in their scope of interest, and continuous contact with local officials not only on their decisions but also on the details of project operations. This requires MPO–multiparty interaction from the point of an entity's inclusion in the MPO's long-range transportation plan to the point where the lines are finally painted on the road surface at the local government level.

Some efforts and regular interactions will extend even beyond the TIF and MPO demands. For example, when a city chooses to expand its existing industrial park, it most likely will involve federal and state funds, state government approvals, local private-sector investors, and the cooperation of county government and other jurisdictions. Each phase of the process (e.g., land acquisition, land improvement or site preparation, regulatory management, building construction, business attraction packages, infrastructure development, human resources development, business attraction, and park operation) will have its own set of steps, including potential collaborations among these various parties (Agranoff 2009, 276–79). This process involves high levels of understanding and working cooperation of an intensity that challenges the most experienced public managers. It is collaborative management in its most ultimate form.

A CASE STUDY OF COGOVERNANCE WITH A CONDUCTIVE AGENCY

In Indiana in the early 2000s, an initiative emerged that is a prime example of what Salamon (2002, 12) refers to as the "new governance," whereby the focus of attention shifts from the internal workings of public agencies to the networks of actors "upon which they depend." The key actors of the Indiana 317 Task Force originally formulated what became Indiana Senate Bill 317 of 1999, which shifted money from state institutions to follow residents into the community. Medicaid funds subsequently bolstered this effort, as programming to assist in transition and community services expanded rapidly. This section carries the intergovernmentalization example forward by looking at the 317 initiative's interlocking partners.

The original 317 committee was a governor's task force that met in the years 1997–98 to develop a comprehensive plan for community-based services. It was chaired by the secretary of the Family and Social Services Administration (FSSA), and it was composed of state government officials, representatives of NGO trade and advocacy associations, representatives of nonprofit and for-profit providers, citizen members, and university representatives. Its meetings were well attended and very open, because each member was able to express his or her views. The process was quite data driven, with reports on financing mechanisms, trends, community service waiting lists, and comparisons with other states. The trade associations supplemented the effort by developing fliers and other public relations materials on deinstitutionalization. A proposal was submitted to the governor and to both legislative houses (FSSA 1998). The essence of the final proposal as submitted included person-centered planning and funding, redirection of funding from larger (state institution and large nursing homes) settings, quality assurance, building community capacity, and securing the necessary financing to meet demand. The lobbying phase was carried out by the CEOs of two major trade associations, Arc of Indiana (formerly the Association for Retarded Citizens) and the Indiana Association of Rehabilitation Facilities (INARF). Key handicapped-citizen leaders and others from the disability community were also involved.

After enactment funding for the 317 plan provided $39.2 million in new state funding, implementation was then assigned to FSSA. Medicaid became an important funder through the state's Home and Community-Based Services waiver. The FSSA secretary formed an informal public- private-sector systems change group that met monthly to go over the numbers, categories, and spending patterns, and to make contract recommendations. The 317 Group emerged from the original task force and the systems change group, a working group to maintain the sustainable elements of the 317 Group both inside and outside government.

The succeeding 317 Group was maintained throughout the decade of the 2000s by those who had an ongoing stake in program continuation. First were the key trade associations, INARF and Arc, plus other groups like the Council of Voluntary Organizations for the Handicapped, Indiana Case Management, and the Indiana Parent Information Network. Second were state officials, including those of the FSSA: the director of the Division of Disability, Aging, and Rehabilitative Services; director of the Bureau of Developmental Disabilities; director of the Bureau of Quality Improvement Services; director of Medicaid; director of the Office of Medicaid Policy and Planning; and director of level of care in the Office of Medicaid Policy and Planning. Third was the director of the Governor's Planning Council for Developmental Disabilities, a federally funded state agency that is independent of the FSSA. Fourth were nonprofit and for-profit provider representatives. Fifth were citizen and consumer representatives. Sixth was the director of Indiana University's Indiana Institute on Disability and Community (IIDC), a research and service unit that is unattached to any particular university academic department or school. It is one of two federally funded university centers in Indiana that seek excellence in information and services for developmental disabilities.

The 317 Group is sustained outside government by the efforts of Arc and INARF, with support from the IIDC and the Governor's Planning Council. Although there was no formal budget, these four entities jointly funded an external study of financing trends in Indiana since 317's inception (Braddock and

Box 5.1   Principles of a Conductive Agency–Stakeholder Partnership for the 317 Group

- Organize some means to bring government, nongovernmental organization (NGO), and citizen associations together to discuss the problem.
- Investigate, in depth, the question at hand, its financing, legal, intergovernmental, and services dimensions by dividing up portions of the work or commissioning a neutral party; data gathering by government and NGOs.
- Develop a working joint public agency–NGO plan that lays out target populations, services levels, responsibilities, and financing.
- Go public and lobby formal policymakers; if supported, have a legislative bill drafted and submitted.
- After authorization formalize the public agency–NGO group; be as inclusive as possible because the need for organized support is just beginning.
- Meet frequently to monitor, evaluate, and discuss the flow of program operations.
- Negotiate data-based and other outstanding program adjustments between the conductive agency and stakeholder group; designate one or two organizations to take the lead.
- Gather long-term data periodically, make results public, and renegotiate potential new program aspects or policies.

Source: Compiled by the author.

Hemp 2004). Arc had staff people dedicated to publicizing 317, and one person who worked with families in institutions to explain community options. These activities were funded by the Governor's Planning Council. INARF sponsored a policy research task force composed of 317 Group members and nonmembers, which investigated such related issues as case management, institutional budgets, best practices in community-based services, and the impact of state budgets on the program. Finally, the IIDC offered a series of 317 focus groups for both consumers and advocates in its Collaborative Work Lab (Agranoff 2007, 72–75).

Since 2005 the 317 effort has become more informal, but it nevertheless still works regularly with the FSSA. These interactions represent the kind of partnerships that are emerging between NGOs and governments when they find themselves working together on similar programs. Box 5.1 summarizes the 317 Group's actions in sequence as a partnership in practice, from organizing to monitoring. This network of agencies and other organizations meets Salamon's (2002, 13) four criteria for those challenged with policy implementation both inside and outside government: (1) *pluriformity*, that a diverse range of organizations are engaged; (2) *self-referentiality*, that each actor has its own interests, frame of reference, and perspectives; (3) *asymmetric interdependencies*, that there is a mutual but not complete sense of dependence or urgency; and (4) *dynamism*, that the other features change over time. This is a prime example of how a conductive agency, the FSSA, and its connected partners can work interactively to design and maintain programs.

THE NONPROFIT AGENCY DELIVERS PUBLIC PROGRAMS

Another way to illustrate the extent of conductive government–partner inter-action is to look at how the US government supports the nonprofit organization sector. In fiscal year 2006 it provided $235 billion of funds to these organizations, as against $1.6 trillion in total nonprofit funds (of which about $300 billion was charitable giving). Of the $235 billion, $145 billion was in the form of fees for services (Medicare, Medicaid), $25 billion was in direct grants, $55 billion was in grants channeled through state governments, and approximately $10 billion was in contracts to nonprofits (as reported by Walters 2011). A survey by the Urban Institute (2010) found that 33,000 nonprofit health and human services agencies now operate nationwide, under nearly 200,000 contracts and grants, to provide a variety of direct services. It is now estimated that nonprofits employ more people than the construction, finance, and insurance industries combined (Walters 2011).

Research on nonprofit–government relationships suggests that neither party completely controls the other. Government support does not eliminate the inde-pendence of nonprofits, but it does guide their priorities. Nonprofits, conversely, have only recently taken an interest in the big picture of the problems that govern-ment is facing. The relationship has been traditionally one of a nominal partner-ship (Salamon 1995, 113); but as the dollars and codependency increase, more formal communication and decision-making arrangements to systematize the flow of information between the two sectors are emerging. Today, both sides try to get a more complete picture of the extent and character of the delivery system.

It is, of course, difficult to characterize a typical voluntary or nonprofit agency because they serve so many missions and vary in the degree to which they are really private or essentially tied to delivering government programs. More than a decade ago Smith and Lipsky (1993, 3) observed that these agencies "play a new political role in representing the welfare state to its citizens, providing a buffer between state policy and service delivery." In many fields—aging, physical reha-bilitation, public health, intellectual and developmental disabilities, youth services, early childhood, community corrections, mental health, substance abuse, domestic violence, rural community development, volunteer fire services—services are largely funded and regulated by government and are delivered by the nonprofit agency, making these NGOs important conduits between the public agency and its various publics.

Many of these nonprofits have become large and rather comprehensive within their fields. In the disabilities field, for example, an "industry" has been illustrated that combines large agencies with multiple functions and some with more limited program foci. The large ones will offer special needs programs for infants and toddlers, development of independent living skills, Medicaid-waiver and other independent living programs, development of less restrictive community living alternatives and group homes, and job training, job placement, and habilitation programs. The smaller agencies feature one or two of these services. In addition to the voluntary sector, a small number at about 15 to 20 percent of agencies offering these services are for-profit in nature. Virtually all the programs under both auspices are direct contractees of some federal–state or state program, with Medicaid and the Medicaid waiver being the single largest programs.

To complicate matters, many of these contract-linked rehabilitation agencies are paid rates at the level where they are expected to subcontract out and/or coordinate with other providers. For example, children in group homes are connected with local school systems and subcontracted for physician, behavior management, dental, assistive devices, and technology and related services. Adults in residential programs need to be linked with contracted vocational programs (if not in-house) and many other services. In other words, as in the example given in chapter 4 of area agencies on aging, the government contracts with the primary service agency, which in turn subcontracts for related services that are paid for by the government but are delivered by a program two or more steps removed.

This makes the subcontracting nonprofit (or for-profit) a directly connected agency of the state, and that it acts as the state's delivery agent and also increasingly in some aspect of a partnership arrangement. It means that funding and program regulations, program standards, and payment/reimbursement mechanisms operate through government channels. Paperwork flows both ways as well. This puts the delivery agency in a position of interacting regularly with various employees of the government agency over such issues as rates of reimbursement; records, audits, and payment schedules; standards or program requirements and violations; and many operational issues, for example, start-ups and delays. This puts the nonprofit in relatively consistent contract and negotiations contact with public agencies. In the disabilities example, regular interaction could well be with the several state agencies on a regular basis, including state vocational rehabilitation, mental disability, Medicaid, and public health offices.

In a large industry like rehabilitation of the intellectually and developmentally disabled, another intermediary entity is also present, because virtually every state has an industry association (i.e., association of rehabilitation facilities), for example, the above-mentioned INARF. These industry groups are important in four ways. First, they provide governmental liaison and advocacy as they communicate, mediate, and buffer between their members and government agencies. They also lobby before state legislatures and join with other state associations of rehabilitation facilities for congressional or federal agency liaison. Second, they offer technical assistance and consultation on management issues and how to operate with government-imposed managerial systems. Third, they undertake education and training for all members of an agency's staff, including how to incorporate state-mandated practices. And fourth, they gather and disseminate professional and educational information related to facility operations and programs, including federal and state initiatives. Although largely composed of nonprofits, a growing number, about 15 to 20 percent are for-profits, are also members of these trade associations.

As a result, relevant trade associations, the collectivity of providers, and the state agencies are now partners in the operation of services as funders/enablers, implementers/caregivers, and as information gatherers and advocates in the new mode of operation. The relationship has served to increase professionalism, expand service capacity, and build a new type of street-level bureaucrat within the rehabilitation field and several other industries. It has not, however, in any way reduced the need for public agency linkages or in any way entirely removed the role of public officials, who remain accountable no matter how diffused responsibility may be (Smith and Lipsky 1993, 118–19).

THE SUPPORT SERVICE CONTRACTEE

Yet another notable actor that now regularly deals with the conductive agency is private firms that carry a portion of the administrative burden that was once shouldered in house. The longest-standing of these are the private information and finance firms that process claims and payments in programs that provide direct payments to clients or vendor services providers, such as welfare payments, Medicaid, Medicare, and rehabilitation funding. Others process government loans or insurance. More recently, these firms have also moved into aspects of the service function, for example, intake and screening, determining eligibility, and managing cases. Here I explore one example that went rather "deep" into externalization—for some, way too deep.

In 2006, the State of Indiana signed a ten-year, $1.34 billion contract with the IBM Corporation and its subcontractor, Affiliated Computer Services, to privatize the processing of food stamps, Medicaid, and cash assistance payments. Under this move, more than 1,500 state employee case workers were transferred to Affiliated Computer Services. The consortium set up several automation moves: telephone call centers, a website, and document imaging. The state faced many problems with introduction, including freezing the innovation in early 2008 at one-third of the caseload, and in late 2009 the state canceled the IBM portion of the contract. It returned state-employee status to the caseworkers in the counties. However, Affiliated Computer Services—which handles the paperwork for welfare payments, food stamps, and Medicaid—continued. Therefore, in 2010 IBM filed a breach-of-contract lawsuit against the FSSA. Although this is an example of heavily extended or "deep" externalization, it demonstrates the reality of contracting for supportive services (Goldsmith and Eggers 2004).

Contract problems aside in the Indiana example, it is important to understand that private, mostly for-profit firms are going beyond the usual non–services procurement and administrative support services to become a part of the service delivery and operations function that was once the exclusive province of government or of nonprofit contractors for the purchase of services. These new firms stand between the externalizing agency and the purchase-of-service agency, a new intervening agent. The firm that manages cases, refers clients, or determines eligibility moves more directly into the services nexus traditionally occupied by government and/or NGO service agencies, the latter previously predominantly nonprofit. The for-profit service firm, and all that bottom-line profit making means, are now part of the network of agencies and programs, adding to the collaborative management challenge. The collaborating for-profit administrative support firm needs to formally and informally interact not only with its government principal but also with the other NGO co-agents that are part of the service delivery system.

SUPPORT STRUCTURES FOR MANAGING PARTNERSHIPS

In an important study of collaborative practices between public and private environmental and natural resource organizations, Wondolleck and Yaffee (2000, 92–98) found that successful efforts to keep various governmental and NGO partners working together required a range of supports to hold the parties together:

1. *Informal relationships*, regularized arrangements between key individuals that allow interaction between different interests (e.g., a multiparty watershed management group).

2. *Coordinators*, or formal positions created to plan, organize, and hold together the activities of multiple partners (e.g., a forest outreach effort to build public and landowner bridges on conservation).
3. *Memoranda of understanding*, formalizing interagency relationships, providing interorganizational structure, capitalizing on expertise, delineating activities, facilitating interactions, and building trust (e.g., to provide structure for forest management collaboration).
4. *Advisory committees*, explicitly involving different interests in discussing, evaluating, and making recommendations (e.g., a fisheries management council).
5. *Nongovernmental organizations*, created to facilitate cooperative activities and ensure implementation (e.g., a natural areas stewardship for habitat management).
6. *New facilities* that provide resources, a focal point, and new place for interaction (e.g., creation of a multicommunity geographic information system center).

Essential to the effectiveness of these structures was that "their core missions included fostering outreach, interchange, and decision making among diverse interests" (Wondolleck and Yaffee 2000, 92), as they established visible and accountable public points of contact, the most important of which forged long-term relationships. These approaches would in many ways be precursors to the organized or structured arrangements identified in chapter 2.

Increased communication can therefore enhance the numerous exchanges that need to be undertaken by a conductive agency and its partners. It requires facilitated cooperation that follows on communication. In a series of intergovernmental relations conclusions regarding cooperation potential among those involved in toxic waste cleanup costs, Kamieniecki, O'Brien, and Clarke (1985, quoted by Wright 1988, 397–98) offer the following suggestions:

1. Cooperation is more likely if there is a perceived sense of urgency about the problem. Greater apparent urgency leads to greater cooperation.
2. The lower the predicted costs that have an impact on the main participants, the greater the probability of cooperation. Conversely, high financial costs and/or major legal liabilities are apt to produce greater conflict. Cost reduction strategies or techniques can contribute to cooperative agreements.
3. Provision of technical expertise and financial assistance can contribute significantly to cooperation. This implies that under conditions of static or declining resources, such as contraction of resources, a higher level of conflict might be expected.

4. Public opinion and organized group pressure are likely to increase the sense of urgency about a problem and thereby enhance the possibility of cooperation. It is also possible that public and political pressure may limit the options and flexibility of leaders in resolving intergovernmental relations disputes.

5. Greater openness and frequency of communication among actors will lead to increased cooperation. Exchanges of information and expressions of interest across intergovernmental boundaries are prerequisites for establishing the trust and respect upon which intergovernmental relations cooperation is normally based.

6. Greater clarity in roles, responsibilities, and boundaries among governments (or actors) is conducive to greater cooperation among the parties dealing with an intergovernmental problem. Seeking this greater clarity or precision is not the same as asking "Who is in charge?" It is unlikely that any *one* is in charge. A more useful approach is to identify which participants have primary responsibility for which tasks are required to solve a particular problem.

These findings, which were taken from case studies involving public agencies and the outside groups with which they interact, present a blueprint for beginning cooperative relationships between agencies and partners. Problem agreement and urgency, cost minimization, seeking expertise/knowledge, public support, frequent and open communication, and establishment of roles and boundaries provide a beginning for making linkages.

GOVERNING TOOLS AS INTERACTIVE VEHICLES

Each tool of governing has a somewhat different pattern of linking between the sponsoring or offering conductive agency and its associated organizations. Table 5.1 looks at some of the major tools of government and potential vehicles of communication. It looks at the formal means of transaction, the types of information gathered, how interactions are transmitted, and how interaction/networking can be improved. To unpack table 5.1, it is useful to take a focused look at the table's second row, contracting. Formally, a contract is a written or structured business arrangement that links the partners, but in a process sense this includes selection–administration–renewal/termination. Information is exchanged by informal conversations; reporting, particularly over formal requirements; and performance monitoring. Transactionally, interaction is likely to occur concerning costs and results, periodic reviews specified in the contract, meeting incentives

TABLE 5.1 Major Vehicles of Governance Tool Communications toward the Improvement of Contacts

Governance Tool	Formal Modes of Transaction	Types of Information	Modes of Transaction	Networking
Social/economic regulation	Legislated controls, rules	Hearings, pricing practices, reporting	Reports on practices/participation rates; networking	Performance standards, negotiation, territories
Contracting	Structure business arrangement, selecting administration, written contracts Renewal, termination	Specify requirements, reporting, performance monitoring, informal conversations	Monitoring cost/performance, discussions, period of review	Contracting agencies and businesses, trade associations
Grant	Cash award based on promised activity application, renewal, termination	Annual reports, monitoring	Informal contact, information and discretion seeking	Periodic meetings
Direct loan	Loan application/review	Fiscal capacity to repay	Repayment/schedule, audit	Postaudit discussions, meetings with recipients
Loan guarantee	Loan application/review	Fiscal capacity to repay	Payment/schedule, audit	Discussions over use of loan
Tax expenditure	Enactment, formal application/forms, compliance	Benefits, tax outlay	Audit	Informal discussions, proof of use
Fees, charges	Legislative authorization, administration levy	Costs, scheduled payments	Monitor, audit; compliance assurance	Fee payer/user meetings, reports on cost, usage
Vouchers	Eligibility, distribution mechanics, degree of choice	Expenditure reports on suppliers, consumer knowledge, find buyers	Audit, performance evaluation	Open meetings, Interactions with suppliers

Source: Compiled by the author.

Box 5.2   Eighteen Interactive Regulatory Compliance Activities

1. Reading, digesting, explaining, and circulating regulatory information to governmental and nongovernmental parties.
2. Holding workshops and information meetings on regulatory programs, standards, guidelines, and compliance.
3. Working with jurisdictions and organizations to draft compliance plans.
4. Developing operating standards and guidelines for the "point source"/regulated.
5. Work with a budget agency and/or task force on compliance costs and (long-term "set-aside" costs for major problems, e.g., storage tanks, inaccessible public buildings).
6. Enforcement; developing a (short-term) system for compliance monitoring.
7. Conducting studies of particular problem areas; feasibility of long-term compliance/mitigation.
8. Working with the most serious violators to encourage change in practices, actions, and to pay for mitigation.
9. Working with jurisdictions and other entities on creating appropriate operating policies.
10. Working with in-house (or out-of-house) legal counsel on issues of compliance, liability limits, feasibility of actions, and other questions of law.
11. Coordinate in-house/consultant preparation of permit application/compliance plan and/or any waiver/exemption/variances (e.g., National Pollution Discharge Elimination System permit required 17,184 person-hours in Columbus).
12. Conduct outreach/education/awareness activities, including the provision of information regarding new technology.
13. Establishing working relationships with federal and state officials through agency contacts (including organizing visits to local governments, sites).
14. Serve as resource center/information line on regulatory program information.
15. Coalition building with other jurisdictions to create demonstrations and innovative methods of compliance, for information and training, and for state and local compliance.
16. Coordinating local responses to proposed regulatory legislation/regulations/guidelines.
17. Networking with professional and technical associations.
18. Promote preventive and long-term solutions.

Source: Compiled by the author.

built into the contract, and interactions over fiscal or other modifications and over claims made for periodic payments. Finally, funder–contractor interaction can be enhanced by joint meetings between multiple contractors and their funder, including prebidding and postbidding conferences; through associations of contractors and trade associations; and with periodic meetings with specified contractor personnel (e.g., chief financial officers or program directors). Thus, in contracting the single meeting of the conductive agency and contractor is a thing of the past, but a constant flow of information and interaction occurs between them. In a similar process way, each of the other tools listed in table 5.1 exhibits many points of information transmissions and interaction beyond the formal mode of transaction between the conductive public agency and its interlocutors. The process involving each of these tools has become highly interactive, even for a regulatory tool that carries no funds or requires no or few formal transactions between the conductive agency and the regulated. As an example, the list of the type of compliance actions in which a local government might engage for environmental regulations is accounted for in box 5.2.

Eighteen different administrative activities are illustrated in box 5.2. Virtually all these actions are by definition collaborative in some way, mostly between the city government and nongovernment businesses and other entities to inventory, convey, and regulate within the city. No city would perhaps undertake all these activities, but the list demonstrates how interactive tools like regulatory compliance can be. In addition to the list given in box 5.2, regulatory interaction would also include those activities related to regulatory negotiation, that is, seeking through interactive appeals or negotiations regulatory adjustment, flexibility in some way, or a waiver from regulations. They are identified in figure 4.2 in the previous chapter. Agranoff and McGuire (2003, 87) found that slightly more than half the 237 cities they surveyed engaged in such activity. This, of course, would entail a whole series of additional contacts between the regulatory agency and the regulated entity, whether it is a local government or an NGO.

Program details and program standards interactions constitute another vehicle of communication. These are additional tools of conductivity. For example, in the Medicaid grant program there is a 1915C Home and Community-Based Services (HCBS) waiver for persons with intellectual and/or developmental disabilities. As mentioned in chapter 2, at one time the HCBS waiver included ten distinct areas of quality management and seventy areas of services that were federally monitored and with state oversight. They had to be maintained by provider agencies. Now they have been succeeded by performance targets. For some states performance measures mean increased interaction on these requirements (Bradley 2009). However less detailed they may be, they remain basically interactive; that is, standards are transistors of conductivity. An interactive system like this requires clearly "delineated roles and responsibilities" and "a commitment to building supporting networks" within an "active learning environment" (Gettings 2003, 224–25).

This is by no means a complete audit of how the conductive agency interacts with its partner organizations. But it does demonstrate that "after the fact" reports or audits no longer constitute the be-all and end-all of communication between government and agents/partners. The tools of governance have become increasingly interactive. These illustrations are symptomatic of activism and electronic government, that is, Government 2.0. Instead of a one-way system in which government hands down laws and provides services, increasingly citizens, corporations, and civil organizations work together with elected officials to develop solutions. This is clearly what happened with regard to the 317 solution in Indiana and in the other situations where the conductive public agency is in regular contact and acts in networked concert with a host of agencies that are part of the scope of implementation.

INTEROPERABILITY

Management between entities can sometimes mean more than interaction by negotiation, reporting, review, approval, audit, and agreement. It can go deeper into multiple agency operations that must take one another's procedures into account. It is a popular response in these situations to suggest that wherever working collaboration between government and NGOs occurs, the magic term is that one must be trained in, be adept at, and be able to practice "bargaining and negotiation." The previous sections of this chapter would suggest that there is much more at stake in opportunities and venues. In the process of collaboration it is possible that bargaining and negotiation constitute merely one set of means to a broader end in "operated collaboration." From a management standpoint a core category of collaborated management has been captured as *interoperability* (Jenkins 2006, 321), which can be defined as reciprocal communication and accommodation to reach interactive operating policy and programming. Interoperable management indeed requires bargaining and negotiation, but it also involves additional actions in making different agencies working on the same issues or programs. There is a need for more studies of public programs to uncover the protracted processes of reaching interoperability, which in turn will more deeply define collaborative management. It needs to be broken down into various cross-agency operational steps.

This form of cross-agency collaboration can be illustrated by the wildland fire policy in the United States, led by several federal agencies that have formed the National Incident Fire Command (NIFC), which has developed an interoperable approach to large fires. This involves the Forest Service of the US Department of Agriculture and the Bureau of Land Management, Bureau of Indian Affairs, Fish and Wildlife Service, and National Park Service of the Department of the Interior.

Box 5.3 contains a mini–case study of the NIFC system and how it is interoperable. It illustrates how the five agencies built on previous collaborations to develop an operating, interagency response system that not only serves the relevant federal agencies but in the case of large fires also works with state forest management and private landowners. The collaborative then developed operating standards and roles and responsibilities, including all the relevant service officers. Common standards, operating policies, and procedures have been considered, for example, for the use of aircraft and for the safe application of aerial and ground suppressants. This process led to the establishment of a leadership council that ensures agency interests and establishes cross-agency—that is, interoperable—policies.

Interoperability must be understood as a form of collaborative management. It refers to public programming when a series of governmental, nonprofit, and for-profit agencies are expected or are attempting to work together, whereby their policies and procedures need to be made to work interactively toward similar and/or common aims that combine policy and administration. In the field of emergency management, Wise (2006) explains how communities engage such a networked approach among federal, state, and local governments that work together with the NGO sector to avoid the more devastating effects of disasters like floods, hurricanes, and forest fires. The same would be true with regard to cleanup and relief after a disaster. By the same token, for public programs to maintain persons with intellectual and developmental disabilities in small group homes in communities, a host of case management, day services, training, medical, and social supports must function in a highly interactive fashion. In the United States they normally require services connections based on federal–state Medicaid, HCBS Medicaid waivers, state program funds, and social services grants that go to nonprofits. At an operating level these agencies obviously need to be integrated (Castellani 2005). It is in this sense that interoperability signifies some level of interactive working policy and management.

Interoperable management can be further distinguished from its close administrative relations, (1) interoperational consultation, which entails effort to seek out information or advice across agency lines about a singular practice; (2) interoperable transactions, such as over a grant or contract of a bi-agency nature; and (3) interoperational coordination, whereby two or more agencies regularly share information or client referrals but do not operate internally on an interactive basis (Agranoff and McGuire 2003). Interoperable management refers to regularized programming involving two or more entities for which operating policies and processes have been articulated and are executed interactively to some considerable degree. This process has been defined by the US Government Accountability

Box 5.3   The National Incident Fire Command's Wildland Fire Policy Interoperability

Wildland fire agencies collaborate to quickly identify and address resource needs for suppressing wildland fires. According to the National Incident Fire Command (NIFC), no single agency is capable of providing the resources needed to respond to especially large fires or to multiple concurrent fires. The NIFC monitors the occurrence of wildland fires and coordinates and mobilizes wildland firefighting resources nationally to suppress those fires. Local and regional federal fire centers unable to meet personnel, equipment, and supply needs contact NIFC in Boise. In response, the NIFC provides certain resources and requests others from the closest available federal agency. For example, the NIFC could request firefighting resources—including aircraft, personnel, telecommunications equipment, and ground and air transportation for equipment and supplies—from the Forest Service, Bureau of Indian Affairs, Fish and Wildlife Service, and the National Park Service to respond to an incident on land under the jurisdiction of the Bureau of Land Management. . . .

The five federal agencies with wildland fire management responsibilities jointly developed and updated the *Interagency Standards for Fire and Fire Aviation Operations*—an operations handbook that defines the roles and responsibilities for all personnel engaged in managing wildland fire operations, regardless of agency affiliation. For example, according to the handbook, the incident commander for a wildland fire is responsible for all incident activities, including developing the fire management strategy and tactics, and ordering, deploying, and releasing resources. The incident commander is supported by an incident command staff, which may include a safety officer, information officer, operations section chief, planning section chief, logistics section chief, finance section chief, and a liaisons officer. . . .

The *Interagency Standards for Fire and Fire Aviation Operations* handbook also specifies common standards, operational policies, and procedures used for wildland fire operations. The interagency handbook includes standards for training and firefighting equipment, as well as policies and procedures for developing a response to wildland fire, aviation operations, and communications. For example, the handbook specifies the standards for the chemicals used to suppress enhancers. It also establishes policies and procedures for the safe application of aerial and ground suppressants in a way that does not harm the ecosystem. . . .

The interagency Wildland Fire Leadership Council was established by the US Department of Agriculture and the US Department of the Interior to facilitate collaboration across agency boundaries by providing leadership and the consistent implementation of wildland fire management goals and policy. The council deals with national policy issues, such as nationwide resource allocation and prioritization that cut across different federal agencies. One official noted that the council members are the ultimate authority within their departments for wildland fire management. As such, they can negotiate and set wildland fire management policy for their respective departments. Council members are to ensure their respective agency's disparate interests, missions, and multiple responsibilities are not adversely affected by policy decisions that the council makes collectively.

Source: GAO (2006, 16, 17, 19).

Office not as an end in itself but as a means to achieve the ability to respond effectively to and mitigate incidents that require coordinated actions. As in the case
of wildland fires, it is based on communicated and agreed-upon goals, planning,
operating principles, operational information, role differentiation, and an operating system that supports communication (GAO 2004).

   Agranoff and McGuire's (2009) case study of interoperability in a networked
public agency found the following sequence of actions to be present: joint agreement on core principles, interactive planning, action exploration and/or mistakes
and failure to launch, governance and reaching key understandings, the routines of
program articulation, reciprocal operations, and feedback and correction. Jenkins
(2006, 321) concludes that such interoperable action is normally taken by personal contact "without sanctions" or requirements, is adaptive in approach, and
requires the meshing of cultural and organizational traditions. He concludes that
with regard to emergency management, a great deal of political and organizational
"castor oil" must be swallowed to overcome the barriers to working together. It is
nevertheless one important means of linking the conductive public agency with
its regular working partners at an operational level.

KNOWLEDGE AND ITS MANAGEMENT AS
THE KEYSTONE OF INTEROPERABILITY

Interactive operating normally flows from various forms of legal, official, technical,
and political exploration of what is known and what must be discovered to make
operations work across organizations. Thus, one of the very common activities of
collaborative efforts among conductive public agencies and their partners is their
quest to create and manage the knowledge that helps collectives arrive at conclusions, reach agreements, and adopt courses of action. The Indiana 317 Group
identified earlier in this chapter works with the state agency, the FSSA, to gather
data on the six major components of the alternative living plan, named DART,
which uses a program called Insight to track Medicaid waivers and intellectual
and developmental disabilities services from the case management program. The
FSSA's Bureau of Quality Improvement Services issues periodic reports on aspects of the program, such as on costs per client and the size of service waiting
lists. Partners in the 317 network provide regular input on the studies, and many
of the service agencies report the raw data that is transformed into information. Meanwhile, the 317 Group itself has periodically commissioned financing
and citizen service surveys. All this makes the work of the FSSA agency with its

partners easier as they attack problems of mutual interest collaboratively through knowledge management.

The movement from data to information to knowledge for interactive operating networks like the 317 partners is at the core. "Data" refers to a set of discrete, objective facts about events, often in organized efforts like structured records of transactions. "Information" is characterized as a message in the form of a document or an audible or visible communication. Information moves around organized bodies through hard networks (wires, satellite dishes, electronic mail boxes) and soft networks (notes, article copies). "Knowledge" is broader, deeper, and richer than data or information. It is, as previously identified, highly mutable and highly contextual, but with greater utility. Davenport and Prusak (2000, 5–6) define it in this way: "Knowledge is a fluid mix of framed experience, values, contextual information, and expert insight that provides a framework for evaluating and incorporating new experiences and information. It originates and is applied in the minds of knowers. In organizations, it often becomes embedded not only in documents or repositories but also in organizational routines, processes, practices, and norms." Knowledge is within people, a part of the assets of the human capital that is so important in contemporary activities. Indeed, it is intrinsically human: "Knowledge derives from information as information derives from data. If information is to become knowledge, humans must do all the work." In effect, knowledge is both a process and an outcome.

The aim of knowledge management is "identifying, extracting, and capturing 'knowledge assets'" in order to fully exploit them toward accomplishing some goal (Newell et al. 2002, 16). In the public sector one would use knowledge to solve problems and thus to add some public value (Moore 1995). Conductive agencies and their partners that work for interagency networks are important vehicles of knowledge management. Knowledge itself depends heavily on collaborative action, or what social network analysts call "connectivity." Problem solving and creative discovery depend heavily on dynamic interactions among people, particularly at strategic points in social networks (Cross et al. 2001). Schrage (1995, 33) defines collaboration activity as *shared creation*, that is, people working interactively on a process, product, or event. As one public official explained, "Work groups on various technical issues is the way we learn and grow; integrate new people into our process . . . and while we don't codify process we rely on the institutional knowledge of a lot of people" (Agranoff 2007, 138).

It is also clear that knowledge blends what can be documented or formulized with the intuitive sense of knowing how to complete a task. Polanyi (1962, 49) concludes that knowledge is "formulae which have a bearing on experience," in the sense that knowledge is "personal knowing," from map reading to piano playing, from bicycle riding to scientific work. This requires "skillful action" based on "personal knowing." Knowledge management is thus thought of as having two analytical components, *explicit* and *tacit* knowledge. Explicit knowledge is what can be codified and communicated easily by documenting in words or numbers, charts, or drawings. It is the more familiar form of knowledge. Tacit knowledge is embedded in the senses, individual perceptions, physical experiences, intuition, and rules of thumb. It is rarely documented but is "frequently communicated through conversations with the use of metaphors." It includes know-how, understanding, mental models, insights, and principles inherent to a discipline; all are tacit knowledge (Saint-Onge and Armstrong 2004, 41).

Tacit and explicit knowledge do not, as some are prone to consider, stand in opposition to one another, but are two sides of the same coin. In the real world of collaborative activity, they are joined. All knowing involves *skillful action*, and the knower "necessarily participates in all acts of understanding" (emphasis in the original; Polanyi and Prosch 1975, 44). Explicit knowledge, for Tsoukas (2005, 158), is always rendered uncertain without tacit knowledge: "It is vectoral—we know the particulars by relying on our awareness of them for attending to some one else."

The tools used in knowledge management are not necessarily highly complicated but are techniques known under other names as information, communication, and human resource practices. Appendixes D and E provide explanatory examples of widely used explicit and tacit knowledge activities that are engaged when agencies work with their partners. If one examines the examples given in appendix D, such approaches that single organizations take as intranets, databases, corporate libraries, information portals, electronic archiving, and decision-support systems in these cases cross agency lines. Less familiar and more associated with collaborate efforts are listservs of discussion groups, virtual organizations, knowledge maps, and the designation of a chief knowledge (as opposed to information) officer. Conversely, those tacit approaches identified in appendix E are almost all similar to activities that take place in single organizations, particularly sharing best practices, mentoring, work groups, apprenticeships, and training and fostering collaboration. These "ordinary" approaches are the most commonly used by collaborative bodies in the public sector (Agranoff 2008), and they differ in degree from the expert systems, artificial intelligence, case-based reasoning, broad knowledge repositories, concentrated knowledge domains, and real-time knowledge systems employed by so-called high-flying corporations (Davenport and Prusak 2000).

Now that some of the techniques of knowledge management have been identified, it remains to be seen how agencies and their partners working collaboratively use knowledge as critical interoperability steps. In a previous work (Agranoff 2007, chap. 7), a five-step process was identified and explained. The sequence includes looking at each agency and partner to seek what information bases exist, converting these data to forms of use to the collective body, then doing a detailed examination to capture the less obvious tacit knowledge-based approaches of core use, and then extending the foregoing as needed by the group and applying them to particular problems. Finally, knowledge is fed back to component organizations as a way to broaden its use. In this quite involved and interorganizationally interactive journey, many products accrue—for example, inventories, map libraries, workshops, best practices books, working manuals, work groups, communities of practice, decision models, cross-agency transactions, and new partner data sources. In contrast to the data/information/knowledge needs of the agency partner organizations, these collective efforts tend to focus on cross-organization joint knowledge needs that are geared to mutually agreed-upon problems.

The conductive agency and its partners can only solve interoperable problems if they step back at some points from a nonadversarial position and try to approach problems as rationally as possible. Mutually based problems often depend heavily on the kind of knowledge base that partners can generate together in order to fashion solutions.

CONCLUSION

Only recently have the regularized, transactional interactions between public conductive agencies and their partners accelerated from those appropriate for the role of grantee, contract agent, or regulated organization to those suited to more program-related collaborating partner relationships in various respects. Contact is no longer intermittent but regularized and on a working basis. Many of these new interactive roles have developed because of the higher stakes in funding flows from government to NGOs, and because problem resolution is a matter of joint ownership as government direct service gives way to implementation by NGOs in many aspects of public service delivery. This raises the quotient considerably in understanding how to manage interactions between the conductive agency and its partners.

This chapter begins the process of explaining how to manage across these boundaries. It has largely been a story of various forms of co-management. After the cases of the TIF and the MPO interactions were presented above, the chapter gave a detailed account of such a comanaging collaborative network in the field of intellectual and developmental disabilities—including its structure, purposes, operating principles, and projects—whereby one state agency works with a host of external actors, particularly service delivery organizations and their trade associations. The tools of governance were compared with a series of potential cooperative practices between the conductive agency and its partners, moving beyond monitoring and auditing. Sometimes in these relationships aspects of interactive operations are necessary, so the principle of interoperability was introduced using the example of the federal government's interagency wildland fire efforts. Because joint decisions are often buttressed by knowledge-informed activities, the process of knowledge management was next introduced. It is a quintessentially collaborative and/or interoperable activity. How to practice effective partner relations, interoperability, and knowledge management are the challenges being faced by today's public managers and professionals, along with NGO staff members and administrators. This chapter has begun to look at these relationships for managing collaboratively. The next chapter undertakes a more intensive look at this process.

CHAPTER 6

Processing Deep Collaboration
Managing in Networks

THE IOWA ENTERPRISE NETWORK (hereafter, Iowa Enterprise) involves a group of federal and state government and university representatives, as well as small business owners, who have attempted to provide consultations and build the skills of people who work in home-based businesses. Its primary work has been in holding conferences and skill-sharing sessions; more recently it has begun to study microbusiness problems, such as business succession in small towns. Iowa Enterprise found it difficult to involve home-based business people over the long run, and in 2005 the network's capacity-building actions were brought under the auspices of the Small Business Committee of the Iowa Rural Development Council.

Iowa Enterprise is managed in a nonbureaucratic fashion. It is organized as a tax-exempt nonprofit corporation under Section 501(c)(3) of the US tax code and is led by one or two university-based staff members from the Small Business Development Center at Iowa State University and the rural council's executive director. It also has a board of officers that nominally includes federal, state, and nongovernmental organization (NGO) representatives but is primarily comprised of small business owners and consultants. This board is supported by an advisory council of state and federal administrators. Although it does not operate with work plans or formal rules, as a 501(c)(3) it has articles of incorporation and by-laws. Its committee structure is topical, mainly focused on specific conferences. Its technical support, in addition to university-based small business consultants and the state association staff, includes outside small business consultants and loan specialists. Thus, though small and informal in appearance, Iowa Enterprise is clearly managed, as are virtually all formalized networks that go beyond occasional contact. As public managers become more involved outside their agencies, one of their challenges is to manage within such bodies.

Iowa Enterprise can count among its successes its location as an important venue for people working from small and home-based businesses to become exposed to new trends and operating practices, particularly through its annual conferences and early evening coaching sessions. It provides its participants with

129

a broad array of information on funding, training, and technical assistance programs. It also allows for access to small business management and development expertise that small owners could not otherwise afford. The sessions provide a venue for exchanging new ideas and a place for interpersonal networking. Its linkage functions makes prospective and actual business owners aware of and how to access the small business development centers located in Iowa at institutions of higher education that are sponsored by the US Department of Commerce, as well as other "how to find" and "where to go" types of assistance for microbusinesses.

Perhaps Iowa Enterprise's crowning achievement was its 2006 partnership with the Iowa Rural Development Council in undertaking a business succession study, to understand the problems of small town main street businesses closings upon owners' retirements, and the subsequent loss of retail outlets because there was no successor or because of successors' failure. The completed study—which emphasized the lack of sufficient capital, nonexistent management and financial training, and the practice of profit dilution by dividing ongoing income flow between buyer and seller—was presented to a panel of state legislators. At the next session the General Assembly enacted legislation that funded a small program housed in the Iowa Department of Economic Development to address these problems head on.

We have seen that public managers work both inside and across the boundaries of their agencies in a variety of modes—grants, contracts, loans, regulations, partnerships, and "self-organizing interorganizational networks" (Rhodes 1997, xi). In particular, these networks have become increasingly important in today's expanded communications age, as potential problems, solutions, and the authority and resources needed to solve them—in both policy and its implementation—are spread across public and nonpublic organizations (Lipnak and Stamps 1994). They have been previously defined as a form of collaborative management: "Networks are structures of interdependence involving multiple organizations or parts thereof, where one unit is not merely the formal subordinate of the others in some larger hierarchical arrangement" (O'Toole 1997). Thus, the processes of managing within such networks need to be examined, because their self-organizing character as networks does not mean there is no need for them to be managed.

Whether legally chartered or more informal but regular in interaction, certain functions and processes within the network need to be carried out. All types of networks share certain characteristics: permanent and/or identifiable status, regular meetings, a definable communication system, leaders and participants, task forces or work groups, a governance structure, specified partners, and some form of division of labor or task allocation. Chartered networks are those that are formally established as organized entities, often by intergovernmental agreement, or by registration as a 501(c)(3) nonprofit organization, by act or resolution of a state legislature, a governor's executive order, and/or through corporate registration with a state government representative, such as the secretary of state. Nonchartered networks have no such formal legal status, but their continuing presence and operations, regular meetings, concrete problem-solving actions, websites, newsletters, and the like are testimony to their existence. Nonchartered networks are often harder to locate in telephone books or at websites than those that have been formalized, but those without chartered status can prove to be equally viable bodies.

The collaborative operational processes and issues that are so important for those who work within structures like these networks are the focus of this chapter. Although the chapter is geared to what is known about networks like Iowa Enterprise, it also seeks to tease out more useful information about how these collaborative processes are related to less formal network activity. Thus the concerns and practices raised in previous chapters are presented in greater depth here. The chapter begins with an account of why organizations might become involved in a network and when not to engage a network. That is followed by a brief overview of what is known about managing within networks. Then the focus turns to the important tasks of network management and who primarily undertakes them—the variegated leadership core. That leads to a discussion of power within networks, that is, its different agency, technical, project, and emergent bases. Then the focus turns to the means of network agreement and the kinds of production or outcomes to which these decisions might lead. The chapter concludes with a series of practical hints for those working within networks.

WHY FORM A NETWORK?

Networks are able to form "cluster organizations" to make decisions jointly and integrate their collaborated efforts "to adjust more rapidly to changing technologies and market conditions, develop new products or services in a shorter time period, and provide more creative solutions in the process," according to Alter and Hage (1993, 2). Public-sector networks bring representatives of public agencies together with NGOs to address problems of common concern that at some point accrue public value for participating organizations and the persons who work with them, helping them to accomplish their missions. As Klijn (2003, 32) suggests, they facilitate interaction, decision making, cooperation, and learning, and thus provide supportive resources, "such as a recognizable interaction patterns, common rules, and organizational forms and sometimes even a common language."

This is not to suggest that a formal network is in order for every collaborative undertaking. Indeed, in other portions of this book I point to grants, contracts for service, regulatory programs, interagency agreements, and even informal accommodation or adjustments as alternative means of collaboration. Many of these devices are two-party or even three-party modes whereas the network normally involves at least three and normally many more organized entities working together. Ansell and Gash (2008, 562) reviewed 137 cases of collaborative governance across a number of policy sectors and found that the time-based legacy of conflict or cooperation, the existence of trust, and interdependence are core contingencies in network formation. This raises the needed agreement quotient considerably higher—one clear drawback of the network approach. The demands and expectations required to successfully form a network are therefore quite high. Box 6.1 highlights the more essential challenges in building such networks. It is clear that without general understandings, organizational support, confrontation of the real issues, mutual respect, and a long-term commitment to reframing and mutual learning, it will be hard for a network to succeed.

Virtually the opposite of these conditions need to be present for the network undertaking to work at success. Box 6.2 highlights when to form a network, and gives sixteen of the more commonly articulated conditions for networking. Among the key forces that make working in networks possible is that the members of a broad group of administrators from different sectors agree that the problems are multifaceted and vexing, that the opportunity for new learning and mutual problem solving presents itself, and that there is potential to approach problems differently, with mutual respect and a willingness to deliberate, grow, and learn—and they also recognize that accommodations might have to be made within each one's organization, and that commitment needs to be made to a process over the long term. Perhaps not every condition needs to be met immediately upon forming a network; but unless a sufficient number of these are fulfilled, it will be difficult to organize and manage the network.

NETWORK MANAGEMENT 101

It is no surprise that management in formal networks somewhat resembles that of organizational management. After all, they are organized and operated by organizational representatives that have shared experiences. In this regard Herranz (2008, 27) found that the strategic orientations of networks differed by their primary composition. Nonprofit community-based networks emphasized "contingent coordination," and entrepreneurial for-profit networks were organized around

Box 6.1   Why Not to Form a Network

- The problem/issues are minor and can be resolved by dyadic or triadic interorganizational contact and accommodation, thus deflating expectations.
- When the focus/orientation is vague or meaningless, for example, to coordinate some unspecified shared problems.
- When key potential partners insist on particular approaches or methods for solving problems.
- Top administrators and decision makers withhold their support or pay lip service to the endeavor.
- Top administrators and decision makers will not delegate authority to their staff to speak for their organizations.
- Potential activist administrators and specialists are unwilling to commit time, energy, and resources to the undertaking.
- Key potential activists refuse to confront core conflict-producing issues and related competitive or historic tensions.
- Inability to overcome conflict, confusion, and disagreement over what "problem(s)" the network is approaching.
- Offensive initial interactions by key potential partners if participants fail to treat one another as entirely equal partners regardless of social, political, or economic strength of individual groups.
- Undue complication of communications, management, or conflict resolution that result in dysfunctional operations.
- Expectations that issues can be resolved in a short time frame instead of an orientation to small yet essential "wins."
- Failure, from the outset, to reframe problems or issues, not based on participants individual perspectives, but rather on new perspectives based in deliberative-based agreements.

Source: Summarized by permission from *Networks That Work* by Paul Vandeventer and Myrna Mandell (2007, 20–22).

market sector values, whereas public-sector-based networks were organized for hierarchical-based directive administration and active coordination. Mixed-sector networks, Herranz speculates, should be based on mixing and adjusting these managerial activities in this "multisectoral trilemma." It is important to restate that these organizational representatives in networks increasingly operate from more "open organizations" that conduct many, many (e.g., grant, contract, regulation) activities that cross boundaries (Saint-Onge and Armstrong 2004). Network activists comprise agency or department heads, second-level managers, program directors, program specialists, local elected officials, and NGO executives and staff members. They bring to the network their changing bureaucratic and NGO

B o x 6.2   When to Form a Network

- Problems are complex, and potential solutions lie with many public agencies, organizations, programs, and services. No single agency or two can approach the problem.
- Top administrators and decision makers recognize the complexity of the problem and are willing to lend their resources (e.g., financial support and staff).
- Problems faced have no or few readily apparent and/or feasible solutions. They have to be worked out by several parties.
- Potential partners see the opportunity to learn and adapt, and to develop new competencies and new approaches to problems.
- Potential to gain the resources—time, money, expertise information, legitimacy, status—from different entities that can be applied to problems.
- Sharing the costs and associated risks of new problem solutions, program, and service approaches.
- Potential to gain influence over policy/program domain, competitive positioning for the problem areas, potentially new clients.
- Potential ability to manage uncertainty, solve complex problems.
- Opportunity to promote mutual support, trust, synergy, and harmonious working relationships.
- Opportunity to jointly develop rapid and efficient responses to changing demands and the introduction of new technologies.
- A willingness to explore new approaches and methods exists within the group.
- Those who control/participate are willing to engage in constructive deliberative dialogue/engagement that leads to the development of new possibilities.
- Participants are willing to confront and manage potential conflict-generating issues.
- A widespread willingness to treat all as equals, regardless of one's hierarchical position in the home agency.
- A willingness among the key partners to commit to a long-term process that involves reframing issues into new perspectives.
- An initial willingness to align services and programs that impact others.

Source: Compiled by the author.

experiences, as Herranz maintains. In this sense, they bring experiences as board officers, followers of organization operating procedures, technical and support staff members, and users of the familiar techniques of organizations (e.g., budgeting and reporting). But in networks activists must go beyond these experiences, developing structures that hold disparate members of groups together so they can decide on mutually determined programs and strategies, seek and distribute knowledge, and define and solve problems collectively.

Box 6.3   Basic Findings for Managing within Networks

1. Not all networks are alike. Some exchange information, some build partner capacity, some "blueprint" strategies and process interorganizational programming, and some make policy and/or program adjustments. Some do more than one of the above!

2. Networks are nonhierarchical but are organized into "collaborarchies" that blend today's conductive bureaucracies with voluntary, organization-like structures. The key is not the official leaders but their champions, vision keepers, technical cores, and staff members. They are mainly organized around work and working groups as communities of practice.

3. The most important function of these communities is to discover, organize, and engage in knowledge management. The knowledge management process binds the network as it approaches problems of a multiorganization, multijurisdictional orientation.

4. Networks are overlays on the hierarchies of participating organizations. They influence but do not control home agency decisions. The core work of the public agency goes on, but in an increasingly conductive manner.

5. Networks do add public value. To varying degrees they help multiple organizations engage in problem identification and information exchange, identify extant knowledge, adapt emergent technologies, engage in knowledge management, build capacity, develop joint strategies and programs, and adjust policies and programs.

Source: Prepared by the author for presentation at the Office of the US Director of National Intelligence, Net Centric Leadership Conference, Herndon, Virginia, June 2007.

These basic issues of network operation are summarized in box 6.3, which provides five basic tenets of the network as an organized form. First, different networks carry different functions, and some carry more than one. Second, networks require distributed leadership, which involves many in different roles. Third, the discovery of useful knowledge is a driving force in these information–society structures. Fourth, networks work parallel to existing organizations, and thus they facilitate issues brought to them by these organizations. Fifth, and finally, in many different ways than just public problem solving, networks can be important contributors to public endeavors.

Network management is seen by a number of scholars as consisting of exercises in managing a set of interorganizational games. According to Kickert and Koppenjan (1997, 47), "network management, conceived as the steering of interaction processes, may involve activating networks to tackle particular problems or issues (network activation), establishing ad hoc organizational arrangements to support interaction (arranging), bringing together solutions, problems and parties (brokerage), promoting favourable conditions for joint action (facilitation) and conflict management (mediation and arbitration)."

In a similar vein, Mandell (2008, 71) points to management as a process that includes relative equality and power among stakeholders, who share an overriding mission, work toward a broad perspective or "view of the whole," establish common values, develop new relationships built on trust, and work toward systems changes. These management interaction processes, conclude Koppenjan and Klijn (2004, 10), "are considered to be searches wherein public and private parties from different organizations, [levels of] government, and networks jointly learn about the nature of the problem, look at the possibility of doing something about it, and identify the characteristics of the strategic and institutional context within which the problem solving develops." To these processes some have added facilitation of coordination among relevant actors, identification of needs and demands, and conflict reduction, particularly through mutual learning (Agger, Sorenson, and Torfing 2008).

MANAGEMENT AND POWER THROUGH THE NETWORK LEADERSHIP CORE

Although participants operate nonhierarchically in networks, the exercise of power is real. Focused research indicates that there usually proves to be a nonhierarchical distributed and differentiated management core. This means that the exercise of power by stakeholder interests and agencies is plural as well as uneven in operation. Barbara Gray (1989, 113) reminds collaborating agents that although it is essentially an exercise in sharing power over defining a problem and solving it, various interests can exert unequal influence and introduce elitist decisions at the access (to political decision makers), agenda setting, and agreement stages. In collaboration, even though the relative power brought to the table may be unequal, "the power dynamics associated with collaboration generally involve a shift from the kind of elitist decision making to more participative, equally shared access to the decision-making arena. Collaboration opens up control over access and agendas to wider participation" (p. 20).

The early work of Provan and Milward (1991, 1995) on network governance structures and outcomes points to the links between lead agencies in mental health networks that are working toward facilitating results. Provan and Kenis (2008) categorize network governance in terms of how they are operated by the participants, by a lead organization, or by a separate administrative entity. More recent work on network control points to several alternative forces: the interacting viability of small groups of managers, bureaucratic rules, and regulations; networks that hold participants accountable to reach successful outputs; the cultural controls

Box 6.4   Power in Rural Development Networks

Lurking behind the overt pretenses of network power sharing was the contesting and some-times contention or compliance enforcing of the most powerful stakeholders. In virtually every state the interest or noninterest of the governor's office proved to be a key force in determining the issues that the councils addressed. In one or two states councils' agendas proved to be their governor's agenda. In other states the work of councils could come to a halt if their governors were uninterested or unwilling to support it. Under very limited circumstances could most councils tread on the turf of an administration's rural agenda, if one existed. Rural policy agendas belonged to the governor, so councils were relegated to marginal cross-jurisdiction discussions, issue papers, and demonstrations. Moreover, at a network operating level most councils have to defer to the power of their two most impor-tant stakeholders, the state departments of economic development (agencies also very close to their governors) and US Department of Agriculture's rural development unit, housed in each state and headed by a presidential appointee. These two agencies constitute the sources of discretionary funding for rural development projects. In one state the power conflict within the council between these two major stakeholders was so intense that the rest of the council tried to mute it by precluding either party from membership on its steering commit-tee. But this was not a deterrent for either one, because they wielded their levers behind the scenes. Most important, in this state the powerful stakeholders limited the council's agenda to issues that did not interfere with their interests.

Source: Agranoff and McGuire (2006, 317).

of the norms and values of cooperation; and the desire of participating organi-zations to achieve control by enhancing their reputation. One or more of these forces has been reported as important aspects of exercising management (Kenis and Provan 2006). Additionally, McGuire (2009, 91) points to the importance of professionalized emergency management agencies in being able to be involved in collaborative management, a field where "control" is as problematic as is working in networks: "A command-and-control model of management . . . is not associated with collaboration."

The rural development council policy dynamics illustrated in box 6.4 suggest that agency or organizational power is real in networks despite the aura of equality of influence (chapter 7). This reality must be faced as the analysis of internal man-agement proceeds. As one reads in box 6.4 about the implications of power being wielded in the context of rural development networks, it is clear that it is a force that either prevents or facilitates action. That is the position taken here. Network collaboration can involve changes in structures of domination or asymmetries of resources employed in the sustaining of power relations (Gray 1989). Schapp and van Twist (1997, 66–67) refer to individual veto power in networks because "ac-tors in the network are able to cut themselves off from the steering interventions of other actors." Such veto power can be used in networks in different ways: to exclude certain actors, to ban certain points of view, to withhold resources, or to close potential actors outside the network.

There is also an enabling component or another side of the coin of network power. The use of power does not always include getting the dominant party to act, or altering its propensity to control. In the social production model identified by Stone and colleagues (1999, 354–55), it is assumed that social forces (and society's most vexing problems) are characterized by a lack of coherence and that many activities are autonomous, with many potential middle-range accommodations instead of a cohesive system of control. Under these conditions, the main concern is how to bring about enough cooperation among disparate community elements to get things done. This is a "power to," so under many conditions of ultracomplexity, this characterizes situations better than "power over." Moreover, the social production model holds out hope of constituting new possibilities under conditions of flexible preferences, or "bringing about a fresh configuration of preferences trough opening up new possibilities." The key task in such power configurations is that of building critical skills within networks of relationships while enlarging the view of what is possible. It is different from mobilization against the powerful, but it entails enlarging ways of thinking about preferences. The social production model juxtaposed against agency power illustrates how two of the core dimensions of power coexist in networks.

The leadership core of the fourteen networks studied in *Managing within Networks* (Agranoff 2007) is depicted in tables 6.1 and 6.2, which summarize a very small amount of all the leadership management data gathered for that study and are presented here for the first time. Table 6.1 covers the seven networks that were not involved in making decisions and developing interagency strategies but that exchanged information and built member capacities. Table 6.2 examines leadership in the seven networks that developed strategies and made program decisions. The actual name of the network is withheld for ease of discussion because the focus on structure and power is more important here. Although these two tables contain many cell entries, they are quite easy to read, particularly if one concentrates on the vertical columns that compare internal network management structures and processes. The horizontal rows, network by network, are of less interest here, inasmuch as what is being demonstrated is that, similar to hierarchical organizations, networks self-organize into particularistic structures. This self-organization is based on (1) what is brought to the network from and by the participating organizations, (2) its internal organization or within network management practices, and (3) the way that its technical work is organized and managed toward the resolution of the issues it faces.

One step that all the organizations that make up the fourteen networks do not all take is to establish some form of legal "chartering" that establishes themselves

TABLE 6.1 Management in Seven Nondecision Networks

Network	Externally Derived Management						Internal Operations			Technical Core	
	Legal Authority	Champion	Key Agencies	Steering Partners	Copartners	Governing Body	Standing Committees	Work Plans, Rules	Work Groups	Technical Composition	Size of Staff
Watershed I	None	1	3 F, 4 S, 4 NP, 4 CO, Univ	State EPA, Nature Conservancy	100+	Informal core group	None	None	By project, stream bank, tree planting	Environmental program specialists, local engineers	2 part-time
State economic development	501(c)(3) nonprofit	None	3S, 21-member nongovernment board	State department of ED, governor's office	100+	Executive committee	3-year ED plan	3-year plan	Plan component, regional advisory	Contract ED planners	5 nontechnical
Watershed II	Interlocal agreement	1	3 SD, 7 S, 2 F	3 natural resource districts	10	Board of executives	None	Project only	Study groups	State agency specialists engineers	1 coordinator
State home/ small business	501(c)(3) nonprofit	None	3 F, 4 S, university NGO, 3 Bus	Univ, rural council	22	Board of officers	Advisory council of state and federal administrators	None	Topical, conference web development	Business and loan specialists	None
State rural council	Intergovernmental agreement, 501(c)(3) non-profit	2	3 F, 5 S, CO, 2 CTY, 2 Univ, 3 NGO, 4 Bus	US Department of Agriculture rural development, lieutenant governor	100+	Governing board	Executive committee, 5 substantive	Annual work plan	Housing, agriculture, business, community development, environment	Rural community ED specialists, interest groups	2 full-time
State geographic information council	501(c)(3) nonprofit	2	1 F, 2 S, CO, CTY, 2 Plan, 5 Univ, 2 Bus	2 University GIS Labs	57	Board of 6 different sectors	7 substantive	Project only	Special workshop task forces	GIS lab staff, GIS users	1 part-time
State rural partnership	Intergovernmental agreement	2	1 F, 1 S, rural council, 2 Univ planning districts	US Department of Agriculture rural development, Univ	11	Governing board, steering committee	Education	Project only	Rural institute, rural development academy	University-based rural researcher, planning staff	1 part-time

Note: S = state government; Univ = university-based; NGO = nongovernmental organization; NP = nonprofit; Bus = business, for-profit; F = federal government; CO = county government; CTY = city government; SD = special district; EPA = environmental protection agency; ED = economic development; GIS = geographic information service.

Source: Compiled by the author; based on research for *Managing within Networks: Adding Value to Public Organizations*, Robert Agranoff (2007).

TABLE 6.2 Management in Seven Decision Networks

Network	Externally Derived Management					Internal Operations				Technical Core	
	Legal Authority	Champion	Key Agencies	Steering Partners	Copartners	Governing Body	Standing Committes	Work Plans, Rules	Work Groups	Technical Composition	Size of Staff
State small town assistance I	None	1	3 F, 6 S, 1 CTY, 2 Univ, 5 NGO, 1 Bus	State water development authority, state public works	113	Coordination committee	Education, finance, technology transfer	Annual objectives	Special (e.g., onsite wastewater)	Conservation engineers, finance specialists, rural specialists	None
US Department of Agriculture state rural development	State unit of federal agency	1	4 F, 3 S, 1 Plan, 1 Univ, 5 NGO, 1 Bus	State department of education, rural cooperatives	50+	State program directors	State field advisory council	Annual work plan	Water, wastewater, housing, agri-business	Grant and loan staff, planners, cooperative staff	1 full-time
State developmental disabilities planning	None (originally Governor's Task Force)	2	2 F, 7 S, 1 CTY, 1 Univ, 8 NGO, 1 Bus	State ID/DD agency/advocacy organizations/trade associations	22	Informal steering group	None	Project only	Funding future, legislative program	Medicaid and DD specialists	None
State communications network	State statutes and code	1	2 F, 8 S, 1 Univ, 1 Bus	Department of administration, legislators	500+	State telecom and technology committee	Education, telecom, telemedicine	Project only	Regional telecom advisory, five others	State agency information officers, educators	20+
State web portal regulator	State code	1	7 S, 2 NGO, 1 Bus, 1 Legislative	Department of administration, state library	9	Voting members under state code	None	For each access fee extension	Project work groups	State agency information officers	3 part-time
Metro transportation I	Intergovernmental agreement, federal statute	1	7 F, 6 S, 4 CO, 4 CTY, 3 Plan, 1 Bus	City-county government, state transportation cabinet, state agency	29	Transportation policy committee	Technical committee	Annual work program, project plans	Bicycle, pedestrian, special transportation pollution attainment	Planning and engineering specialists, local government officials	10 full-time and 6 part-time
Metro transportation II	Intergovernmental agreement, federal statute	1	2 F, 1 S, 1 CO, 6 CTY, 2 Plan	Core city government, state department of transportation	24	Transportation policy committee	Technical, transportation advisory	Annual work program, project plans	Transit, freight, bicycle	Planning and engineering specialists, local government officials	7 full-time

Note: S = state government; Univ = university-based; NGO = nongovernmental organization; NP = nonprofit; Bus = business, for-profit; F = federal government; Plan = regional planning agency; CO = county government; CTY = city government; SD = special district; ID/DD = intellectual disability/developmental disability.

Source: Compiled by the author; based on research for *Managing within Networks: Adding Value to Public Organizations*, Robert Agranoff (2007).

as a recognized entity. A look at the second column of each table reveals that three are nonchartered, that is, they have no form of authorization. That includes the longest-standing of the fourteen, the small town water assistance network in table 6.2. More commonly, networks seek some form of legal authorization or recognition that gives them "status" as an official body. The most common routes, as identified, are through an intergovernmental agreement and registration with their state governments or as a 501(c)(3) nonprofit organization under the federal tax code. Others are publicly launched by executive order, state code (or statutes), or federal legislation. No matter how they are authorized, most of these networks seek some form of standing in the sphere of public enterprises to do what they do, which gives them an aspect of legitimacy equivalent in some way to that of public agencies or NGOs. The latter, of course, automatically receive some measure of legitimacy when they are legislatively enabled and/or chartered.

More central to management are those properties that involve what public agencies and NGOs bring to the network. The first broad field in tables 6.1 and 6.2, externally derived management, depicts a profile of the organizational properties necessary to form and maintain the network. Within this first field is documented the presence or absence of a "champion(s)," a person or persons most responsible for establishing, orchestrating, and maintaining the network; a catalytic leader who passionately supports the network purpose, promotes its work, and protects it when it is politically or otherwise threatened. Holbeche (2005, 179) regards champions to be vital at an early stage, but also in sustaining commitment to the joint efforts. All but two of the networks experience a champion, and four have two champions. In every single case but the two without champions, these persons are high-ranking administrative (e.g., governor's cabinet) officials or heads of programs at the core of the networks in which they work, and they are usually substantial funders of the network's agencies and/or projects.

In the next column in each table are the representatives of the key agencies that form the network. These were usually department or program heads in state and federal agencies and executive directors. For example, in table 6.1 watershed I's core includes officials from three federal, four state, and four nonprofit environmental associations; a university faculty member; and a planning agency director. A look down the line to other networks—regardless of decision mode—reveals a similar mix of representatives of federal and state agencies, except in the few cases where the network's focus is more state oriented. A few networks also feature private-sector or business representation. These key agency representatives keep their networks going, have agency knowledge, engage in information sharing and have the ability to speak for and make any necessary decisions on behalf of their agencies. In one network, this group was referred to as vision keepers.

Within this group were normally one or two agencies that formed the "steering partners" (the third column in the field in both tables) who guided the work of the network and provided needed staff and program resources to maintain the operation. Holbeche (2005, 179) calls these "alliance managers." They provide the important "glue" across organizations because they represent broad interests. In the case of the state rural council (table 6.1), it was the state office of the US Department of Agriculture for rural development and its director and the deputy commissioner of agriculture in the lieutenant governor's office (the latter is commissioner in that state). In the small town water assistance network, it is the state water development authority director and the state public works commission chief of staff, both important funding bodies. Both these directors and their staffs organize the meetings, prepare reports, put their agencies behind new programs, loan the most technical staff, and engage other partners with the greatest frequency.

The last column in the externally derived management field in both tables is a numerical listing of the number of nonnetwork copartners or entities that are called upon from time to time to work with them. For example, the state home/small business network (table 6.1) works frequently through the community colleges, the state vocational rehabilitation office, the rural electrification cooperative association, the chamber of commerce, the municipal league, and the county association. The US Department of Agriculture's state rural development network (table 6.2) works with lending institutions, rural cooperatives, university technology transfer programs, university rural extension programs, and many others. These partners tend to be project oriented, and their representatives are not part of the operating core of the network.

This brings us to the second major field in tables 6.1 and 6.2, internal operations, which highlights how the networks are organized, one leg of the core of their internal management. First is the existence or absence of a governing body. Note that most have some form of board, executive committee, policy committee, or steering committee. Only two, one in each table, rely on informal steering groups. The other twelve obviously find a need for formality in structure, albeit nonhierarchically, that signifies that it is organized under (for most) their charter. The officers of these groups almost always rotate. Second is the presence or absence of standing committees, which were adopted by ten of the fourteen networks. Some of these are administrative (e.g., executive), although most are technical—for example, to organize a plan, to perform education functions, or in some way look at technical issues. The third looks at whether each network employs "work plans and/or guiding rules." Most employ some form of advance planning, albeit for specific projects or on an annual basis for the network as a whole. Indeed, five incorporate annual work plans and eight plan around projects. In the case of the two transportation networks, they regularly engage in both, a requirement for their federal funding.

This leaves the third and last field in tables 6.1 and 6.2, the emergence of a technical core, which is present in every network. The concept was introduced by Thompson (1967, 19–20) as the attempt by organizations to "translate the abstractions called technologies into action." He argues that organizations buffer their technical cores. Used in an interorganizational sense, Thomas (2003) indicates that organizations collaborate because technical solutions related to solving difficult problems require such interaction. This means that networks are better served by managing technical concerns into the joint effort. The core emerges because knowledge-building and problem resolution work normally requires a level of expertise and commitment of time that goes far beyond the capacities of the administrators who are part of the management core. Networks also need professional specialists. As a result networks build technical working groups that serve in program capacities for their agencies or organizations as well as bring in other specialists who are not part of the network's core organizations. Thus, the first column in the last field of each table, technical core, enumerates the work groups that form the heart of each network's more substantive or problem-oriented function. Some of these technical groups are standing—for example, metro transportation I (table 6.2) has bicycle/pedestrian, special, and pollution abatement work groups. Others are project oriented—for example, watershed II (table 6.1) has had one on its geographic information service website. All operate with some combination of these standing or project-related work groups.

The second column in this field in both tables, technical composition, depicts who belongs to these work groups. It is clear that these are nonadministrators: program specialists, consulting engineers, conservation biologists, business consultants, university planners, geographic information service laboratory technicians, hydrologists, finance specialists, buyers, information technical people, transportation planners, and city engineers. On network projects, these are normally the people who spend hours sitting at the "multidisciplinary" table with a variety of different technical specialists, looking at problems and exploring the feasibility of solutions that ultimately will go back to the key agencies and/or executive boards.

The third column, size of staff, enumerates the number of persons who help move both administrative and technical processes along; they organize meetings, find space, prepare reports, and so on. Although the staff serves both internal operations and the technical core, it normally spends much more time on the day-to-day work of the technical staff than that of the quarterly or bimonthly meeting of the network board. The last column in tables 6.1 and 6.2 reveals the considerable staff size range, from three networks that have no staff (normally pro bono with steering partners) to sixteen, and more than twenty for one. Typically one part-time staff member or the equivalent of one or two full-time persons constitutes the network staff. For all the networks but the three listed in table 6.2 that have a large staff—the state communications network and the two metro transportation networks—there is no doubt that as much staffing is actually done within the key agencies as is done by network staff. In short, each administrator in these core agencies carries some of the burden within their home structures.

This glance at network composition, operations, and groupings of work suggests that whereas networks may be self-organized, they are formally organized. Interestingly, minor differences emerge between those two types, those that share information and build capabilities in a nondecision framework, in table 6.1, and those that are more directly involved in decisions and program adjustments, in table 6.2. However, in the first field, externally derived management, differences do show up in their internal operations (the second field), where the decision networks shown in table 6.2 have more defined committee structures, have more standing committees, and, with two exceptions, have designated work projects. Although virtually all the networks have extensive technical cores and all but two decision networks listed in table 6.2 are permanently staffed, with up to ten to twenty deep for two of them (the last column in table 6.2), the nondecision networks in table 6.1 are more thinly staffed. As a result, one can see that regardless of the decision standing of various of types of networks, they are led neither by hierarchical authority nor by some random form of leaderless direction. They have defined structures.

Each of the fourteen networks thus has a definable set of leaders, organizational contributors, and associated partners. Most have a designated core of officers who legitimize decisions designate and organize the work. All have the ability to mobilize specialized task-related specialists. Both the "power over" and the "power to" are wielded within these structures. In many ways networks organize by blending participants' experiences in both large bureaucracies and voluntary organizations. They structure and function to organize interaction and agreement with very loose but nevertheless defined management practices suitable to flexible problem solving.

WHAT NETWORKS DO

Now that network structures have been identified, their activities are introduced. Here network communication, outcomes, and deliberative processes are analyzed.

Communication within Networks

Networks depend heavily on frequent interaction, as do organizations. Face-to-face contact, however, is considerably less frequent than it is within organizations, particularly those housed at common sites. Networks normally meet face-to-face monthly or quarterly at best. Fortunately, networks have emerged in the same era as that of rapid electronic communication, that is, through information and communication technology (ICT). Networks can therefore use ICT as exchange vehicles and learning entities. In this respect, "the information used for communication among the stakeholders in network processes is as important as how information is collected, stored, and shared among network participants" (Agranoff and Yildiz 2007, 332).

Communication within the network must of course compete with the administrator's or specialist's other contacts—home, organization, and personal—which stretch the limits of interaction. Anthropologists such as Robin Dunbar have concluded that the size of the human brain allows stable interpersonal and social network limits of about 150 persons, with the upper limits of all contacts somewhat higher. But what is important is the "social core" of networks, a small number of individuals among whom one can discuss important matters. One sociological researcher at Facebook reports that whereas the average number of friends is 120 (ranging up to 500), consistent with the "Dunbar number" (i.e., the upper limit of persons one may reasonably contact), actual contact is made with smaller numbers of two-way interactions, 4 persons for chats or e-mails by men and 6 for women. As the Facebook users approach 500, the number is 10 for men and 16 for women who engage in two-way communication. As the *Economist* (2009, 85–86) concludes, "People who are members of online social networks are not so much 'networking' as they are 'broadcasting' their lives to another tier of acquaintances who aren't necessarily inside the Dunbar circle." It is more "advertising" than a smaller interactive circle.

This puts a notable burden on self-organizing networks because they must exceed the demands of broadcasting. They do not have the communication advantages of hierarchy or rarely co-location to facilitate partner communication. ICT is essential here not only for "broadcasts" but also for working interactions. Social networking within the network also helps create knowledge, facilitate interaction, and encourage agreements. Agranoff and Yildiz (2007, 333–34) identify seven different uses of ICT in the kind of goal-directed public networks analyzed here. They range from their use in broadcasting for low-cost "one-to-many" links and means of overcoming restrictive two- or three-person contacts to its use for electronic decision making, mega–data/information/knowledge projects that cut across partners and are geared to solving common problems, and decision models, for example, intelligent transportation demand models:

1. Information via web pages, e-mails, teleconferencing, encouraging contacts.
2. Coordination through "one-to-many" media, e-mail, teleconferencing, website presence, electronic document transfer, and interactive "chatrooms."

3. Interaction among administrators and specialists, by electronically arranging meetings, distribution, advanced materials, organizing exercises and simulations, and/or otherwise sharing technical, legal, and financial information.
4. Task groups, work groups, seminars, and conferences to arrange results and findings into usable information and knowledge.
5. Electronic decision-making software to broker feasible processes and decisions (e.g., web-based geographic information systems, groupware).
6. Information/databases from partner agencies and organizations joined in a problem-oriented format across users to enhance the network knowledge base.
7. Management information systems/software packages decision-making models using data from several network partners (e.g., intelligent transportation demand models, client service flows, stream bank remediation planning, and related uses).

Virtually all networks use the first four items, whereas fewer become engaged in the more involved decision tools (Agranoff 2007, 102–3).

ICT also supports most networks' modest (so as not to overshadow partners) public relations efforts, most of which are undertaken through electronic venues along with an occasional printed brochure and newsletter. For example, most newsletters are electronic. Products of development and maintenance, such as research reports and the publicizing of new technical tools, are the major elements of public promotion. Contacting of nonnetwork, like-minded agency managers, specialists, and knowledge holders regarding commonly held aims or interests moves network activists to engage in a defined involvement that brings in others. Those who benefit personally, professionally, and/or organizationally will come forward and add their participation. Although rarely used by networks, media advertisements, news releases, newspaper and magazine articles, and other aspects of mass publicity can also create visibility. The ICT modes seem to be at the core of the limited amount of publicity and promoted public involvements that networks undertake.

The level and frequency of ICT use by network members depends on a number of factors. First are the heavy schedules of public managers and agency heads who must devote most of their time to the "home organization" and take part in networks. Under these busy circumstances, sending one e-mail that reaches many network members simultaneously is much easier, faster, and more cost-effective than traditional methods of communication. Second is whether network members perceive ICT use to be easy or difficult. This may partially be a generational issue. One may expect that, as a rule, the older a network member is, the less likely that he or she uses ICTs regularly in network settings. Of course, there are exceptions to this rule. Also, older network members may benefit from ICT use with the help of younger staff members who work for them in their home agencies. Third is the issue of the digital divide. Different network members might have unequal levels of access to ICTs and ability to use them. The digital divide literature (Bikson and Panos 1999, 31–41; Neu, Anderson, and Bikson 1999, xxii) tells us that geographical location, income, and educational level are important determinants of the level of ICT access and use. It thus can be that network members from remote areas and with less income and education are more likely to experience the negative effects of any digital divide, and are less likely to fully benefit from ICTs during their experience with the network structure.

A third ICT issue relates to power in networks. Inasmuch as there are strong and weak power wielders in networks, and some members even have extensive powers due to their strategic position or resources (Kenis and Provan 2006), some groupware products may lessen the negative consequences of unequal power as reflected in the social pressures of dominant network members and groupthink. The use of such software provides network members with anonymity and the ability to simultaneously participate online during meetings, so that they would not know the number of participants supporting a certain idea or the magnitude of their support.

A fourth and final problem is that of bounded rationality due to the complexity and uncertainty inherent in those issues being dealt with by networks. Agranoff and McGuire (2001) note that the wider participation and agreement that typically characterizes the decision-making process in networks may partially overcome the bounded rationality problem and produce better or new alternatives to consider, which could not be produced by bureaucracies. ICTs may also help network members manage the problem of bounded rationality by summarizing and visually representing vast amounts of data with technologies such as geographic information systems, and by making connections between different sets of data easier for human beings to comprehend, such as the use of global positioning systems for transportation, land use, soil and agriculture, and environmental management.

In conclusion, ICT approaches are important management supports for holding networks together. They are well suited to these new "meta-organizations." They facilitate the accomplishment of the real results of network activity.

Adding Value in Networks

One finding that was introduced in box 6.3 is that not all networks perform the same functions. Some only exchange information, others perform that function and build member capabilities, still others perform these functions and agreed-upon policy and program solutions, and yet others not only engage in these tasks but also make program and policy decisions that cut across organizations. A collaborative outcome, as mentioned in chapter 1, is often necessary because rarely does a single government or agency have a monopoly on potential solutions to difficult problems, or the resources or programs to deal with them. Some problems, such as nonpoint source pollution, involve a wide range of actors—environmental activists, public agency managers, and specialists, along with farmers and ranchers. These broad categories of activities can be broken down into a series of outcomes that demonstrate how public networks add value to public and private undertakings. Twenty-two of these are identified in appendix F. It was found in the original study that the more a network is involved in the kind of strategy or policy development and/or policymaking, the more of these functions will be undertaken. On the contrary, those involved in only exchanging information will normally confine their activities, in particular, to the first, second, and fourth categories (Agranoff 2007, 184) listed in appendix F.

The first category shown in appendix F is that of problem identification and information exchange. The most basic information function in networks is core to its operations because multiple parties must be convened to explore the various dimensions of a problem, to become aware of the technology used to deal with each facet of a problem, and to ultimately learn the various agencies' plans to take action with regard to these technical solutions. Thus the key to the network information process is bringing in those stakeholders that are necessary to approach an issue. A network can pool the information and decide that the problem has been insufficiently researched. It can then look more deeply into the problem. For example, conservation networks can explore the advantages and disadvantages of different kinds of nitrite-based fertilizers and their use, application amounts, time of application, and so on. Networks can also take the next step of seeing how actors in other areas have tried to solve similar problems. An inventory of potential solutions can be taken, and network meetings and workshops can be used to learn more about the most feasible solutions. One watershed network in Ohio, the Darby Partnership, has undertaken all these means (see chapter 7). Finally, the stakeholders can be educated about how to implement a given solution, and how any potential action will intersect with other stakeholders' actions. The hope here is that the relevant network participants will voluntarily take action.

The next broad category involves finding and understanding existing technologies. How is extant technology found and revealed? This flow of information is generated within the technical expertise reach of network participants, or it is sought outside the network, such as from researchers and vendors. This has been the primary function of the state geographic information council identified in table 6.1. Many different transfer vehicles exist: roundtable presentations, attendance at regional and national conferences, speakers invited to network meetings, Web postings, and e-mail transmissions. A number of networks have technology committees devoted to finding and bringing the latest developments to the entire network. A number of networks have full-time technical staff (contracted staff members, in some cases) who are subject matter specialists primarily responsible for finding and presenting solutions. This flow of technical knowledge is part of the ongoing operations of most networks. As needs are exchanged and programs are adjusted within networks, valuable expertise is accessed and exchanged. Whether formal or informal, technical knowledge is accessed and enhanced by transactional contacts within the network.

Adaptation of technologies is the next broad category. In most cases it involves some form of extension of technology findings. Often there are situations in the life of a network where someone else's technology is not feasible. Moreover, the network cannot make the necessary incremental adjustments to make it fit the situation at hand. Analytical thinking must then be supplemented with "more creativity and vision, more mental flexibility, and more *intuition*" in order to meet the challenges of information societies in an increasingly chaotic and complex world (emphasis in the original; Franz and Pattakos 1996, 638). In effect, the network must collaboratively transfer or create a technical solution that is adapted from existing research and technology. For example, the state small town water assistance network identified in table 6.1 pioneered the development and financing of wastewater reuse processes. The network studied how a small village could establish cluster permits to install, operate, and comply with the US Environmental Protection Agency's regulations for a set of nearby settlements and villages. The network's technology committee had already looked at the existing technology and had developed its own model for constructing such a creative system. This entailed an extended process of research and development by a group of network hydrologists and engineers. The network's finance committee was then charged with exploring the costs and financing potential for such a system, and to report back to the steering committee. State environmental officials were charged with consulting with the US Environmental Protection Agency regarding the process of obtaining operational permits for cluster systems. Finally, the entire process was put together—construction, financing, and securing permits—and the project was then piloted. This is not an atypical challenge: transforming and extending existing knowledge through collaborative efforts.

Knowledge infrastructure is the next broad category, inasmuch as being able to "move" knowledge is essential. Networks lack the same hierarchical transmission channels as organizations with their legal and moral authority; nor do participants frequently meet on a face-to-face basis. Network actors are infrequently in direct working contact with one another and/or with the clients or populations they are trying to assist. As a result, such ICT transmission vehicles as e-mail, websites, and electronic bulletin boards are important supplements to meetings and telephone calls. The need for information exchange among busy administrators and program managers in different organizations places increased pressures on the adaptation of ICT communication approaches. Most networks look for new ways to transform information into usable knowledge. For example, the rural development networks studied are very conscious that many of the people they are trying to serve live in remote locations, and they try to ascertain the extent of lack of accessibility, including generational and income barriers, to the Internet. As a result, they work harder to extend electronic communication to the informal outreach networks that serve rural people: county extension, higher education rural institutes, community colleges, high schools, local libraries, state agency offices at the county level, chambers of commerce, and other voluntary associations. They also work on transmitting tacit or experiential knowledge through community leaders in these institutions. By the same token, the two transportation metropolitan planning organizations (MPOs) studied base their decisions on highly developed databases, information sets, models, and other forms of tacit and explicit knowledge.

The next category, capacity building, involves the ability to help participating component agencies or organizations and staffs anticipate and influence change; make informed and intelligent policy decisions; attract, absorb, and manage resources; and evaluate current activities in order to guide future action (Honadle 1981). Networks are heavily engaged in this type of activity, particularly to develop and transmit knowledge architectures for subsequent solution-based activity and adaptation by its partners and clients, a form of knowledge management. This is the core function of some networks, for example, the public policy and information-based study created by the Lower Platte River watershed network discussed in chapter 2. They are interested not only in the transmission of knowledge but also in its creation and utilization by its participants, collectively and within their organizations. This requires capability. Annual meetings, technology seminars, technical assistance, and cross-training on a cross-organization basis are thus important to networks in this respect. Participating organizations need to do more than acquire knowledge; they want to be able to use knowledge. Implementing knowledge into internal action requires a level of capability that is fostered by most networks.

One function that stops just short of joint policymaking–program adjustment for some networks is "blueprinting" interactive strategies that the participating agencies and/or organizations respectively carry out. This type of networking is commonly found among interagency human services funding and services bodies at the metropolitan or interlocal level (Agranoff 1986). As collaborative bodies, networks involve a variety of agencies and programs when addressing problems, and they chart agreed-on courses of action that are implemented elsewhere, normally by the major partners. These strategic and programmatic approaches can be institutionalized or blueprinted, such as with a common interagency funding application form, or they can be tailored to a particular situation, such as to attract a business. They can be ad hoc, such as when a network helps a particular community access funds to improve a central business district, or they can be strategically policy oriented, such as the actions of a state-level multiagency/organization plan for maintaining the developmentally disabled outside the large institutions identified in table 6.1. Reciprocal programming for strategy making can thus be either a formal or an informal activity for some networks. These agreed-upon strategic approaches constitute important collaborative results for a number of networks that lack some "final decision authority" to act on behalf of the participating stakeholders but can act by mutual understanding.

The final category, joint policymaking, is the one most commonly associated with networks (e.g., Koppenjan and Klijn 2004; Sorenson and Torfing 2007). But in reality only a small number of networks—for example, the transportation MPOs—have the kind of authority needed to act in such capacities. For example, in table 6.1, only the last four networks identified possess such authority, inasmuch as they hold either federal or state authorization to make decisions in their charters, and in the case of the MPOs, both levels authorize such decisions. Even when these networks have such powers, they are different from representative bodies of elected officials where formal votes are taken, the majority rules, and political considerations are paramount. These networks are also different from rigid hierarchies, where someone is ultimately the legally responsible decision maker. In decision networks heavy doses of research and technical knowledge enter into the proceedings and decisions, deliberations are as likely to be as technical as they are political, and voting is more of an enablement formality after a negotiated agreement is reached (Gray 1989; Forester 2009). In practice most decision networks need to find a way to respect component members yet adopt the necessary collaboration-supportive technical and quasi- (or pseudo-) parliamentary moves that allow them to blend knowledge with a joint policy or activity. After extended network discussion many constantly send agency proposals back until an agreement can be reached. These component administrators and executives come together as representatives of different government, quasi-government, and nongovernmental organizations, with all their attendant aims, legal mandates and rules, and internal operating procedures. They represent different needs, organizational cultures, and political interests. They must make decisions, but they do not have the same hierarchical authority as in their home organization. Instead, the kind of action they take is based on negotiated adjustment while applying extant knowledge, as the partners simultaneously go through a learning process. These are very open, deliberative decision-making processes.

Deliberation in Networks: Collaborative Power

In the discussions above of table 6.1, several multifaceted faces of network power were identified, including network champions, the key agency-based administrator core, the internal operational core, and the technical core. Each of these constitutes a facet of power within a network, to move network activities along or to somehow resist their activities. Also introduced was the social production model, or "power to" possibilities.

This tradition of opening new possibilities emanates from the civic engagement field that scholars like Innes (2004) identify as (1) including the full range of stakeholders, (2) dividing meaningful tasks, (3) entails participants setting their own ground rules, (4) mutual understanding and avoidance of positional bargaining, (5) self-organizing processes, (6) information that is accessible and fully shared, (7) a consensus that is reached when all interests are explored, (8) following explicit and transparent implementation steps, and (9) there is opportunity for a public review of draft agreements by stakeholders and the public.

Booher (2008, 128–29) adapts this tradition to network process by pointing to six essential deliberative features:

1. Network structures need to be dynamic, and they change over time.
2. System information is encoded as data and dynamics of patterns.
3. Agents' interactions are geared toward multiple possible responses whereby diverse possible actions can be explored and potentially amplified.
4. The network system carries out a fine-grained, parallel search for possible options.
5. The network system exhibits a constant interplay of bottom-up and top-down processes.
6. The profound uncertainty in the world creates pressures to constantly expand diversity within networks.

These rules of engagement place a high premium on networks as they search for even greater possibilities to solve problems.

It is also clear that the managers who represent agencies can play distinctive roles with regard to promoting these deliberative processes. Chapter 3 identifies nine rules of collaborative management engagement—cogoverning, structuring lateral processes, information and knowledge orientation, and so on. They involve activity in promoting network activity geared toward forging new possibilities, ranging from promoting inclusiveness to measuring and monitoring collaborative activity. The process factors in deliberative power identified here underscore the importance of mutual learning, advancing knowledge, building communities, and employing interactive processes. Along with the rules of engagement, they constitute the important roles that managers can play in building networks.

OPERATIONAL ADVICE FROM NETWORK PRACTITIONERS

The last section of this chapter summarizes a large amount of practical advice offered by collaborating administrators and network participants, that is, the agency and NGO organization administrators and specialists who have played these games extensively. These observations have been gathered by the author during about thirty years of interviews, structured discussions, and, most important, interactions and group reports at dozens of workshops and conferences. They appear as bullet points in boxes 6.5 through 6.9 and are highlighted here, although most of these points speak for themselves.

Every participant is in a dual role as network actor and home agency or organization representative. This important distinction is like that of the "two bosses" concept in single organizations, and though there are not two bosses in networks, dual loyalty to the home organization and the network brings on a totally new mindset and value stance for participants (Weiner 1990, 459). Box 6.5 offers eight distinct tips. It is clear that one should not hold back the home agency's interest in a project or issue, and as a representative one must either know the agency or find knowledgeable representatives. Hierarchical leadership support, if you are not the executive, is essential, and any network actions will demand some form of delegated authority. The list given in box 6.6 clearly demonstrates the dualism between being an agency representative and a full collaborative participant.

To some extent the same dualism is present in box 6.6, working within the network. Participants are challenged to balance advocacy and inquiry. One is there to see that your agency's brief is advanced and that agreements constitute these interests heard, respected, and to some degree accommodated. There is much more to this role as an internal operative, for example, to deal with the different aspects of power and find solution barriers. Time and patience are useful qualities, as is lateral thinking based on knowledge and learning. Results, however small, help build trust, as does doing your share in dividing the tasks. Finally, technology and

Box 6.5   Representing Your Agency or Organization in the Network

- Explain your agency's interest in the network, and in all its deliberations.
- Maintain constant communication with the key program people in your home organization or agency.
- Know all facets of your home organization—as a boundary spanner, you are its spokesperson.
- Enlist the top leadership's support for your network involvement and reach a basic understanding of your role as a boundary spanner.
- Secure delegated authority to make preliminary or final commitments on behalf of the home organization and recheck on major decisions and commitments.
- Be prepared to report all activities or programs within your organization, not only those with which you are most familiar; if in doubt, check internally.
- When an issue or concern is beyond your technical expertise as an agency boundary spanner, bring in the right expert person from your organization.
- Recruit other specialists and/or volunteers from your organization to network with work groups and committees.

Source: Compiled by the author.

communication aids will help the work of the collaborative, as does the search for knowledge, wherever it might be found.

As box 6.7 suggests, networks are self-managed but in a nonhierarchical way that requires different kinds of leadership. The authority within moves from external agencies and organizations (although power often flows from participating organizations) to the self-organized structure. The work of the network is, as indicated above, exploratory and deliberative, with a lot of work in subsidiary work groups, and the work is flexible, adaptive, and depends heavily on its human capital. In this process, participants need to see both the forest and the trees. The network almost always implements its programs through its component agencies and organizations.

The network is not without its costs, and it is always important for participants to be somewhat cognizant of these forces. Most practitioners initially point to the first two in box 6.8, resistance to and loss of agency domain or turf, as accommodations are made and the blocks of time and other demands impinge on the home organization as a result of network involvement. Also, time invested in processes tends to be protracted in networks and a rush to find a consensus may deflect the network from its core challenges. Other costs include power games by powerful partners that can thwart agreements or limit agendas, plus agency withholding of needed complementary resources or services can have considerable costs. Finally,

Box 6.6   Working within the Network

- Never be silent; you are at the table to contribute your experience, knowledge, and organization's perspective.
- Be a decision broker by helping to form a consensus.
- Confront power; work to convert "power over" to the "power to"—open up new possibilities.
- Identify the barriers to collaborative solutions and creatively work to overcome them one by one.
- Be patient; moving multiple partners to decisions and actions has very long timelines.
- Ride the wave of the network as a "learning organization" for new technologies, human resources management, and problem solutions.
- Think outside the box; wicked problems often require solutions that are not easily transferred but can be adapted; if adaptation is not in order, find a wholly new solution.
- Constantly expand the network's technological base.
- Build trust by working together over long periods of time.
- Progressive accomplishment works well; start small, achieve some results, and gradually build in larger programs.
- Divide the work into specialized work committees, groups, and task forces.
- When you agree to undertake an activity, deliver at the specified time or you will hold up others whose time is as valuable as yours.
- Find expertise wherever it may be and enlist it—from consultants, universities and colleges, vendors, governments, think tanks, and within your own organization.
- Develop multiple communication vehicles: e-mail, electronic bulletin boards, conferences and workshops, publications, and more.

Source: Compiled by the author.

a poorly understood "cost" is one presented by restrictive public policies. The network as a collaborative body may agree on a course of action that is contrary to existing policy, or legislative and/or executive policymakers will not support such actions, nor will they commit the resources to approach the problem.

Finally, box 6.9 concludes with a series of in-network tips for those who are involved in networks. These tips relate to network organization, management, and "behavior." These points come with a reminder that in network work one also represents the home agency. Inside the network, smaller nonpermanent staffing available means that participants must do some of the administrative work, all must explore and broaden the agenda and deliberations, and all have a potential to contribute, in an inclusive atmosphere that convey mutual benefit. It is also

Box 6.7   Keys to Managing in Networks

- Delegate authority from the home agency, "pooled" within the group.
- Reach decisions that are based on mutual agreement after discussion, discovery, adjustments, and reaching a consensus.
- Engage in planning that is driven by vision and problems—normally, with a work plan around projects from a consensus.
- Implement agreements through partner organizations that "step up" and agree to the task.
- Organize by work groups or a series of mostly "standing committees" of agency representatives.
- Promote networks; they don't "just happen" and include (1) champions or workhorses, (2) promoters or vision keepers, and (3) activists or sustainers.
- Dynamically expand involvement as the need for human capital and other resources becomes apparent.
- Maintain steady flows of communication in order to sustain networks.

Source: Compiled by the author.

important that the network work within its bounds or mission, whether that is only information exchange, capacity building, or blueprinting multiagency strategies. Finally, network success can be leveraged by pointing out to participants the advantages that will accrue to them and their agencies along with the overall purpose for which the network is organized.

Box 6.8   The "Costs" of Networking

- The agency's or organization's "turf" or domain is protected by administrators and officers.
- There is accumulated time and lost opportunity from internal efforts.
- Involved human relations processes consume even more energy than in the home organization or agency.
- Consensus building drives networks toward risk-aversive agendas.
- Power; despite a consensus, stronger partners can and do control weaker partners.
- Because of resource hoarding, there is an unwillingness to contribute needed resources to the collaborative enterprise.
- Policy barriers result in a course of action that may be agreed to, but the real policymakers are unlikely or unwilling to change.

Source: Compiled by the author.

Box 6.9   Ten Leveraging Lessons for Network Activists

1. Be a representative of your agency and the network.
2. Take a share of the network administrative burden.
3. Operate by agenda orchestration; focus on purpose and vision.
4. Recognize shared expertise-based authority or interdisciplinary expertise.
5. Stay within the decision bounds of your network.
6. Accommodate and adjust while maintaining purpose.
7. Be as creative as possible.
8. Be patient and use your best interpersonal skills.
9. Recruit constantly.
10. Emphasize incentives and benefits to overcome the costs.

Source: Compiled by the author.

CONCLUSION

However incomplete it may be, in many ways this chapter and the next, where overcoming collaborative barriers is examined, represent a short course in network management. Much more could be said here about how these emergent entities foster collaboration, and more will no doubt be said by others because there is much greater interest in this subject. At least seven important conclusions should be taken away from this overview.

First, an effort to form a network should not be the first line of collaboration, but it should be undertaken when problems and conditions point to concerted activity by many entities. Other, easier alternatives are available to meet ordinary concerns.

Second, to form a network is a "long haul" undertaking, where heavy investments in deliberation, growth, learning, and the emergence of new ideas form the operational considerations. These activities require considerable investments.

Third, self-organized networks are structured, organized, planned, and tasked toward a set of agreed-upon aims. People from agencies and organizations do not just sit around the table and ask "How can we coordinate better?"

Fourth, networks can add significant public value that bridges across partner agencies and organizations. The ability to achieve these values varies considerably depending on the mission and charter of each network, whereby some are proscribed from policy and program adjustments.

Fifth, successful networks deliberate and redefine the problems they face in a trust-based and respectful manner that honors the widest range of concerns possible. This allows for the development of new possibilities and different ways of looking at problems.

Sixth, public managers have potentially important roles in promoting the process of governing by network. As representatives of legal authority and purveyors of resources, they can create platforms for different interests to come together.

Seventh, and finally, all agency organization representatives who work in networks carry a dual burden of explaining, advancing, and accommodating their home organization's interests and of participating in, growing and learning, and contributing to the maintenance and outcomes of the network. This dualism is both technical and managerial. Moreover, the network effort will only be as good as the skills, experience, and knowledge of the persons sent by organizations to be at the table.

These shared experiences demonstrate that public service in formal networks requires considerable knowledge and commitment to a process that is different from that of hierarchical management. Yet it is nevertheless management, across the boundaries of organizations. This look at formal networks is, then, a laboratory for understanding less formal network activity as well as deeper forms of collaborative management. It will hopefully enhance collaboration and make network activity more salient.

CHAPTER 7

Identifying and Overcoming the Barriers to Collaboration

ONE OF THE NETTLESOME PROBLEMS identified in chapter 1 that brought on the need for collaboration was the North Carolina mental disability contract system. Between 2001 and 2006 the General Assembly of North Carolina essentially removed local services delivery authority for all types of mental disability services from county-level units and put them in charge of services planning, provider network development, service management, financial management, evaluation, oversight, and coordination. Session Law 2006-142, 122C3 (20b), identified a local management entity (LME) as "an area authority, county program, or consolidated human services agency that refers to functions/responsibilities rather than government structure." These reforms were designed to take local entities out of direct services in government mental health, intellectual and developmental disabilities, and substance abuse services and to get local entities into resource priority setting, operating under a state plan, increasing consumer voices, and most important "separating management functions from provider functions and creating local governance with strong county linkage" (Lin 2007, 14).

An independent study of the LME system revealed many system difficulties, particularly with collaborative management. Among them were fatigue in local planning with basic system issues overlooked, along with a lack of comprehensive documentation; core service areas underaddressed in several areas of the state; difficulty in divestiture of direct services involvement, particularly in rural areas where there were no alternatives; gaps in developing tools for consumer access and consumer waiting lists; needs assessments and service gaps analysis being either delayed or ignored; difficulties in bringing in some new providers because of delayed state government payments; scarcity of professionals suitable to provide services; fraud and abuse by some service providers, related to the level of service and the providers' qualifications; and slow consolidation of services (Lin 2007, chap. 3). This is quite an extensive indictment of collaborative breakdown.

It should come as no surprise that agencies and nongovernmental organizations (NGOs) do not automatically collaborate or naturally form networks, even when they are mandated to work together. Very early in the process of integrating disparate human services in the 1960s and 1970s, it was found that the serious business of getting agencies to work together entailed a complex set of interacting forces, including overcoming separate agency or program legal mandates and missions, absent technical capacities to solve problems, power configurations in communities that thwarted coalescence, and a lack of service provider agreement on the need to relate different services around the client (Agranoff and Pattakos 1979; Agranoff 1991). Barriers to collaboration like these are shown in full force in the case of mandated coordination and contracting in North Carolina, where problems similar to the earlier services integration issues came out as the system of the 2000s was studied. The players learned that despite notable progress in moving toward a collaborative model, administrators involved in the North Carolina experiment must, as in all collaborative endeavors, understand and deal with obstacles that are put in the way of collaborative results, the concern at this stage of analyzing collaboration.

The fact is that in many situations a harmonious atmosphere that leads to easy joint agreement does not always prevail, even in successful collaborations. The reality of harmony can also prove to be the opposite: acrimony, power domination, disagreement over aims, difficulties in reaching agreement, and a lack of ability to make solutions work. This is the other side of collaborative management, so to speak, where real obstacles thwart and often prevent any level of collaborative success. Management must also account for and learn to deal with these atmospheric realities.

There are probably as many examples of unsuccessful collaborations as there are successes. A key agency in a human service network withholds critical services resources. Important stakeholders—for example, local governments—refuse to zone their land so as to control suburban growth. Farmers are reluctant to risk yields by reducing their fertilizer amounts, thus mitigating soil degradation. A proposed business startup cannot proceed because key lending institutions have not come through. After three-plus years trying to develop a common funding application for nonprofit social services agencies, the allied agencies give up in frustration, agreeing to "share information" from individual forms. The county emergency services manager discovers that she does not have the legal authority under state law to coordinate emergency vehicle/ambulance dispatch in cases of a real disaster.

There are many reasons for failures to collaborate; to paraphrase the famous line from the movie *Hud*, in which someone said "What we have here is a failure to communicate" as a chain gang prisoner was being beaten by penitentiary staff. Sue Goss (2001) contends that four sets of forces that have undermined cross-boundary work go to the heart of policy and governmental systems. First, professional specialization and professional isolation narrow the scope of intervention. Second, the creation of isolated public organizations that connect by grant/contract or other arrangements with outside agents create performance cultures and reinforce organizational boundaries. Third, departmental separation at higher levels (national and state in the United States) creates boundaries that undermine the scope for local negotiations and compromise. And fourth, cross-boundary efforts are notoriously underfunded, normally through pilots or projects requiring competition and bidding. These obstacles must be overcome in the twenty-first century; Goss (2001, 112) argues that "a failure to make networks and partnerships function effectively will necessarily be a failure of governance."

Collaborative failure and its avoidance are the focus of this chapter. To illustrate the obstacles it returns briefly to the case of a government legislated collaboration in North Carolina mental disabilities programming and the difficulties in achieving these aims. An identification of the preconditions for collaboration follows. Then the role of power—positive and negative—in collaborative management is introduced. Next, the focus is on seven basic obstacles to collaboration, ranging from agency domination or "turf" to public policy barriers. After the obstacles are introduced, the issues of how to facilitate public agency stewardship contracting and overcome obstacles through deliberative bargaining and negotiation are discussed. The important concerns of trust in facilitating collaborative management are covered next. The concept of collaborative advantage, or collaborative inertia, and how to combat it is introduced at the end of the chapter.

LEARNING FROM THE EXPERIENCES OF LOCAL MANAGEMENT ENTITIES

The LME system is not a total failure. The experience in North Carolina presents an account of the collaboration barriers faced in the real world. The state is no doubt in the early steps of building a system. It is going through some of the collaborative pains that other states have experienced. The interim assessment report reached several important conclusions with regard to how to face the obstacles to collaboration:

1. Most system reforms take time and effort, and the results may not be realized during the initial years.
2. Managing gaps in provider networks requires strong state authority intervention, whether or not the local/regional authority is in place.

3. The involvement of counties, especially in funding the administrative in-frastructure and services, goes a long way to assure ownership of the public disability system.

4. The state and local authorities have had to learn how to navigate in a new environment when public–private partnership is the dominant mode of service delivery.

5. As more private providers enter the system, serious attention should be paid to how all providers are being paid and monitored, to ensure equity in services offered.

6. Past roles and functions, along with the culture of past practices, cast a long shadow on the public system; some habits do not disappear (Lin 2007, 45–48).

The report makes clear that LMEs are making a start at understanding and developing local networks, and that they are feeding back lessons learned into action.

In this respect many areas that found gaps in core services are seeking new providers. Divestiture no doubt could not have happened overnight, particularly in rural areas where no service alternatives existed. The local public providers were expected immediately to go from clinical work to become contract managers and network builders. Limited resources, even if federal Medicaid dollars are at stake, are the reality of meeting client needs. Many local public agencies that would be expected to work with the LMEs—vocational rehabilitation, schools, public health, transportation, employment and training—would normally not be expected to automatically cooperate with these "new kids on the block." Finally, though local providers no doubt would like to expand additional service contracting, it is clear that an extended time frame is involved in building relationships. It is probably safer to conclude that the LMEs have faced many initial obstacles, but in this situation "failure" is not the correct conclusion; instead, LMEs have achieved small measures of "success" as they have identified and overcome the obstacles to collaborative outcomes.

PRECONDITIONS FOR COLLABORATION

Certain situations or antecedents have been associated with collaborative success, and the absence of these conditions is associated with collaborative breakdown. Cigler (2001, 78–81) found that these situations emerged from her multiple case study research on cross-community organizing involving sets of small towns and counties. They suggest practical strategies for beginning and facilitating partnership formation and for how to avert collaborative failure. Initially, a perceived system failure like that in North Carolina, a disaster occurrence such as a farm crisis, massive funding cuts, a flood, or the loss of a large business triggers events that lead to exchange relationships among community actors. In a related fashion, the fiscal or perceived stress that results from these crises triggers thinking about resource dependence.

Still other preconditions relate to capacity building by external agents: "Without the 'push' of public opinion calling for behavior, leaders may need the 'pull' or incentives such as technical or financial assistance in order to hone the skills necessary to mobilize for action and to harness resources needed for collective action" Cigler (2001, 79). In such situations external capacity building—by, for example, state government, foundations, and professional associations—was needed to strengthen and broaden leadership, for example, in the rural leadership programs mentioned above.

Internally, the presence of collaborative skills-building leadership in the community was also an important precondition—particularly the various voluntary organization board members or local government committee members who possess skills in such areas as planning and finance, but also participation in government-sponsored visioning and strategic planning exercises. These, of course, can build on trust-building relationships.

Collaboration is also facilitated by the existence of a policy entrepreneur or group of entrepreneurs. These, of course, would be similar to the network champions identified in the previous chapter. Their energies and talents started the undertakings of the organized effort, along with an asset-based perspective on the area and its problems. Also, they had the skills to blend the political, analytical, and people skills that were needed to mobilize key support.

These leaders were then able to build a political constituency for cooperation. In many policy or problem areas, politics really does matter. As a result, garnering political support is necessary. Such broad-based political constituencies do not readily exist or are rare. They must be cultivated—or, as suggested by Agranoff and McGuire (2001), they require activation skills to tap knowledge and resources to obtain the needed money, information, and expertise to manage across agencies and organizations.

Additionally, early and continued support by elected local officials facilitates collaboration. They not only know but can also broker the necessary politics. Most collaborative solutions ultimately need the support of some authority-NGO board, city or county council, state legislature, or the like—for actions, and often neglect, involving one or more key officials in collaborative processes on a proactive basis can lead to a lack of support down the line.

Finally, Cigler found two legitimacy-raising and related preconditions that facilitate cooperation. One is attempts by leadership to demonstrate to broader publics the advantages gained by collaborative action. It allows the many actors to see the early positive results, which spurs on subsequent links in the partnerships. The other is early focus on visible, effective strategies. This, in turn, "helped build interested and supportive constituencies" (Cigler 2001, 81).

Cigler (2001, 83) concludes that although future collaborative ventures will rely on interorganizational actors that will be expected to chart their own courses, it does not necessarily mean that they do not need external help or that the existence of a catalyst is enough. Politics, public support, and process experience can be as important as technical expertise. Opportunity, capability, and process development are also essential preconditions for failures to launch collaborative efforts.

INTERORGANIZATIONAL POWER

The discussion of preconditions is an explicit reminder that a necessary condition in collaboration is that of unequal power (Agranoff and McGuire 2001). Power dynamics exist within an array of collaborating organizations. This brings on the power dependence relationship. Among other scholars, Rhodes (1997, 9) argues that organizations depend on each other for resources and therefore enter into exchange relationships, where they maneuver with one another. Power dependence explains why different entities interact and variations in the distribution of power within networks. Rhodes (1997, 36–37) goes on to say that such entities are usually controlled by dominant coalitions, which employ strategies within rules of the game to regulate the processes of exchange. In this respect power can be seen as a force to both facilitate and hinder network processes. Agency organization power is a very real barrier when lead organizations serve to keep certain problems off agendas, withhold support for key network strategies or decisions, or withhold required agency-controlled resources. These are the key power dependence barriers to network results. Conversely, here I indicate in some detail that various kinds of collaborative power, introduced in the previous chapter as the social production model of power, can lead to more positive results. I argue there that power is not always understood as a negative force.

In my study of fourteen networks (Agranoff 2007, chap. 6), I found four different types of interactive power, each of which can be a positive or negative force for collaborative outcomes. The first is the familiar agency power, or the ability to play the power dependence game to thwart or enhance results: "We cannot ignore the facade of trust and the rhetoric of collaboration used to promote vested interest through manipulation and capitulation of weaker partners" (Clegg and Hardy 1996, 679). The second type is operational power within the collaborative enterprise, and how it is structured and operated. Klijn (2001, 36) defines this dimension as generalizable procedures that are adopted and, in the production of games, both "arena rules" that determine the nature of the game and "interaction rules" that define internal behavior. The third type is knowledge-based power that emerges when technical actors work together to identify and solve problems about which they are initially uncertain. Power accrues as technical experts blend "framed experiences, values, contextual information and expert insight that provides a framework for evaluating and incorporating new experiences and information" (Davenport and Prusak 2000, 7). And the fourth type is a deliberative power, which is employed as new technical information is infused and new possibilities emerge as a result of discussions and multiparty engagement. It involves sort of finding "good answers through process" (Innes and Booher 1999, 5), based on the concept of collaboration as power sharing (Gray 1989).

This fourth type of power is perhaps the least understood but most central to engaging in collaborative management. Deliberative power is most closely associated with the community power/community development social production model of Stone (1989) and Stone and colleagues (1999). It is based on urban regime theory (Stoker and Mossberger 1994), the assumption that society is characterized mainly by a lack of coherence, not by a single system of domination or coordination (i.e., power over some form). Instead, society is a loose network of institutional arrangements, with many autonomous activities and midrange agreements: "The issue is how to bring about enough cooperation among disparate community elements to get things done" (Stone 1989, 227). Another part of the social production model involves preferences. If one assumes that they are not fixed but can be modified as situations change and new options open up, power is no longer about the terms on which fixed preferences are adjusted to one another. Thus social production can be a matter of bringing about new sets of preferential configuration through "opening up new possibilities" in a sense of "an enlarged view of what is possible" (Stone et al. 1999, 354–55). Box 7.1 provides several hypothetical illustrations of deliberative power, complied from environmental improvement situations. They demonstrate situations where power is "expanded" to facilitate reaching various types of joint agreements within various collaborative arrangements.

It needs to be understood that, as illustrated in box 7.1, conceptually both a "power over" and a "power to" are exhibited in collaborative management. Of particular importance, partner agencies bring much more than positive or negative power to the table. The power dimension needs to be expanded to include

Box 7.1   Possible Dimensions of the "Power To" (P2): The Enabling Dimensions in Collaborative Settings

Hypothetical illustrations of "power to" that flows from the synergistic operation of environmental networks:

P2a = power of discovery of new ideas; synergy of solution—collectively, a task group or agency finds a new way to research, propose, and develop a comparative environmental risk program for the community.

P2b = power of technical solutions; brought to the fore that can be used by a partnership; e.g., an intergovernmental estuary partnership learns about a new way of mitigating fertilizer runoff.

P2c = power of feasibility; e.g., the US Environmental Protection Agency and/or a state environmental protection agency agrees that a proposed watershed mitigation proposal, using waivers and statutory relief, jointly proposed by a network is agreed to "in principle" and now the details are to be negotiated.

P2d = power of willingness to accommodate; e.g., two influential and large manufacturers, DuPont and General Motors, and the City of Cleveland agree that they are potentially responsible parties in a contaminated landfill and are willing to discuss mitigation costs and measures with the Cuyahoga County Brownfields Task Force.

P2e = power rebalancing; newly introduced network partners change the formula; e.g., the Iowa sustainable Agriculture Strategic Network (state agencies, agribusiness, producer organizations, farm organizations, universities) adds the Sierra Club, Citizens Environmental Council, and three other environmental advocacy groups to its membership.

P2f = resource dependency change; e.g., a power shift due to the expansion of an interagency coordinating council beyond the US Environmental Protection Agency brings in the US Army Corps of Engineers, Soil Conservation Service, Agricultural Research Service, Federal-State Extension Service, Rural Development Administration, and Economic Development Administration as other federal agencies that can legally, politically, and financially support joint research and operations.

Source: Compiled by the author.

the power dynamics inside the collaborative undertaking itself, a principle that is not well understood. In sum, in collaborative activity the four power dimensions often appear to manifest themselves in overlapping form: (1) the familiar power the partner brings to the agency, (2) the internal operational power that results from agency inputs and interactive processes within the collaborative process related to its maintenance and operations, along with (3) knowledge-based power pursued by each cross-organization operating technical core, and (4) the deliberative power of generating new agreement possibilities generated by the search for technical solutions and outcomes that address multiorganization and interagency problems. Because analytically all four of these dimensions are likely to be present in collaborative processes, they can serve as positive forces to facilitate overcoming those negative synergies of agency power used in resisting joint agreement or action. Any of these processes can be understood to jump-start and maintain power needs in collaborative processes.

UNDERSTANDING AND RESOLVING SEVEN COMMON COLLABORATIVE BARRIERS

There also are interagency forces that operate "less naturally" to forge collaborative outcomes, that emanate not from the nature of programs that are designed to encourage collaboration (professionalism, isolated public agencies, departmental separation, and low resource effort) but from the collaborative interactions themselves. Among them are an agency's protection of its turf, risk aversion, lost time and opportunity costs, human relations costs, the exertion of power by agencies and publics, resource hoarding, and public policy barriers.

When in a collaborative mode, agencies (i.e., their representatives) have to think of their own "home" organization concerns as well as those issues related to collaboration. If the balance is entirely or too far in favor of the former, protection of agency turf can be a barrier. Bardach (1998, 164) defines turf as "the domain of problems, opportunities and actions over which an agency exercises legitimate authority." Agencies can try to protect their turf by fashioning distinctive competencies, or managers may resist collaboration to protect their autonomy (Bardach 1998, 179–80). Thomas (2003, 35) suggests that agency managers (1) may be convinced that they know best, and therefore decide how to carry out agency tasks; (2) may seek to control one's own space in order to avert loss (or failure) in new territory if it involves perceived loss of control; and (3) because autonomy reduces uncertainty, managers must be careful not to encourage too many threats to their organizational environments. Turf can clearly block network action.

How can turf barriers be overcome? Various mechanisms are available. For example, such cooperation strategies as contractual relationships, cooperative agreements, coordinating councils, and joint ventures can overcome some protective fears (Mandell and Steelman 2003). Another important means of overcoming turf is the practice whereby management networks generally avoid becoming program implementers but leave program administration to partner agency services (Agranoff 2007, chap. 9). Most important, Koppenjan and Klijn (2004, 162) point to three key managerial strategies for "managing content" that shift from barriers like turf to common ground: (1) avoidance of early fixations, furthering awareness of plurality of perceptions and preferences; (2) furthering substantive variety and favorable conditions for learning and intermediate adoptions; and (3) joint image building, that is, a search for common ground for joint interactions despite recognition of enduring differences. Clearly, there is no guarantee of success in eliminating turf, but the implication is that investments in process can reduce its most pernicious impacts.

Risk aversion may be a by-product of the consensus pursued in collaborative endeavors. Often, agendas sink to less ambitious aims as parties weigh in on their concerns. This is particularly true when there are multiple conflicting stakeholders, for example, in the Lower Platte River watershed network discussed in chapter 2. Landowners, farmers, local governments, state environmental agencies and natural resource advocacy organizations all have different interests in watersheds. This has kept many issues off the decision agenda, particularly those related to land use. However, watershed affiliates all over the country normally agree at some level that they will rise above partner objections to look together at degradation, usually through scientific study, and identify mitigation strategies that might be adapted. Hopefully, jurisdictions and landowners will take these on by themselves in the long run. Meanwhile, the collaborative body is still at work on this and other issues. Sometimes it is important to back up and deal with what can be done rather than let ideals jeopardize the ongoing effort.

Managers involved in collaborative ventures often note the time and opportunity costs lost in work for the home organization because of devotion to collaborative activity. Every administrative hour spent on interorganizational collaboration is an hour taken away from internal management, accumulated time that at some point takes its toll. Collaborative decisions and managers' reports normally take more time within network and partnerships than in their home hierarchical organizations. Local government managers who are not full-time boundary spanners once estimated that between 10 and 20 percent of their time is spent working across organizations, with a large portion spent taking intergovernmental joint actions and on projects (Agranoff and McGuire 2003). Much of this collaborative time is spent in formal networks and/or in interagency committees and task forces. The formal meetings of the networks and their operating committees normally take a small proportion of this time, at most a 2- to 4-hour commitment monthly or quarterly. It is the project work of the collaborative efforts that take the major portion of time commitments, often up to 120 person-hours per project. These efforts may represent crucial time and expertise enhancement needs, but nevertheless they detract from time spent on home agency efforts.

Managers involved in this kind of work report that as a result of the pull of collaborative work, they leave some work at home unfinished or need to delegate it to other staff. The more likely scenario would be to absorb extra professional time on the job, thus expanding the work role. The problem with delegation is that staff members are often already committed to other more technical collaborative work and thus are not available. One managerial practice that can avoid extended collaborative time is well-planned and organized meetings, with prior staff work and study reports, so that interactive time is not wasted. It is also important that all partners be prepared to report on their portions of the shared workload when expected or another's time will be wasted. Prior circulation of documents and reports by e-mail is essential. Also, for example, the Iowa Geographic Information Council, a formal network, holds three of its four quarterly meetings on full-motion video closed circuit television to decrease travel time and facilitate full attendance.

There are clearly barriers presented by the multiorganizational and multicultural nature of collaborative activity. Organizations that devote efforts to processes that lead to learning-based agreements, joint production, or other types of negotiated results have the advantage within the organization hierarchy, and authority to ultimately decide and move things along. Collaborative bodies or efforts do not. Whereas similar human relations or group processes unfold, mutuality in decision making between organization participants is a paramount value. The process is also "multicultural" in that different agency or organization traditions and practices need to be recognized and worked through, and sometimes worked around. Respect for the "other" is not only highly valued, it is essential to ultimately move an organization representative toward agreement. Trust, an essential ingredient in network processing, takes a great deal of time and experience to build up. Consensus, the only way that agreement or decisions can be reached, does not come easily. Program success normally requires a complex overlay of process and mutual agreements that combine political, technical, and financial considerations. The result is generally satisfying to stakeholders but involves human relations energy (and more time costs) that far exceed that of a training program in a single organization. More will be said about these concerns as collaborative inertia is discussed at the end of this chapter.

Power exertion as a barrier has already been identified. In the study of fourteen networks power issues often arose above other barriers. For example, in the two transportation networks large jurisdictions—central city and metropolitan area counties—often were dominant forces, sometimes for resisting joint efforts and sometimes for promoting them. More important, they used their positions of power to advance their core concerns at the expense of a metropolitan-wide view, setting aside area-based concerns on the collective table. The Des Moines city delegation had nine of thirty-one votes on the body's transportation policy committee during the study period, normally voted as a block, and often tried to thwart area-wide efforts in the interest of core city projects. Conversely, the west (Polk County, Iowa) suburban block of twelve often tried to counterweigh this power game in a metropolitan direction. The point is that in the networks, activists reported that raw power in many forms—withholding agreement, withholding resources, exercising effectual vetoes, or temporary withdrawal from an anticipated agreement—is a barrier that must often be overcome.

The practice of holding back needed resources or failure to contribute needed resources to collaborative agreements was reported in the network study as a frequent barrier. Although withholding of agreement on a plan is the most common example of thwarted decision making, held-back resources in the face of recognized interdependent conditions comes close in frequency. It can include withholding contributed time, denial of access to an agency's programs or services, refusal to make financial allocations or contributions, nonsupply of information or technology, or holding back key political and organizational support. As mentioned above, in the states numerous innovative rural development projects are normally funded by two agencies, the US Department of Agriculture's rural development agency state-based office and the state government's economic development department. When these sources demur, the remaining representatives of rural collaborative efforts and formal networks must dig deeper into their own resource pools, try to evoke a change of heart, find new alternative resources, or go without critical support. Holding back resources can make reaching collaborated decisions and actions difficult, and often impossible.

Finally, but hardly the least important, sometimes a collaborated solution is blocked because there are policy barriers to a solution. For example, the Darby Creek watershed network in Ohio faces the challenging barrier of maintaining the creek's stream banks within incorporated city limits, because the Ohio Constitution puts the regulation of riparian boundaries within incorporated city limits under the exclusive jurisdiction of city governments. This policy barrier is particularly acute because whereas the Darby group may find and agree upon a solution, it does not make any decisions. Policy prevents resolution in this case because some city governments along the creek will not go along with jointly agreed-upon plans.

Although some collaboratives do find ways around such policy problems or forge ad hoc multiagency solutions to problems (Kickert and Koppenjan 1997), they sometimes will still hit brick walls. For example, the Indiana 317 Group (see chapter 5) encountered an intellectual and developmental disabilities policy barrier to its goal of expanding services for deinstitutionalization beyond the minimum needed to sustain clients outside institutional settings. The state, along with all other states, is facing the US Supreme Court's *Olmstead* decision (see chapter 2), which requires state governments to provide community services for those institutionalized handicapped individuals who are clinically ready and choose to be discharged. However, the 317 Group faced a huge obstacle to the facilitation of community services: allowing Medicaid to finance personal assistance services. The state legislature has the final word on this issue and has thus far taken a very careful approach to Medicaid-funded services, which has led to reduced benefits in recent years. So in this case the collaborative body knows what to do but cannot do it because it cannot change the policy.

The 317 Group has tried to overcome this barrier by involving key legislators in its deliberative processes; providing hard data on service levels, waiting lists, and funding trends; and educating the interim legislative commission that sifts through proposals between regular sessions. By the same token, city governments along Darby Creek have been educated about stream bank erosion, and the Darby collaborative network has tried to influence city planning commissions. In other words, overcoming the policy barrier requires various types of knowledge and also long-term educational and lobbying processes that may or may not work. This and other barriers can also be served by engaging in various forms of negotiations, particularly through engaged deliberation.

PREPARING THE PUBLIC AGENCY FOR COLLABORATIVE MANAGING

In chapter 4 the idea of stewardship contracting was introduced as a means of moving agent models to more collaborative government-to-contractor relationships (Van Slyke 2007). The idea of building relationships in collaboration, like stewardship in contracting, was first crystallized by Bardach (1998). Based on an examination of multiple case studies, he identifies a set of building blocks in interagency operation that, when combined, build "interagency collaborative capacity," a concept that builds toward stewardship. One pillar of such "craftsmanship" involves creative opportunity, intellectual capital, an implementation network, and supportive advocacy groups. The other platform involves trust, acceptance of leadership, and a communications network. These platforms then combine to lead to improved steering capacity, an operating subsystem, and continuous learning (Bardach 1998, 274). In a sense these forces lead to stewardship in moving contracting toward building networks.

Since the 1990s senior executives of two federal agencies, the US Forest Service (in the Department of Agriculture) and the Bureau of Land Management (Department of the Interior), have encouraged their staffs in the field to engage diverse groups of stakeholders (e.g., timber interests, environmental groups, local governments, conservation districts) to work together to resolve conflicts, solve nettlesome problems, and leverage technical and financial resources for land management problems. This is called stewardship contracting (Moseley 2010, 10), and it has led to hundreds of different land management collaboratives that are effective on the ground in enabling the two federal agencies to forge new agreements. Although some of these efforts are more successful than others, their experiences in dealing with collaborative obstacles offers important practice lessons.

Collaboratives like the federal stewardship effort present many difficulties: "The demands of vertical hierarchies in an organization and horizontal collaboration with third parties are often different from one another. Hierarchies have clear lines of authority and reporting, whereas collaborative networks are each unique and can be quite fluid" (Moseley 2010, 10). Having been in place for decades, the culture and staff work habits of a government agency are deeply ingrained. This can lead to many barriers. The first type are legal ones. For example, the Federal Advisory Committee Act requires federal agencies to secure a formal charter if they are to take the lead in a collaborative process, which often means that federal officials must leave the formal leadership to others. Other regulations on civil servants and civic activity may make attending some meetings problematic, particularly politically charged sessions. Also, formal mechanisms such as memoranda of understanding, cooperative agreements, and service contracts may only be devised after protracted sets of negotiations, which may cover only a part of the collaborative's effort. Next, top executives in government agencies could find themselves between the interests/standards/resources of their own agency—hierarchical obligations—and those of the collaborative. Moreover, line officials may not have the complete authority or "decision space" to act on behalf of the agency affecting the power and efficacy of collaborative operations to reach agreement. Finally, a not uncommon situation reported by Moseley (2010, 11) is that "in some instances, federal agencies, their community partners, and citizens may find themselves having spent months reaching common ground, only to have the rules changed, priorities shifted, funding removed, or staff reassigned." Any one of these events can cause a public agency to back out of any commitments it has made. In sum, potential obstacles must be contemplated and approached.

The land management stewardship contracting experiences studied by Moseley lead her to suggest four strategies for government executives to support field-level coordination. First, it is important to create time and space for collaboration to develop. Line staff members need to be able to build common ground through conversations, meetings, field tours, and work on small-scale projects. This means that executives need to provide funding and staff time, to engage partners.

Second, executives can change the rules to encourage collaboration. Several means are available: allocating money that supports implementation, creating the decision space so that meaningful decisions can be made, pushing authority downward, engaging oversight approaches that do not hamper flexibility, and reviewing and possibly eliminating long-standing procedures that provide cumbersome barriers.

Third, incentives for staff to collaborate can be created or consequences can be created if they do not engage other interests. This turns collaboration into an agencywide priority like encouraging stewardship contracting itself, which encourages adaptation to local circumstances, encourages staff exchanges of ideas and experiences, provides guidance and assistance in helping staff members understand how they are allowed to engage various publics, leads by example through executive involvement in collaboration, and creates performance measures, (e.g., the number of stewardship contracts) that promote collaboration.

Fourth and finally, agencies can invest in building the capacities of both governmental and nongovernmental partners. This involves various forms of training and orientation, technical assistance, encouraging peer-to-peer learning, and liaison work with support staff in the agency contracts and finance offices (Moseley 2010, 30–35).

An agency's executives can do many things to "shake the hierarchy" by shifting the structures, tools, resources, and incentives to collaborate. The matter, as Williams (1980, 262) once concluded, "is whether the agency can be reoriented and reorganized to shift more toward field performance and whether a strategy that has increasing local commitment and capacity as a central objective can provide a decision and action framework that fits the agency's particular situation."

DELIBERATIVE NEGOTIATIONS AND INTERGOVERNMENTAL BARGAINING

The concern for various forms of collaborative exchange vis-à-vis agencies' ability to make program decisions and adjustments through bargaining and negotiation comes from two venerable traditions in public affairs: intergovernmental grants and related adjustments, and efforts to encourage true citizen engagement with deliberative negotiations and directions. It is clear from both these antecedents that the standard two-party, win/lose orientation (Fisher, Ury, and Patton 1991, cited by Bingham and O'Leary 2008; Lax and Sebenius 2006) gives way in collaborative management not only to multiple party involvement but also to the process becoming more open. There is an attempt for all or most involved parties to achieve measures of joint agreement after a sequence of delving deeply into an issue, whereby they look for mutually satisfactory solutions while meeting the concerns of multiple interests.

Bargaining and related forms of negotiations have become standard features of intergovernmental management since the exposure of grants-in-aid and regulatory programs. This topic was introduced in chapter 4, where the work of Pressman (1975), Ingram (1977), Liebschutz (1991), Elmore (1985), Williams (1980), and Grodzins (1966) was discussed. For Grodzins bargaining occurred within a story of growing expertise, growing professionalization, and growing complexities; it is a story most of all of ever-increasing contact between officials at several levels of government within the federal system. Contact points bring disagreements and produce misunderstanding and enmity. But most of all, they have produced cooperation, collaboration, and effectiveness in programming and steering the multiple programs of modern government (Grodzins 1966, 373). Grodzins's last point about the mutuality of the process, as opposed to hard two-party bargaining, laid important groundwork for the idea of multidimensional negotiations.

Agranoff and McGuire (2003) empirically tested these ideas regarding cities' interactions with governments and NGOs in their area and in state and federal government contact. They found high levels of negotiation; nearly three out of four governments regularly engaged in contacts and sought changes. They also found many different styles of interaction, defined by the extensiveness of their collaborative activities and strategies. Bargaining in the traditional sense identified here was only one of several stances (e.g., abstention, strict compliance, reactive). Most important was a jurisdiction-based approach to collaboration, whereby strategic action was taken with multiple actors and agencies to advance their cause interactively, based on local or own-source goals and objectives in the intergovernmental system. From this study, box 7.2 presents a mini–case study of jurisdiction-based managerial bargaining in Cincinnati. Goal achievement in complex settings "requires interaction and adjustment with critically positioned or endowed actors" (Agranoff and McGuire 2003, 48). These findings indicate that the intergovernmental system has brought forth a more deliberative form of collaborative negotiation in jurisdiction-based activity in addition to two-party bargaining.

Negotiations that transcend the standard win/lose or zero-sum postures have been developed over the years by the members of the Harvard Negotiation Project (Fisher, Ury, and Patton 1991; Fisher and Brown 1988). They urge actions that nurture and continue relationships oriented around problem solving, as being "unconditionally constructive. This means that in a relationship with you, I should do those things that are both good for the relationship and good for me—whether

BOX 7.2   Jurisdiction-Based Negotiation in Cincinnati

Cincinnati became heavily involved in both political and administrative bargaining and negotiation with state government while under pressure in the mid-1990s by both its major professional sport franchises (the baseball Reds and football Bengals) to build new playing facilities to improve financial arrangements with the city. The city government, including the city manager, was under heavy fire to broker a deal that would keep both franchises in town. Cincinnati saw the opportunity to negotiate with the State of Ohio regarding its Capital Improvement Project (CIP) funds. The CIP program is primarily designed to help communities revitalize their physical infrastructures, particularly either those of general public use or those that connect with state projects through the Ohio Division of Natural Resources, the Ohio Building Authority, the Board of Regents (university), or agencies in the governor's administrative cabinet. Although the CIP is not explicitly designed for retaining sports franchises, city staff initially generated additional local funding criteria to state criteria and then sought local public input on projects. Though the original public hearing list of nine priorities included an aquarium, a park, and conservatory improvements, in the end the city was able to place heavy emphasis on the projects designed to help retain the sports franchises, particularly riverfront improvements near the proposed stadia and for nearby downtown recreation and entertainment. The next stage involved extended back-and-forth negotiations with state officials, who were not initially receptive. After a great deal of give and take, a total of $13.9 million in CIP money was approved, the largest award in the city's history. The city was able to direct a substantial proportion of this state program, primarily intended for other purposes, toward its most pressing priorities at the riverfront site. It would not have happened without mobilization of local support, sublimation of other priorities, and most important the confidence in formulating proposals and experience-based ability to engage in protracted bargaining with the state government.

Source: Agranoff and McGuire (2006, 504–5).

or not you reciprocate" (Fisher and Brown 1988, xiv). In their well-known manual *Getting to Yes,* Fisher, Ury, and Patton (1991, 11–14) offer the following advice: (1) Separate the people from the problem; (2) focus on interests, not positions; (3) invent options for mutual gain; and (4) insist on using objective criteria. They suggest that parties begin analysis by gathering information, organize it, and think about it, and this is followed by planning and organizing ideas and deciding what to do, and then the discussion stage, which involves communication toward an agreement. Through these strategies, the four elements they identify should pervade the discussion.

In relationship bargaining they remind us that in dealing with those with whom we differ, outright rejection creates physical obstacles to problem solving; that rejection creates psychological obstacles, about the importance of demonstrating a willingness to hear others and give their ideas due process; to deal with respect; to give others' interests the respect they deserve; to treat parties as equals, in basic respects; to work with not against other parties; and to behave as if we care, because changing the way we behave changes the way we think (Fisher and Brown 1988, chap. 9). "The method permits you to reach a gradual consensus on a joint decision *efficiently* without all of the transactional costs of digging into positions only to have to dig yourself out of them" (emphasis in the original; Fisher, Ury, and Patton 1991, 14).

A closely related stream of tactics that emerged out of two-party negotiations is that of alternative dispute resolution. As Bingham (2008) relates, this emerged from priority justice systems in labor relations, but it grew from interest-based and collaborative modes rather than positional or competitive bargaining. These modes, which are identified and described in appendix G, compiled by Bingham, include negotiation, conciliation, facilitation, mediation, fact-finding, mini-trials, arbitration, and ombudsperson programs. She points out that these processes are not actually new—they have existed in virtually every culture throughout history, for example, in the work of village elders and informal judges: "What evolved was the notion of institutionalizing them either outside of government orientation to civil society's way of enhancing community, its problem-solving capacity, social capital, and justice. People involved in alternative dispute resolution generally subscribe to the concept of procedural justice, that people will assess the outcome of a dispute process to be fair if they judge the process of reaching that outcome to be fair and that they are given a participatory voice and respectful treatment" (Bingham 2008, 251–52).

Deliberative negotiations have strengthened the core effort within the civic engagement movement. After identifying other means—adversarial, electoral, information exchange, and interest association (civil society) engagement—Cooper, Bryer, and Meek (2006, 82) identify deliberative approaches as including a full and open discussion of ideas, particularly efforts to foster joint action across sectors of society, classes of people, and types of individuals: "They seek consensus in action through lengthy, sometimes tedious deliberation. The core components of these approaches to engagement are dialogue among different types of people, joint action, and shared responsibility for outcomes."

In the same vein, Fung (2006, 69) calls this decision making by deliberation and negotiation. Participants may not reach a consensus, but the process is as follows: "Participants deliberate to figure out what they want individually and as a group. In mechanisms designed to create deliberation, participants typically absorb educational background materials and exchange perspectives, experiences, and reasons with one another to develop their views and discover their interests. In the course of developing their individual views in a group context, deliberative mechanisms often employ procedures to facilitate the emergence of principled agreement, the clarification of persisting disagreements, and the discovery of new options that better advance what participants value." In other words, it is a process of learning by interaction, exchange, and the pursuit of edification before group choices are made.

As the process of deliberative negotiation proceeds, according to Booher (2008), two important issues of stakeholder agreement are essential. First, the process encourages participants to invent approaches that respond to all the interests of stakeholders instead of deliberating the merits of various positions. They should resort to old-fashioned distributive bargaining if they fail to find mutual gain solutions, again blending in deliberation and bargaining. Second, the process entails seeking a consensus, with complete efforts made to find solutions that all stakeholders can support. Outcomes should be geared to situations where participants can continue to deliberate: "During deliberation and negotiation the stakeholders draw on their networks to test options for agreement, generate still more options and build support for future agreement" (Booher 2008, 124). Innes and Booher (1999) offer a three-order framework for the effects of this type of deliberative negotiation. Their continuum ranges from such first-order effects as trust building and agreements to longer-time-frame, third-order effects; to new collaborations; institutions, and partnerships; and the like.

Most challenging among collaborative deliberative negotiations are the needs to recognize and deal with cultural differences when multiple stakeholders are involved. Too much conflict over cultural differences can lead to cultural polarization; too little may lead to cultural isolation. The productive confrontation of differences involves multicultural negotiation or problem solving (Brown 1983, 167–68). Several strategies are suggested by Brown (1983, 198–200) to reduce such conflict:

1. Alter stakeholder perceptions (change views, educate one another).
2. Alter communications (increase contact, expand communication capacity).
3. Alter actions (separate out symbolic issues, propose alternative face-saving positions, recruit and train persons who can depolarize.
4. Alter the interface (define the culture more closely, organize the process more tightly, close interaction boundaries, encourage facilitative norms).
5. Alter one or both parties (clarify party interests, reduce group-based pressures for conformity, create representative roles that encourage moderation).
6. Alter the context (encourage the recognition of cultural issues, solicit hierarchical support, employ rewards and punishments that reduce polarization,

redesign operating structures, invite external allies that support depolarization, involve external parties, monitor increasing cultural differences to anticipate future problems).

Brown (1983, 212) concludes that cultural differences are deeply rooted in the historical experiences of individuals and groups and fundamentally shape social identities, yet can often be peripheral to the task at hand. As a result, interventions are often necessary to "moderate the effects of cultural shock and polarization." As Forester (2009, 186) concludes, dealing with differences "does not abolish differences or deny them so much as honor and build upon them."

Finally, perhaps no set process template or fixed schedule for collaborative-based deliberative negotiation exists. Parties need to feel their own way and create their own sequence as they go along. One possible scenario is reported in Chisholm's (2001, 110) work on deliberative change in a school system, where interorganizationally multiple interests promoted Martin Luther King Jr.'s birthday as a holiday, an agenda that represented the results of a series of workshops and county human relations council deliberations. The action steps sequenced include identification of the problem, gaining a shared understanding of the issue, envisioning the future, decision making, building community support, implantation and action steps, and feedback by survey. This process put deliberative negotiations into a broader context of deliberative participation. The three workshops then led to implementation, that is, to action steps that culminated in a favorable school board decision. The entire process was a demonstration of adaptation: "These entities of political mobilization and social capital, together with administrative agencies, are the nodes that can be connected through complex adaptive networks to deliberate together about our future" (Booher 2008, 142). Such sequences represent true efforts at deliberative negotiations.

TRUST AND TRUST BUILDING

In collaborative activity trust has proved to be an important equivalent for the traditional role of the manager in enforcing legal authority. One widely held belief is that trust in multiagency collaborative activity is a key substitute for such mandated authority. Trust in collective behavior is linked to fiduciary obligation; such responsibilities are essential in holding organizational representatives together because they impose the obligation to broadly attend to the concerns of others beyond the boundaries of specific, measurable transactions (Barber 1983). Trust does not require common belief, but obligation and expectation. In an insightful review of trust in the public sector, Thomas (1998) identifies three dimensions of trust: fiduciary trust, in which an individual places trust in another to act in his or her capacity; mutual trust, based on interpersonal reciprocity rooted in social exchange; and social trust that occurs within social systems, a form of social capital that gradually accumulates through the microlevel interactions of individuals. Although analytically separate, these three aspects are interwoven and mutually supportive. Mutual trust is generated through microlevel interpersonal relationships and gives rise to and shapes the character of social trust. In turn, social trust enhances the ability to develop mutual trust. Social trust in turn supports the sense of moral obligation that sustains mutual trust and provides the requisite context for stable, concerted interaction.

How are these ideas converted into collaboration-related action? A notable formulation is presented by Ferguson and Stoutland (1999, 44), who break down such expectations in collaborative activity into four trust questions:

- Trust 1: What are the *motives* of current or potential allies? For example, can they be trusted not to exploit me and not to betray the purposes that are the basis of my interest in the alliance?
- Trust 2: Are they *competent*? For example, do they have the knowledge and skills to do the jobs that the alliance will require of them? Do they really understand the issues? If not, are they willing and able to learn?
- Trust 3: Will they be *dependable* in fulfilling their responsibilities? For example, even if they have the best of motives, do they have the necessary resources to follow through on their promises?
- Trust 4: Will they be *collegial*? Respectful? Fair? Or, for example, will they be condescending? Confrontational? Accusatory?

Ferguson and Stoutland suggest that the success of community development alliances depends heavily on the answers to these four questions. These aspects of trust, they argue, are the foundation for alliances, where trust is a positive expectation about the future behavior and performance of allies.

Trust is required as organizations in networks and participants in joint ventures attempt to redefine and work with their legal-based (hierarchical, contractual) relationships (Nohria 1992). Sabel (1992, 67) suggests that mutual obligation and expectation are key: "Trust-based governance structures have rich, consultative institutional structures whose very existence belies the assumption that the agents expect their actions automatically to be harmonized by the confluence of belief." Indeed, Fountain (1994) suggests that trust as a social relation may be on par with exchange as a lubricant in network behavior.

In the fourteen-network study, trust mainly developed in three major ways.[1] First, most of the regular players had already worked with one another, over a period of years. People working in their respective fields in intellectual disabilities, environmental management, or transportation have much working experience in interagency or association-agency work. Some have moved from agency to agency, or organization to agency, or the reverse. One longtime state agency deputy director related that he had a project history with some people that spanned many (gubernatorial) administrations.

Second, most managers who span boundaries have numerous experiences with counterparts from other agencies and organizations in dyadic or triadic collaborative ventures outside the network or other formal collaborations themselves. Beyond these dyadic/triadic contracts are state, federal, and association officials working with one another in other collaborative settings—on interagency funding awards committees, task forces, councils, and consortia, as well as the other bodies.

Third, both technical and program work within the collaborative undertaking builds on the two previous forces and reinforces the trust process. As each agency pursues its designated work and results are produced, people representing different organizations develop the respect needed to foster additional trust. Even if people might disagree, it is usually done with respect for one another. Participants learn to participate and address one another's concerns and projects. Others remark that with regard to trust, "we hold together because we know that if we show concern for everybody's agendas and needs, we will be able to build up the kind of results that advance the overall good that we are really here for" (Agranoff 2007, 120).

Trust is not guaranteed by action. As mentioned above, the Des Moines transportation network has had some difficulty getting representatives to think from a metropolitan perspective rather than from that of their own jurisdiction's interests. Their policymaking body, composed of elected officials and local managers, finds this particularly difficult. They also suffer from a turnover of local elected officials on the transportation policy committee. The organization's technical committee finds this to be less of a problem, because it is composed of appointed administrators who have worked together over time. The two natural resource networks also find it difficult to promote mutual respect among conflicting interests. In these cases trust is harder to develop, though it appears to exist among the core of administrators. In the other cases a level of working familiarity if not trust is evident; however, they rely heavily on their interactive processes to orchestrate mutual obligation.

It was found, by contrast, that for all the networks the process of mutual learning through exploration contributes to additional trust: "As we educate one another, we take advantage of diverse backgrounds." When participants hear technical presentations by colleagues or learn about others' programs, they develop more than a passing level of understanding. They not only learn about the other agency and its programs but also are able to make deeper judgments regarding the competency of the agency, along with its potential contribution to the overall mission. As participation increases over time, individuals demonstrate an increase in key technical and managerial abilities, which in turn builds the group's collective confidence. Indeed, the more knowledge that is extended, the greater the opportunity to increase trust in others' abilities.

Virtually all network participants agreed that the consensus-building process increases trust: "We give up some autonomy for a new paradigm shift, collaboration. This leads to mutual understanding and a passion about partnering." As the details and positions are put on the table and adjustments are made, people feel more comfortable about one another. One federal official stated that a great group dynamic means "don't let your power get in the way" (Agranoff 2007, 121). Each instance of consensus cements this obligation-based trust.

Another operating rule in many collaboratives is that trust is maintained by nonencroachment on any participating agency's domain. One state official in a network put it bluntly: "Let each agency put their details and concerns on the table; respect each agency's needs and interests. They come first" (Agranoff 2007, 121). Most network actors state that it is better to keep agency agendas in the open; but when agendas do come forward, it may be impossible to force an agency to change. Mild persuasion and minor adjustment may follow, but intransigence on the part of an agency, particularly a powerful one, usually means that a network/ collaborative venture must pull away from a controversial issue. Individual agency information sharing among collaborating organizations also cements relationships in a very subtle way. In some networks a key portion of every meeting is the time allotted for agencies to share their own experiences and agendas; this unfolds before they tackle any joint or mutual outreach activities. Most meetings can also include an around-the-table report on those issues relevant to other agencies or programs. Through this process, partners come to know what others are undertaking; agendas are upfront. These exchange sessions allow all members time and effort to represent their organizations. This process of opening up one's agency to others also advances trust.

Extended time frame conferences or meetings are also important social platforms. For example, the Iowa Enterprise Network has a biannual conference at a university where prepared papers and panel presentations are exchanged. The network also holds periodic conferences where self-help projects are demonstrated, along with useful presentations on maintaining small businesses. One of the rural partnerships holds an annual rural institute, planned by its component partners, which is an established trust builder. These meetings bring the key actors together to plan the sessions; and the sessions, formally and informally, provide the type of social intellectual bonding that reinforces preexisting trust.

Finally, the fourteen-network study demonstrated a long-standing principle of collaborative activity: Trust can also be built through progressive results. "Start with something small and build from there" was a sentiment echoed by a number of participants. Another suggested that it helps to start with low-risk efforts. As each network carves out the possible, results accrue that prove to the group that they can work together. Committee and work group efforts are critical here. When small groups work together on focused projects, it leads to a higher level of intimacy. If the work gets done, it breeds deeper understanding. Failure to do committee work, to deliver a promised information component at a set date, or to do some other work necessary for network operation contributes to loss of trust. Because collaboratives rely primarily on the volunteer contribution of full-time administrators and professionals from organizations, each member is expected to do his or her share and come through with any commitments made to the group.

Trust in public-sector activity can be produced and maintained, proposes Thomas (1998), through three primary strategies. The first is by valuing the personal skills of administrative and professional staff and encouraging their participation in activities outside the agency, particularly professional communities. Second, the interactive processes of working with one another over regulations, oversight, and standard practices, including the promotion of ethical behavior in transactions, enhances fiduciary redundancy and thus reinforces trust. Third, with the increase in detailed contracting, which is largely a trust-building deterrent, other social exchanges between parties—for example, through participation in consensus-building groups made up of multiple interests—is essential. Together, these forces can serve to build cultures of trust.

Trust building is thus at the core of efforts to overcome many agency-based barriers to collaborative agreement. It is an important way to work around power issues and to facilitate deliberative negotiations (Thompson and Perry 2006). Such trust building proved to be a "work in progress" in the fourteen-network study, as it is in most collaborative ventures. It included taking advantage of long-term working familiarity, prior dyadic/triadic experiences across boundaries, joint technical and program work, mutual learning opportunities, engaging in consensus building, respect for other organizations' boundaries, information sharing, extended time frame meetings, and by progressively achieving results. Might all this effort lead to process fatigue and a lack of results? It is important to address this concern here.

OVERCOMING COLLABORATIVE INERTIA

Collaborative overprocessing does have its own trade-off costs, which are normally thought of as transaction costs, that sometimes prevent agreements or other outcomes, inasmuch as a consensus has its price (McGuire and Agranoff 2011, 269). In what is known as "collaborative inertia," Huxham and Vangen (2005, 3) identify the need to pay such transaction costs as the other side of network success, that is, collaborative advantage. This lack of advantage occurs when collaboration is marked by slow progress, painful experience, a lack of achievements, and sometimes network collapse. They point to many different social forces that can lead to collaborative inertia. One is often mixed aims, when partners sit down to collaborate and discover the complexities between explicit, assumed, and hidden aims that occur on three distinct levels of aims: collaborative, partner organizations, and individual actor. Another is the predominance and power generated by those partners who hold the purse strings. Then there is the other side of trust—suspicion—which can be generated by a lack of collaborative trust building.

One related process dimension is what Huxham and Vangen (2005, 72) call "partnership fatigue," coupled with a lack of clarity about the one with whom one is collaborating, that is, the challenge of managing ambiguity and complexity. Constant change can also lead to inertia as relationships between partners become increasingly fluid. Displaced leadership—or a shift from expected group-oriented, task-focused give-and-take to a situation where one or a few leaders do most of the work—can make the collaboration "move out of the control of their membership" (p. 78). Finally, leadership activities are continually facing obstacles to success and removing them in a less than collaborative fashion (e.g., by pushing partners out or isolating agencies), sort of collaborative thuggery as a substitute for process facilitation.

Huxham and Vangen present seven valuable inertia-related perspectives on collaborative management:

1. We must have common aims, but we cannot agree on them.
2. Sharing power is important, but people behave as if it is all in the purse strings.
3. Trust is necessary for successful collaboration, but we are suspicious of each other.
4. We are partnership-fatigued and tired of being pulled in all directions.
5. Everything keeps changing.
6. Leadership is not always in the hands of the members.
7. Leadership activities continually meet with dilemmas and difficulties.

Huxham and Vangen (2005, 224) conclude that finding ways to avoid collaborative inertia is an essential part of network leadership. It is a continuing process of adjusting in different ways and styles to ensure that the agenda moves forward, sometimes calling on the "need to lead when you are not in charge" (p. 225). They conclude that participants need to jump in and establish their own means of overcoming these inertia-causing factors. Three forces are most important: (1) active management of the process, (2) selective identification of projects that have a prospect of success, and (3) doing it *well enough* (emphasis in the original). The third force means accepting that although things may not turn out perfectly, always working toward beneficial results can be worthwhile (pp. 256–57).

CONCLUSION

This chapter cannot conclude with an easy formula for resisting collaborative barriers. Successful outcomes in collaboration are multidimensional, complicated, and protracted. They involve dealing with the complexities of public policy, divided jurisdictional responsibility, legal contracting, public finance rules, agency power, technical limitations, intercultural norms, conflicting ideas and stakeholders, and many more concerns. Given that situations are different, understanding, patience, and a willingness to make adjustments are needed to overcome barriers in reaching collaborative success. The forces introduced here need to be thought about, understood, and dealt with as multiparty processes unfold as they are wrapped around the intricacies of particular nettlesome problems.

Therefore, this chapter has attempted to alert interorganizational actors in the process of collaborative public management to what they may be up against. After introducing a real-world case of an agency that tried to do too much at once in the realm of collaborative management, the chapter identified collaborative preconditions and power bases and the use of power in reaching a collaborative agreement, along with the major obstacles to collaborative success and how public agencies can use stewardship to overcome them, deliberative bargaining and negotiation, the role of trust and trust building in collaboration, and, finally, the problem of collaborative inertia. These ideas are not abstract but everyday challenges in identifying and overcoming collaborative barriers that require complex thinking and acting among partners.

NOTE

1. This section relies heavily on Agranoff (2007, 119–22).

CHAPTER 8

The New Public Organization

METRO HIGH SCHOOL IN COLUMBUS (hereafter, Metro) is an accelerated science, technology, engineering, and mathematics (STEM) undertaking that is uniquely operated by a set of public and private agencies. Metro's major learning partners include the Educational Council (EC), which is composed of the superintendents of the sixteen county school districts in surrounding Franklin County, Ohio; Ohio State University (OSU); national and state coalitions for essential schools (in Ohio, this is KnowledgeWorks); and Battelle Corporation. In addition, other nonpartners are involved: learning sites where students experience internships, projects, field placements, and classes; the PAST Foundation, which organizes research, field learning, and the dissemination of STEM learning to the sixteen school districts; contractual arrangements with OSU for student counseling; OSU's leadership and educational resources; and such other community resources as industry/educator curricula task forces and the use of OSU library as the Metro Library.

Metro's governance is done by a combination of the EC, upon the advice by Metropolitan Partnership Group, a steering body, and is administered by the Metro administration and the EC staff. The school admits about a hundred students for each class, by interview and lottery, who are apportioned by school population from among the sixteen districts, and it operates on an accelerated basis and by subject mastery. Students must master the eighteen subject-related credits required for Ohio high school graduation, normally in their first two years, after which they attend classes at OSU for credit. In addition to the network that undergirds the school's operation, a community of students, teachers, and parents is involved in many aspects of the school experience (Hunter et al. 2008).

Metro is a public school that has a principal and teachers who do not answer to a school system hierarchy or school board but instead to a combined council of school administrators, business leaders, university deans, and education experts. It immerses its students in dynamic interactive relationships among community organizations, businesses, public agencies, OSU, and Battelle Laboratories. Among its keys to success are the relationships that it generates.

Public agencies today have had to become more concerned about their "relationships," as has been maintained throughout, as they conductively engage other organizations and deal with their external publics: political officials, external service delivery agents, interest associations, clientele advocates, and recipients of government services. In this respect, Goss (2001, 84) maintains that as the public agency is connected outward, it needs to think about its roles and responsibilities to the wider community and see the big picture—that is, how things interconnect—and make judgments about the best ways to sustain relationships to achieve goals: "If public organizations have to develop a capacity to establish relationships, then organizational forms must be developed that enable managers and staff to listen and respond, and to make and keep promises. A relationship organization will be one where staff are capable of reciprocity."

The new public agency is much more than one that efficiently and effectively delivers services. It must operate in a sphere of governance, working together with other entities in contractual and forms of collaborative relations to seek the kind of public value expected of them. In this sense, the agency is a reflective coproducer. But increasingly more is being expected of public organizations. Administrators, managers, and citizens must reflect on public value, listening to citizens/representatives and partner organizations, while being responsive to political leadership. In these interactive discoveries, discussions, deliberations, and decisions, the new public manager must be able to speak for the agency, using "negotiated exchanges of policy and practice to serve the whole community" (Goss 2001, 87). The new agency needs to be capable of rapid action, trying as best as administrators can to overcome internal or legal resistance as well as engage in fast and effective communication. Finally, the new agency works with partners and the public and uses information and communications technology and knowledge to reflexively generate solutions.

This chapter explores some of the core features of the new bureaucratic organization, those that are highly conductive, beyond those identified in chapter 3. The chapter begins by returning to Metro as an illustration of a new "Organizing 2.0" public agency, a networked entity that has eschewed the lines and boxes of hierarchy, and thus constitutes a quintessentially conductive agency. Then the key emergent features of public agency management suggested by this 2.0 model are introduced, ranging from an open organizing structure to multiple accountability functions. This is followed by an introduction of some of the newer approaches to citizen government interaction at the local level, as employed in Western Europe and the United States, another feature of relationship public agencies. The chapter concludes with some speculations about the public agencies of the future.

METRO AS A 2.0 ORGANIZATION

The development of Metro is an interesting story in itself, but because it is not directly of concern here, its formative events are summarized and highlighted in appendix H. These milestones—from initial contacts with Battelle, OSU, and small school specialists to the startup of the first entering class of one hundred—fit well into the network developmental framework originally posited by Agranoff and McGuire (2001): *activation*, or identifying and incorporating key persons and resources; *framing*, or arranging and integrating a structure that will facilitate respective roles, rules, and network values; *mobilizing*, or developing support for network processes from participants and external stakeholders; and *synthesizing*, by creating an environment and enhancing conditions for favorable, productive interactions among participants. What is important here is that Metro's founders did not set out to create the network structure, nor is the network approach the only route to community involvement in school reform (Stone 2005), but like many such entities, it began as a form of a loose partnership among Battelle, OSU, and the Educational Council. As the group proceeded, its operating principles were built on three ideas: (1): Start small/stay small; (2) autonomy from a hierarchy/school district; and (3) the small school movement principles of personalized, performance-based development of habits of the mind. This led the steering group toward a 2.0 organization, that is, a networked organizational structure.

What does the Metro operational structure look like? Figure 8.1 depicts the entire Metro network structure. The structure is actually less complicated than it appears. Legally, Metro is not a school but an entity that is officially a project of the EC, which is its official governing body but in essence ratifies official decisions normally worked out by the Partnership Group, which deals with formulation of policies and holds the entity together. It is also the most involved with school oversight, except for fiscal and budget matters, which are handled by the EC's executive director. Moving counterclockwise in figure 8.1, there is close interaction with the sixteen school districts, which are responsible for enforcing Ohio high school graduation requirements and maintain career counseling services for Metro students. Then there is the consultation/coaching work of the Coalition for Essential Schools and KnowledgeWorks, a commitment of more than $1.1 million during the first four years of the school's existence. OSU is also committed

TABLE **8.1**   Organizing 1.0 and 2.0 Compared, as Reflected by Metro

Features	Organizing 1.0	Organizing 2.0
Auspices	Government entity, relatively closed and identifiable boundaries	Conductive entity, open and flexible boundaries
Boundary-spanning activity and resources	Supportive effort	Core effort
Oversight monitoring	After-the-fact auditing, periodic oversight	Continuous feedback
Principal–agent contact	Periodic review	Constant interaction
Procedural adaptation	Principally by managers	By all administrative, operating and support personnel
Decision participants and style	Managers and administrators, at points in time	By all operatives, when issues emerge
Resource acquisition	Legislative authorized budget, agency delivery of agents	Multiple sources, wherever they can be accessed
Organizational structure	Hierarchical, based on authority	Adaptive, based on connective need

to Metro for more than $1 million per year in space contribution, and three OSU colleges allocate and pay for the mentoring and tutoring work at Metro of about ten graduate students each year, an expenditure of about $1 million. The other major partner, Battelle, a research laboratory (at about 2:00 p.m. in fig. 8.1) provides seed money, is a major learning partner for STEM, and is a major field site. Back to the other side of the figure, at about eight o'clock are agreements with OSU for student psychological counseling and library use. The PAST Foundation plays an important role in transmitting STEM and small school learning to the school districts, and it has worked with a research team sponsored by the Battelle Center for Science and Math Education at OSU. Then there are the learning centers, where students apply their knowledge and build mastery portfolios that lead to credit. Also supporting the school's work are OSU classes, after-school activities (journalism, engineering clubs), parent involvement, and a series of industry and educator curricular task forces.

The characteristics of Metro as a 2.0 public organization are highlighted in table 8.1. First and foremost, it is a conductive organization, not a boundaried government agency. A STEM school like Metro does not have to be organized as a network; it could be a charter school, a special unit of local government, or some other special unit carved out of a school district. It adapted into the network model because it needed open boundaries with high degrees of connectivity to build working relationships and to find learning resources.

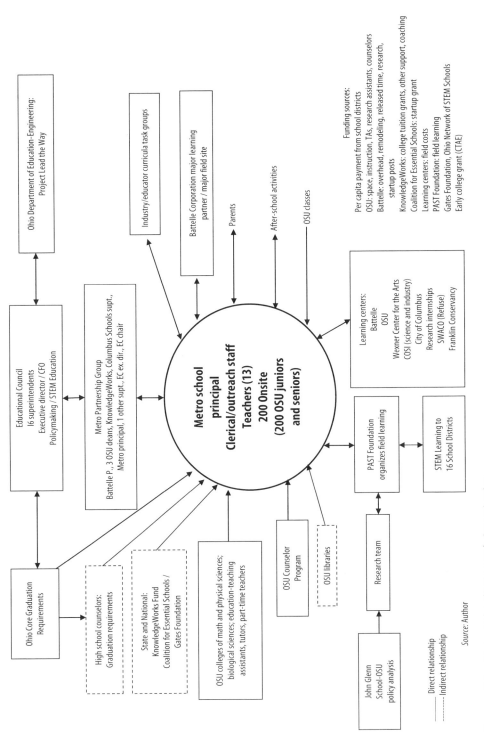

Ohio Department of Education–Engineering: Project Lead the Way

Industry/educator curricula task groups

Battelle Corporation major learning partner / major field site

Parents

After-school activities

OSU classes

Funding sources:
Per capita payment from school districts
OSU: space, instruction, TAs, research assistants, counselors
Battelle: overhead, remodeling, released time, research, startup posts
KnowledgeWorks: college tuition grants, other support, coaching
Coalition for Essential Schools: startup grant
Learning centers: field costs
PAST Foundation: field learning
Gates Foundation, Ohio Network of STEM Schools
Early college grant (CTAE)

Educational Council
16 superintendents
Executive director / CFO
Policymaking / STEM Education

Metro Partnership Group
Battelle P., 3 OSU deans, KnowledgeWorks, Columbus Schools supt.,
Metro principal, 1 other supt., EC ex. dir., EC chair

Metro school principal
Clerical/outreach staff
Teachers (13)
200 Onsite
(200 OSU juniors and seniors)

Learning centers:
Battelle
OSU
Wexner Center for the Arts
COSI (science and industry)
City of Columbus
Research internships
SWACO (Refuse)
Franklin Conservancy

PAST Foundation organizes field learning

STEM Learning to 16 School Districts

Ohio Core Graduation Requirements

High school counselors: Graduation requirements

State and National: KnowledgeWorks Fund
Coalition for Essential Schools /
Gates Foundation

OSU colleges of math and physical sciences; biological sciences; education–teaching assistants, tutors, part-time teachers

OSU Counselor Program

OSU libraries

Research team

John Glenn School–OSU policy analysis

Source: Author

——— Direct relationship
·········· Indirect relationship

FIGURE **8.1**   Metro School's Network Organization

Second, it is an entity that invests heavily in resources by boundary spanning that maintain these connections, including key personnel to maintain collaborative, curricular, and learning site linkages. Working across organizations is not some add-on or minor effort. For example, one Battelle staff person is assigned to the school for scientific learning experiences at Battelle Laboratories and other sites, and another person serves as a liaison with the state education agency, the sixteen school districts, and mixed-source curricular task forces. Part of the connectivity is infrastructure maintenance through continuing partner dedication of key resources.

Third, Metro's structure is designed for oversight and monitoring via continuous feedback about its structure, operations, achievements, and culture. Its challenges cannot handle occasional monitoring or postauditing. Input is regularly provided laterally by key partner representatives, learning site coordinators, consultants, and coaches, as well as from administrators, teachers, students, and parents. Information is funneled through the school principal, the Metro Partnership Group, and ultimately to the EC.

Fourth, principal–agent resource links are reinforced by participants who have learned that the "devil can be in the details." Periodic review will not be sufficient. Issues such as mastery portfolios, pedagogical methods, learning milestones, and individual student pacing are articulated between Metro, learning sites, and the school districts. This, of course, amounts to a great deal of interoperability.

Fifth, procedural adaptation is a constant task not only for managers but also for all operating and support personnel—teachers, learning site coordinators, parents, supporting associations, curricular task force members—who play a role in the development of operating policies and procedures. Their developmental work then finds its way to the administration and ultimately to the governance bodies. It is neither top-down nor bottom-up—but sort of sideways into the administrative/governance structures.

Sixth, more essential than a hierarchical structure are partnership affiliations in decision involvement, in this case for STEM education by industry and higher education representatives, which structurally requires flexibility that allows for rapid inputs of information, knowledge, and resource potential, and for the ability to make or defer decisions on the fly. Its decision style followed a partnership-oriented mode by consensus, and rather than adopting a long-range plan or plans, as issues arose they were approached on a singular basis. Decisions cannot involve only managers.

Seventh, resource acquisition, including financial support and learning—real dollars, organizational dollar commitments, and in-kind contributions—is found wherever it may lie. Metro does not have a budget from some school administration or a learning resource directory. Beyond modest base tax funding from the sixteen districts, its funding sources come and go—as do learning sites in the community. So Metro must be continuously collaborative as it pursues ways to meet its resource needs from a variety of sources.

Eighth, and finally, Metro's organizational structure is not only nonhierarchical but is also built to suit its challenges as they are faced and to accommodate its collaborative nature. Instead of being codified in an organization chart, its structure—with the exception of a formal (EC) and informal (partnership) governance structure—involves depictions of partner, learning resource, and support relationships, which are more appropriate when there is high adaptability based on connective need.

The Metro arrangement continues to evolve over time. The development and maintenance of Metro are done through the interactive network of students, parents, teachers, school administrators, partner representatives, learning site representatives, and others. Ideas and practices are filtered into school and EC administration, teachers' meetings, student town hall meetings, and, most important, through the informal interactive dynamics of the extensive Metro network. The existence of these pieces—plus the activities of students, parents, and intermittent learning resources—makes it difficult to call Metro an organization in the Weberian or modern sense. Legally, again, Metro is not even a school. It is a networked entity.

Metro is thus not an *organization* in the standard, hierarchical sense. But it nonetheless has an unusual standing as a public agency. Metro was initially made possible by the dedicated energies of key community leaders, particularly the former president of OSU and the CEO of Battelle, whose support and resource commitments moved others to support the concept of a STEM plus a small school. Several identifiable levels now combine to constitute Metro as a hypercollaborative: the EC, the Metro Partnership Group, KnowledgeWorks, the Metro principal, and Battelle. As the school continues operations, layers of teachers, learning site representatives, and support personnel from OSU have also become network participants. Metro's operations extend well beyond the walls and staff of the school, and thus involve the active learning and support activities of many partner resources and learning centers throughout the Columbus metropolitan area.

EMERGENT ORGANIZATIONAL FEATURES

An entity like Metro is a proven conductive alternative to a single-organization hierarchy. Like a true hierarchy, Metro includes a governing body (EC) and a governance and advisory structure (Metro Partnership Group and administrators),

TABLE 8.2   Emergent Features of 1.0 and 2.0 Organizations Compared

Feature	1.0 Organizations	2.0 Organizations
Organizational structure	Divisionalized	Nondivisionalized overlays of collaborating staff working externally
Organizational governance	Closed hierarchy	Flexible collaborarchies
Operational enablement	Legal authority	Transfer of partial authority from participating organizations
Professionalization	Specialization in bureaus, disciplinary orientation	Epistemic communities based on shared beliefs
Planning and organizing of operations	Program and project oriented in a single unit	Interactive, discursive, and sequential across units of different organizations
Problem solving and decision making	Within the unit, forward looking	Across units, complex, and ad hoc
Strategy/boundary spanning interactions	Agency strategies and inter-departmental accommodations	Sets of joint strategies by multiple agencies
Operations	Executed by divisions and departments	Interoperability
Accountability	Single or limited points, other indirect	Multiple direct points
Legitimacy	Legislative authorization of bureau and program	Self-built through continuous contact efforts

but it is not *divisionalized* or specialized. The network exists with overlays of students, parents, teachers, administrators, learning site representatives, and learning partners. Instead of command and control, Metro as a network features consensus-based decision models. Its participants experience role differentiation but operate with a fluid, participatory, agreement-seeking orientation. Authority is thus found in many places. Theoretically, this makes this hyperconductive agency very different from that of a classic hierarchy. An additional series of features beyond the Metro characteristics identified in the previous section, which are summarized in table 8.2, appear to be hallmarks of relational organizing. Whereas all are suggested by the Metro experience, they are existent in many postmodern organizing situations.

Like Metro, an increasing number of organizations will be governed more openly in a nondivisionalized mode to one degree or another, with network-like, highly flexible collaborarchies. The author's study of fourteen networks (Agranoff 2007) defined them as self-managed bodies of officials who employed self-imposed rules that used consensus building to develop collaborative capacity (Bardach 1998, 307), which encouraged exchanges and the development of cooperative dispositions and mutual understanding between the individuals trying to work together on common tasks. The Metro study demonstrated that the principle of "soft guidance" by the multiple focal nodes is an accurate description of the way decisions are made and actions are taken (Windhoff-Héntier 1992). Such guidance is the network equivalent to direct supervision in hierarchical organizations. The most central administrators—the Metro principal and the CEO of the EC—apparently are significant for information flow and planning, but they do not dominate the network's operations. The principal is indeed the center of the Metro universe, but substantial evidence from previous network research suggests a focal "hub" or hubs can be critical to network success (Meier and O'Toole 2003). Although the classical approach views networks as being flat, self-organizing, completely interdependent entities, it has been found that, in practice, a network center is not uncommon. Case studies of community mental health networks, for example, demonstrate that their effectiveness was based in part on the extent to which the network was coordinated centrally through a core agency (Provan and Milward 1995). At Metro, the principal appears to be that hub, although other nodes have been, and remain, indispensable to Metro's operation.

Another principle of emergent organizing appears to be alternative to legal authority by *transferred governance*. To avoid states of complete anarchy and a lack of accountability, partnerships, networks, and related collaborative bodies need to have some body of legitimate authority and rulemaking. Given their interorganizational nature, legally based executive authority is not a good fit. Instead, these bodies are more comfortable with the transformation of *partial authority* from the hierarchical organizations they represent to more collegial bodies that receive input from below, seek a consensus, and decide. The Metro EC operates very much in this fashion. It has some overlapping representation on the Partnership Group, including the key superintendent who sends almost 60 percent of the students, but it listens on most policy issues to the Partnership Group, which in turn overlaps with the administration, which relies on multiple lateral inputs. In a sense, the governance is based in the ability of key partners to shift (minor) portions of their hierarchical authority to the collaborative structure.

It is also evident from the Metro experience that specialization is blurred. A 2.0 organization is commonly led and staffed by highly professionalized *epistemic communities* that have a high propensity to collaborate (McGuire 2009). This type of community comprises professionals from different disciplines who share common outlooks and possess similar solution orientations, and also share normative and principled beliefs that can provide a value-based rationale for social action (Haas 1992, 3). The Metro group came together this way from high school educators, higher education professors, industry researchers, business employers, and small school advocates. As they worked together for a reasonable period of time, they evolved into a community of practice. Wenger (2000) defines such entities as self-organizing systems that share the capacity to create and use knowledge through informal learning and mutual engagement. Indeed, adherence to the principles of engagement, learning, and knowledge development on an interdisciplinary basis is a hallmark of the emergent organizing experience.

Another experience is that planning and organizing are less unitized and are project or program oriented but problem focused. It normally is flexible and springs from multiparty agreements that are *interactive, discursive,* and *sequential.* The Metro network was built piece by piece, not as an externally created, finely tuned machine that was completely ready to operate from the outset with a five-year plan. Just as it did during its formation, the Metro network meets its challenges as they emerge, almost on a case-by-case, one-by-one basis. For example, it did not have a four-year high school graduation template for two years, but took on each issue as it needed to be faced. Physical education was not addressed until almost the third year. Algebra II was taught before algebra I in the first year because of a need to link students with projects in the field. Social studies teachers were added only in the second year. Metro has operated without a uniform discipline code, but it relies on the codes of the student's home districts (which, incidentally, create occasional inconsistency problems). As needs arise, plans follow to meet a particular need. This nonlinear mode appears to be characteristic of flexible organizing.

In a similar fashion to most conductive organizations, Metro's operations are not necessarily forward oriented but are complex, with series upon series of multinetworked interactions and transactions. A succession sequence of problem emergence, problem delay, and problem solution at Metro demonstrates how adaptive structures need to anticipate challenges but often delay solving them until they have put together the multiple agreements and resources required for earlier, more pressing concerns. The space issue at Metro is an example. Metro first had to find a space, with prime cooperation from Battelle and OSU. When the students arrived, Metro had to find learning sites outside the school. As the first class was about to enter OSU in Metro's third year of operation, a new space issue arose: where classes would be held besides at OSU, because the original site is limited to a total of two hundred students. Like many other networks, both small and large problems are solved as they need to be faced, by collaborative agreement, not when they are uncovered (Agranoff 2007).

In turn, the key network strategic interactions are regularized or patterned into "sets" of joint strategies that are the equivalent to interdepartmental operations in bureaucracies. In contrast to agency strategies, they are approached as negotiations–adjustments–accommodations–decisions by partners between major participating organizations. For example, annually the EC receives input and decides how much to "levy" each school district per pupil (it is roughly the amount of state assistance) for the coming year. Also, the school districts, upon the advice of the Partnership Group, have agreed to accredit student portfolios (individually, not group prepared) as credit equivalents. The school districts, through these superintendents, resisted paying for low-income school lunches, special education services, and early college tuition, so the school has absorbed these costs in the first two situations and received a grant for the third. Each of these major issues became an operating policy, but they are built one by one between organizations, are consensus based, and are not legally mandated, and they form one important set of operational "rubrics."

An additional key set of organizational concerns involves programming, which in 2.0 organizations are at the core of interorganizational conductivity. Instead of divisional departmental execution, high conductivity demands more detailed, articulation-based *interoperability* (Jenkins 2006, 321), which increasingly must be part of collaborative management. This practice is a means of bridging organizations and operations at a more detailed level; it was defined in chapter 5 as "reciprocal communication and accommodation in order to reach interactive operating policy and programming." The Metro process of awarding *each* student credit for work done in the classroom, field, or laboratory fits this process, because the Metro curriculum coordinator and/or principal and a school district professional look at records and portfolios. As suggested, it involves considerably more than the standard "bargaining and negotiation" often used in the literature: joint agreement on core principles, interactive planning, exploration of mistakes or a failure to launch, reaching key understandings, program articulation routines, reciprocal operations, and feedback and correction. Interoperability is a quintessential boundary spanning activity that will draw increasing interest as organizations accelerate their collaborative stances.

Moving more externally, organizations like the Metro network face multiple and direct performance accountability points—to the partners, to external stakeholders in industry and business, to the scientific community, to public agencies, to the small schools movement, and to students and to their families. In general organizations are thought of as having single or a limited number of direct-accountability points and other secondary points. To the 2.0 organization, virtually all points are indirect. Esmark (2007, 283, 287, 293–94) suggests that there are three challenges vis-à-vis network accountability. First, networks need to be considered as representative forums, to be inclusive in scope, and to be concerned with relevant stakeholders outside the network's formal membership. Second, networks need to institutionalize procedures for publicly assuming responsibility and give explanations according to basic standards of communication to the stakeholders or moral constituency outside the network. Third, in networks recognition must be given internally to different types of mandates or sanctions from representative organizations at the same time that they pay attention to unorganized stakeholders. This is a difficult order for multiorganizational entities, and it makes the performance quotient quite difficult. As Robert Behn (2001, 77) concludes, collaborative operations mean that "the one-bill, one policy, one organization, one accountability holdee principle doesn't work for performance."

Finally, any multiple partner networked entity like Metro will need to build its own legitimacy. It will rarely have the traditional public agency legislative authorization to enable its existence, and even if it does have such a legal charter, it will still need to prove its mettle. How a network or collaborative structure grows and evolves into public acceptance is important (Human and Provan 2000). Maintaining the legitimacy of the Metro network as a recognizable identity, particularly for outsiders, is one mechanism for growth and acceptance. Building legitimacy also means that internal network participants find value in their membership and continue to provide resources and support. A great deal of collaborative capacity was built among the major partners, but the social network analyses and the interviews with teachers and parents revealed a marked gap in the degree of connectivity with the learning partners (Hunter et al. 2008). Metro is now finding a way for these potentially influential entities to become viable participants in information sharing and planning. This will remain a critical component of Metro's growth and adaptation, and cement its legitimacy. Once again, these emergent features are summarized and compared with more traditional organizing in table 8.2.

The Metro networked structure is therefore very much a 2.0 type of organized entity, which in many ways follows a new science or quantum approach as opposed to a Newtonian approach. Many modern organizations are Newtonian, in that they are boundaried entities that grew to legitimacy as bureaucracies under legal authority, with divisional structures, rules, responsibilities, and so on. These organizations are Newtonian not only in the machine imagery sense but also in a materialistic sense, with a focus on that which can be known through our physical senses. In the same way that scientists sought building blocks of matter, organizations were explained by their components, such as functions, staff, standards, and personnel.

The new science, by contrast, focuses on holism rather than parts, whereby systems are complete and attention is on relationship building, bringing on a whole new set of connections that cannot be easily reduced or explained by studying the parts in isolation. For example, the quantum mechanical view startles us out of common realities where "relationship is the key determination of everything. Subatomic particles come into form and are observed only as they are in relationship to something else. They do not exist as independent 'things.' There are no basic 'building blocks'" (Wheatley 1999, 11).

In a similar quantum mode, the emergent organized entities can be seen as potentially boundaryless, making relational adjustments to their systemic needs, and as highly unmachinelike as they face strategic challenges in a more unconventional way (Clegg 1990). This type of organizing is very much a matter of resistance to standard control of people and rationalization of process models in organizing, "focusing on the constructed nature of people and reality" (Alvesson and Deetz 1996, 192). This is clearly the way to understand the network relationships that built and sustain Metro school.

NEW APPROACHES TO OPENING GOVERNMENT AGENCIES

Yet another layer of emergent concern is the cross-national movement to ratchet up the involvement of citizen representatives and citizen groups in twenty-first-century organizing. It builds on to the dynamics of organizing for collaborative endeavors, or what Emerson, Nabatchi, and Balogh (2012, 11) identify as principled engagement. Although the organizing modes are transferable to state and federal program concerns, in most cases we are referring to an organized local citizenry, which most often works with local governments and local organizations. Among the more visible emergent approaches are citizen juries, community workshops, and interactive conferences, along with the more traditional boards and conferences. What is different about these approaches is that they are designed to go beyond the gathering of opinions to "offer spaces in which managers and citizens can engage together in active thinking, where citizens acquire new knowledge, test assumptions and prejudices, explore different ways of doing things, [and] propose solutions" (Goss 2001, 144). As Stone (2005, 228) maintains, "to the extent that democracy is about problem solving the community in its various segments needs to develop and utilize a framework of action; . . . building civic capacity also involves enhancing the abilities of those previously excluded." These processes bring on what David Booher (2008, 113) identifies as complex adaptive networks, wherein agents interact dynamically and nonlinearly in an open system so as to generate novelty and emergent adaptive patterns; in this regard, "democratic change isn't so much about building something as it is about nurturing learning networks and communities of networks that are both robust and capable of adapting."

Along with such mixed participation, there are efforts to move local government organization into the contemporary era so that it can transcend traditional bureaucratic organizing: efforts to strengthen the powers of chief executives, the

New Public Management (NPM), encouraging partnerships, and civic engagement. Initiatives to empower local governments to anticipate area-based problems and to gain the ability to coordinate the various forces needed to solve them are now at the core of such reforms.

In Canada the general response to such problems in metropolitan areas is either the provincial government's assumption of local services or consolidation. Under the latter approach, small municipal governments are combined into larger units or special regional authorities are created (Sancton 2002), which thus takes powers away from local governments. The United States tends to rely more on competitive multigovernment networks of local public choice. State and local concepts of home rule, fiscal independence, and the legal strength of most forms of local government and executive powers actually allow for broader approaches. In the United Kingdom and other countries, where local powers have been weak, there has been a move to strengthen the executive in similar fashion to that of the United States' directions, either by directly electing mayors or by giving local councils enhanced powers over disparate local agencies and special governments (John 2004). Other changes in this arena fall into the category of strengthening mayors' executive responsibilities, the professionalization of executive department leadership, reduction in the size of local executive bodies, and the employment of hired executives who manage under the mayor or council, that is, the city manager–city council–coordinator form in the United States. These moves are designed to enhance the "power of general competence that endows municipalities with the right to undertake policy initiatives in all areas that are not explicitly precluded or defined as the exclusive responsibility of another layer of government" (Denters and Rose 2005, 247).

The reform of local public administration has largely followed the NPM movement. NPM, which generally has been imprinted from business, focuses on inside operations and broadly includes three major foci: (1) a shift from government to governance, invoking a host of nongovernmental organizations in the work of government; (2) a shift from direct service provision or "rowing" to enabling outside competition by government "steering"; and (3) a shift refocusing government from itself to the "customer" and "user" of services (Snape 2004, 63). Once identified as a "new public management for all seasons" (Hood 1991, 3), NPM invokes at least seven identifiable approaches: hands-on professional management, explicit standards and measures of performance, a greater emphasis on output controls, a shift to external forces like nongovernmental organizations (NGOs) that involve disaggregation of the public sector, a shift to greater competition in the public sector, an emphasis on private-sector management practices, and greater concern for discipline in resource use.

Among the direct instruments of NPM are services privatization; increased managerial flexibility and deregulation; competitive bidding for services delivery by government agencies and NGOs; performance-based contracting by government agents; citizen input into management decisions; municipal companies that are self-sustaining and off budget; and the use of performance benchmarks, performance evaluation, an imposition of national minimum standards of service, the internal devolution of power and decision making to services departments, and strategic (cross-entity) local management. Obviously no one country or even single government has instituted all these approaches, but they have become important means of making public organizations work at the local level. One survey concluded that a number of these NPM approaches—performance measurement, control of results, benchmarking—along with management information systems will be considered by public management experts to be even more valuable in the future (Prueller 2006, 21).

Local government, in partnership with other entities, is yet another influence. As Denters and Rose (2005, 253) conclude, what a "local council does has to be replaced with a conception that local public decision making increasingly involves multiagency working, partnerships, and policy networks which cut across organizational boundaries—in essence governance." These interorganizational or cross-entity moves include partnerships and alliances with both nonprofit and for-profit private organizations, cooperation in services delivery among adjacent governments, the establishment of quasi-NGOs (e.g., local housing authorities, hospital trusts), local community neighborhood public–NGO partnerships, joint public–private nonprofit associations, public–private economic development corporations, intergovernmental partnerships and networks, public–private strategic planning partnerships, and private joint development corporations. Innes (2004) identifies a series of necessary conditions for such partnership-based collaborative planning and decision making: broad inclusion, meaningful tasks, self-generated rules for operation and decisions, self-organized processes, and explicit and transparent steps to implementation. Such interdependencies introduce newer dimensions, conclude Blanco and Gomá (2002, 29). In orchestrating these cooperative partnerships and networks, local government does not lose functional responsibility but takes on the additional role: "City governments and their officials possess some legal and fiscal levers that can keep governmental units at the center of collaborative transactions . . . that outweigh NGOs" (Agranoff and McGuire 2003, 43).

One of the most widespread current trends in public–private partnerships is the movement to social innovation, where public service delivery taps into the ingenuity of the private sector through a social entrepreneur, that is, someone who develops an innovative and cost-effective answer to a social problem and thus brings business ideas into the social sector. These include ideas like encouraging the poor to be vaccinated or pass examinations in exchange for cash, the payment of college tuition and fees in exchange for high grades, and job training in exchange for not repeating certain crimes (*Economist* 2010a, 56). One of the more notable social innovation projects is the Circles program, which employs social capital to eliminate poverty in the United States. Circles is based on building "bonding social capital within the community, bridging social capital to access resources contained by higher income networks, and linking social capital that connects the first two with public institutions." It involves a family living in poverty that works with volunteer middle- and upper-income allies who lend support and work with a volunteer Circle leader who directs a program that includes a comprehensive curriculum, community training, financial literacy planning and training, and many support meetings. At the community level each Circles program is developed by building a coalition of public and NGO officials, low-income families, and volunteers, with the guidance of a lead agency (Circles 2010). Like other examples of social innovation, Circles is funded by a combination of public funds and private social investment financing. Obviously, social innovation, if it is to become widespread, will depend on a combination of open public organizations, public and private funding, and a great deal of public volunteering.

A final trend involves enhancing local democracy by strengthening alternatives to the electoral channel through civic engagement. In many countries there has been a steady downward turn in electoral turnout rates for local elections, and in other countries turnout is traditionally low. Nevertheless, interest in other forms of local political participation has not necessarily waned, because globalizing forces have encouraged "rooted cosmopolitans" to take contentious and/or concerted action at the local level (Tarrow 2005). This has led to the implementation of a series of local democracy instruments in different countries: local referenda, petitions that are transformed into council agenda items, services user boards, citizens' written motions that go on local ballots, hearings for prior appraisal of actions, permanent consultative forums (disabled, women, immigrants), future (planning) scenario workshops that involve citizens, multistage—look, appraise, act—citizen dialogues, partnership boards to encourage social integration, youth councils, opinion surveys, consultation via the Internet, and calculations of an electronic democracy balance sheet. These new approaches, which obviously have been influenced by the NPM customer orientation, "defines the citizen as a 'consumer,' making choices about the kind of services he or she wishes to avail of" (Loughlin 2001, 391). These mechanisms, which are designed to improve relationships between local government and the general public, have to some degree also been introduced—for example, in Spain's local governments (Font, Font, and Subirats 2002).

Initiatives to promote participation and related partnerships, along with community building and process orientation to management, are among the changes that have emerged for local city managers and mayors, as delineated by Nalbandian (1999). Such changes have also been part of the school reform movement in the United States, where disadvantaged urban populations have been encouraged to take directives in reconstructing family–school system interactions (Stone 2005). In a related approach, Kathi and Cooper (2005) develop a model of citizen participation that brings neighborhood and city councils into a collaborative partnership. It is centered on an interactive process for building trust and creating mutual understanding and agreement. In terms of city responsiveness to neighborhood organization interaction, five possible determining factors may be at work: organizational culture, organizational leadership, organizational rules and structure, dependence on stakeholder demands, and the extent of external control placed on the agency (Bryer and Cooper 2007).

Cooper, Bryer, and Meek (2006, 76) emphasize the role of the public in collaborative management processes and advance the argument that "deliberative and collective action strategies of civic engagement hold the promise in achieving a public-involving, citizen-centered collaborative public management." They offer a conceptual model of civic engagement to demonstrate five basic dimensions to civic engagement: who is involved, who initiates the engagement, why citizens are involved, where the engagement takes place, and how citizens are involved. They thus make a case that collaborative public management processes and structures must necessarily include citizens in deliberations. An empirical study of neighborhood councils in Los Angeles, the Collaborative Learning Project, focuses on the responsiveness of government bureaucracy to citizens in the collaborative process (Bryer 2009). The study's primary finding is that "administrator and citizen perceptions of their own and the other party's roles may influence the quality of responsive behavior in collaborative activity."

In a similar vein, Fung (2006) looks at collaborative engagement along three interacting dimensions: who participates, how participants communicate with one another and make decisions together, and how participants are linked with public action. In this regard, a number of citizen-based, quasi-legislative, and quasi-judicial processes of engagement have been identified, such as deliberative democracy, e-democracy, public conversations, participatory budgeting, citizen juries, study circles, collaborative policymaking, and alternative dispute resolution (Bingham, Nabachi, and O'Leary 2005). The use of these best practices contributes to the citizen engagement phases of collaborative public management.

The emergent mechanisms for local government organizational partnerships and citizen connections are numerous. Making them work is the key to future organizing. Illustrative lists of partnerships and connections are given in boxes

Box 8.1   Organizational Partnerships

- Interlocal intergovernmental partnerships/agreements
- Partnerships and alliances with private organizations—nonprofit
- Partnerships and alliances with private organizations—for-profit
- Cooperation in services delivery among adjacent governments
- Citizen–NGO–government networks
- Quasi-NGOs
- Neighborhood council–NGO partnerships
- Public–private nonprofit associations
- Vertical intergovernmental partnerships
- Private–public joint development corporations.

Source: Compiled by the author.

8.1 and 8.2, respectively. These devices can be used to look outward, at the big picture, and with reflexiveness, and thus possess a capacity for engendering self-learning. They foster effective communication and promote reciprocity (Goss 2001, 113). As Booher (2008, 127) states, such systems will succeed under five conditions: (1) Large numbers of individual agents are connecting; (2) agents are interacting dynamically; (3) interactions are nonlinear, iterative, recursive,

Box 8.2   Citizen–Local Government Connections

- Local referenda
- Petitions for council agendas
- Citizen-written ballot motions
- Neighborhood panels
- Citizen juries
- Prior appraisal hearings
- Permanent consultative forums
- Future planning scenario participation
- Multistage look–appraise–act dialogue
- Partnership boards for social integration
- Youth councils
- Opinion surveys
- Internet consultation
- Electronic democracy balance sheet.

Source: Compiled by the author.

and self-referential; (4) open systems are being experienced, whereby behavior is determined by the interactions; and (5) the system has a capacity to maintain its viability and to evolve. In other words, these systems involve mutual citizen–group–NGO–government searches for new possibilities in the information age, whereby citizens can gain access to various types of information and the skills to put this information to effective use. It also requires what Boyte (1989, 5) refers to as public-serving wisdom—"the ability to guide and frame action with integrative concepts and a clear, if flexible and evolving, set of values and purposes."

The internationally influenced local government improvement movement has been introduced in the United States both by local advocates and by state and federal government programs. In this sense, reform has been both bottom-up and top-down. Top-down encouragement has come from political forces concerned to strengthen financial management and managerial efficiency and to increase the democratic quotient. Bottom-up engagement has been engendered by a more informed and digitally engaged citizenry. In a complementary way, central influences have been coupled with efforts to encourage political decentralization, that is, through regionalization and greater nongovernmental involvement. In sum, the reasons for these institutional reforms appear to be a mix of actions to (1) impose emergent neoliberal agendas, which include offloading central and intermediate-level functions; (2) overhaul overcentralized and inefficient systems of public administration; and (3) involve genuine attempts to enhance regional and local democracy (Loughlin 2001, 394). The extent to which these citizen-based tendencies have taken hold is of central importance in understanding the development of organizing in the future.

FUTURE ORGANIZING

The immediate frontier of government organizing will no doubt be the employment of digital tools. The Internet is becoming increasingly powerful. YouTube serves more than 2 billion videos a day. Those that Twitter employ this mode 750 times a second. The Internet's traffic is growing by 40 percent a year, and it has morphed into a social medium. People post 2.5 billion photos on Facebook every month. And it is not only people who log on to the Internet these days. One company has produced a prototype of an "ecosensor" telephone that can detect radiation and pollution (*Economist* 2010b, 82). During the 2008 US presidential campaign, candidate Barack Obama built an online community of more than 1 million people. Instead of the usual controlling of the message from campaign headquarters, individuals in the community had the digital tools to organize themselves, share information, and create campaign events on their own. These campaigners were later turned into voters. In fact the current generation of young people, sometimes called the Net Generation, amounted to 15 percent of the electorate, and are projected to form up to one-third of the population by 2015 (Tapscott 2009, 244).

Now, in office, President Obama is deploying the information resources he developed during the campaign. He is using contact details from his campaign's 10 million donors, supporters, and volunteers to garner support for his policies. Millions of e-mails are being sent to these individuals urging them to support the White House agenda. This "permanent campaign" in effect sends messages like these: "In the next few weeks we'll be asking you to do some of the same things we asked of you during the campaign—talking directly to people in your communities about the president's ideas for long-term prosperity" (*Economist* 2009, 85). This digital connection is well suited to the politics and government of the future.

The author of *Grown Up Digital: How the Next Generation Is Changing Your World*, Don Tapscott (2009, 244) describes the Net Geners' approach to government and politics as follows:

> As they get more and more political, they will no doubt sweep away the conventional broadcast model of politics with its "you vote, we rule" style of operating. In this old system, citizens listen to speeches, debates, and television ads, give money, and vote—but when it comes to having input into policy and real decisions, they are relegated to the sidelines. They are supposed to sit passively watching while the real powers—the politicians, their financial supporters, and the lobbyists—make all the decisions, often according to their own interests. But this generation won't settle for that model. Having grown up digital, they expect to collaborate with politicians—not just to listen to their grandstanding speeches. They want to be involved directly: to interact with them, contribute ideas, scrutinize their actions, work to catalyze initiatives not just during elections but as they govern. And they will insist on integrity from politicians—they will know very quickly if a politician says one thing and does another. They are going to shake up both politics and government.

Clearly, the mechanisms of involvement and citizen engagement introduced in the previous section are well suited to meeting the expectations of citizens at the local level, whereas more digital approaches will have their greatest impact at state and national levels.

Electronic government has great potential not only to eliminate mountains of paper but also to change the way people contact their governments. Many governmental units—for example, city and state governments in the United States—offer a host of online services for permit processing, licensing, and paying taxes and fees. Seoul's Cyber Policy Forum provides a vehicle for citizens to debate urban policy online with city administrators, whereas web-based information services facilitate citizens' efforts to find housing, child care, and travel assistance. The open data initiative in the United Kingdom gave citizens access to the massive Treasury database, allowing citizens to access a host of information, from civil servants' salaries to hospital problems. Neighborhood Knowledge California (NKCA) is an online tool that provides easy access to a vast collection of property and neighborhood data. It integrates databases from federal, state, city, and county government sources and private investment and pollution sources that can be transferred to an interactive neighborhood monitoring system, which uses a mapping interface to plot real-time information on city maps posted on NKCA's website. This function allows neighborhood residents to monitor housing complaints and promote code enforcement, and to otherwise participate in neighborhood improvements: "For communities left out of the high-technology boom in particular, open platforms and well-designed Web services can provide real hope when they are applied to concrete social problems" (Tapscott and Williams 2006, 205). According to Marc Holzer of Rutgers University (quoted by Margolis 2010), "There's a huge amount of pressure for improving services around the world, and the Web is the best place to empower people at low cost." This is a world where open government will be at a premium, as the growing availability of high-speed Internet, increased democratic impulses, and the emerging demands of an educated population reshape public services and break down older bureaucratic cultures.

Government itself operates differently in the digital era, and thus increases the conductivity of agencies. Taxation agencies are improving their means of identifying delinquent payments (e.g., by flagging people who apply for benefits). Publicly funded health services use clinical data to determine the effectiveness of certain treatments and drugs. For instance, electronic data studies enabled the German Federal Labor Agency to reduce spending by €10 billion during a three-year period while also reducing the amount of time people spend out of work (*Economist* 2011, 74). The Estonian government used volunteers and global positioning systems to locate more than 10,000 illegal dumps and then electronically enlisted 50,000 people to clean them up. Governments can use the Web as a base for interacting with their employees, for example, with GovLoop.org (*Economist* 2010b, 52).

Also on the electronic horizon is a type of partial replacement or supplement for local newspapers: community-focused blogs, which are run by journalists but rely heavily on citizen news gatherers and commentators. Many of these local websites are sponsored by larger organizations—Patch.com by AOL, Local.com by the *New York Times*, EveryBlock.com by MSNBC, Topix.com by three newspaper chains, and PlaceBlogger.com and Rural News Network by the Knight Foundation. The interest of the big players in these new games is that they see potential in local advertising in hyperlocal coverage, a model that virtually eliminates big city newspapers' huge printing and delivery costs. These sites typically employ one or two experienced reporters, supplemented by mostly unpaid amateur commentators and interns. For local government, this means a new form of extremely close coverage, where every potential or actual move by city hall is communicated at a much earlier stage than before. One town manager reviews the local blog and informs his council so they hear it from the administrator, not the blog. For decades the typical small town or suburb got its news from a slow-paced weekly newspaper, normally well after the council acted. With the blogs, virtually everything is up for public review, even trivial issues like the conversion of parking meters to tokens, well before it is considered. For government, it means "allowing a new generation of watchdogs to walk the beat" (Roberts 2009, 50; *Newsweek* 2009).

Several forces point to the future of the public agency and its public and organizational contacts as ultraconductive in nature (see chapter 3). They will be similarly linked in many different forms of citizen involvement, for example, social entrepreneurship. NetSquared, a nonprofit NGO, has introduced prizes for the best ideas about social entrepreneurship. In the future, it is expected that "app stores" carrying Web, smart phone, and tablet computer applications for the public sector will be created (*Economist* 2010b, 82). Civic engagement in collaborative management with the public will also accelerate. Bottom-up local efforts, citizen boards, joint administrator–private agency–executive/citizen efforts, and multiorganization alliances, partnerships, and networks will increasingly use information and communications technology to help break down the "towering bureaucracies of elites and experts" in government and nonprofits that have vested interests in the nationalization of community (Schambra 1998, 48). Today citizens can employ publicly available data to demand better public services. In the United Kingdom the Open Knowledge Foundation has used government databases to develop a site called WhereDoesMyMoneyGo.org (*Economist* 2011, 74). In hundreds of communities, small groups and organizations are battling problems like inadequate housing, teen gangs, substance abuse, how best to educate children, and the need to develop neighborhood economies. Using online databases appears imperative if these interests are to advance their causes by engaging and partnering with government.

Efforts to reach consensus are also essential. In engaging the conductive public agency, the agency's mission and legal requirements need to be blended with those organized self-interests. As Wolf (1999) has pointed out, despite high-level political divisiveness in public life, a vibrant civil society flourishes as people focus on mutual problem solving. This means that efforts must be made to find that line between self-interest and those of others: "That is what civil society means—it is the place where people, neighborhoods, and communities define, mediate, and argue as they work to forge consensus. The common theme in all of the struggles is empowerment, both for the individual and the community as a whole" (Solo and Pressberg 1998, 83). Problem solving cannot be left to government alone, because enhanced policies emerge from collaborative efforts between conductive agencies and the interests of citizens and communities.

The privatization of government services raises additional burdens on engagement. For example, third-party organizations such as managed care firms that contract with government or garbage collection firms have little incentive to involve citizen and community interests. Many are part of large for-profit chains, which make the relationship between government and citizens more indirect (Smith and Ingram 2002). As a result, engagement and decision influence are difficult and put extra burdens on citizens' organizations despite the fact that such contracting makes the public agency more conductive. Nonprofit contracting, voucher programs, and other government-to-community organization linkages enlist new constituencies in public service delivery. Many nonprofits and community organizations have developed a "keen stake in government funding and regulatory policy" (Smith and Ingram 2002, 57). This in turn has led to trade associations of service providers, which organize politically on individual and collective bases and may have a stake and role in policy development. As mentioned above, this is the case with regard to state associations of agencies that serve the intellectually and developmentally disabled. Public agencies are now used to dealing with this type of advocacy or coparticipation.

Recognition of the learning component of engagement with government is a related future concern. This issue, which has been identified as the "new citizenship" by Rimmerman (2005, 5), is based on the idea that people are not born citizens but require education and training and experience through regular community participation, grassroots mobilization, service learning, and the use of the Internet as a participatory vehicle: "The new citizenship is also an important means for bridging the ever increasing gap between the public sphere (the area of the intersection between an individual's interests and those of the larger community) and the private sphere (the locus of the individual's own interests." Clearly, the youngest adult generation has already bought into this model.

Participation in public dialogue will then flow more naturally. To engage in deliberation involves joint learning and multiple flows of communication, which involve "the degree to which they include the general public, occur in a public space, foster genuine deliberation, privilege different forms of discourse, are empowered by government, and focus on policy-specific outcomes" (Booher 2005, 65). Public dialogue is critical in forming policy, argues Matthews (1994, 42), because people need time to reflect, listen, digest, and be exposed to many sides of a question: "A public dialogue is a natural home for democratic politics. It is a home that people feel forced out of and want back into." Leadership for connectivity with the conductive public agency is part of this dialogue. There are clearly no magic formulas for organized interests that seek to deal with the new public sector. Tapscott (2009, 212–64) identifies several of the more electronic/digital modes of contact with public agencies: Internet-based dialogue, e-petitions, electronic virtual town hall meetings, online citizen panels, virtual question periods, and simulated scenario planning.

Finally, one must understand that despite a public agency's increased conductivity, it remains an administrative unit of government. The government is the authoritative repository of values. Its decisions, regulations, and codes, though potentially malleable, represent current legitimization. As Michael Walzer (1998, 138) reminds us, "I want to warn against the antipolitical tendencies that commonly accompany the celebration of civil society. The network of associations incorporates, but it cannot dispense with, the agencies of state power." This, then, is what he calls the paradox of civil society: "Citizenship is one of the many roles that members play, but the state itself is unlike all other associations. It both frames civil society and occupies space within it, fixing the boundary conditions and the basic rules of associational activity, compelling association members to think about the common good." As Himmelfarb (1998, 121) concludes, "The appeal to civil society is a salutary corrective to big government but should not be taken as in invitation to demean government itself."

CONCLUSION

No one can predict with exactitude what public organizations and civic engagement will look like in the future. Current trends point to increasingly problem-focused and networked arrangements, multiple information and communication flows, multiple governments interacting, and a desire by large groups of citizens to have a voice in policy at both the formulation and implementation stages. For example, this is clearly the case with regard to planning and mitigating traffic congestion (Koliba, Campbell, and Zia 2011). Taking the logics of individualization, collaboration, and networking one step further, Zuboff and Maxim (2002, 372–73) predict the breakdown of hierarchical structures as "managerial practices based on collaborative coordination would have to replace command-and-control management as it evolved in the twentieth century; [this is]... a new management canon based on very different social relations, in which peer-to-peer collaboration replaces hierarchical supervision and multidimensional coordination replaces executive administration and direction."

The consequence of this accelerated collaboration is what Tapscott and Williams (2006, 44) identify as "emergence," the creation of attributes, structures, and capabilities that are not inherent in any single node in the network. We are seeing sophisticated artifacts and outcomes emerging from relatively diffuse, loosely coupled activities of collaborating agents supported by Web-based tools. As such, this chapter has showcased what a real-world, nonbureaucratic, highly conductive public agency looks like. It has also identified some of the key features of collaborative organizing, with a sort of the-present-is-the-future approach. Then the analysis began to look at how these holistic entities link people and government agencies.

These conductive shifts clearly move public organizations further into governance postures. To engage in governance includes but is more than citizen engagement. It also involves organized interests: public agencies, nonprofit and for-profit NGOs, contractors, grantees, suppliers, trade associations, interest groups, and neighborhood councils operating in a dynamic, overlapping, almost chaotic fashion. In this chapter I have tried to capture how this seeming confusion is "organized"—or at least might be "organized."

CHAPTER 9

Conclusion: Collaboration Works!

THERE IS NO DOUBT that we live in interesting and confusing times. The technology of communication, both broadcast and personal, continues to advance at a furious pace. Social interconnections increase exponentially, now existing at levels ranging from village and neighborhood to global. As Tapscott and Williams (2006, 290) conclude, organizations experience open and porous boundaries and compete by reaching outside their walls to harness external knowledge, resources, and capabilities. They seek innovative ways of doing things, attempt to attract qualified minds, are concerned to add value. This is "a new type of collaborative enterprise—an ecosystem of peers that is constantly shaping and reshaping clusters of knowledge and capability." Moreover, economic ownership is complicated, for example, unions own businesses, there are joint ventures between different kinds of companies, and there are public–private partnerships and government ownership of parts of private corporations. Standard boundaried organizations remain but operate alongside myriad networked or multiorganizational forms. Governments offer direct services on a more limited basis because they increasingly rely on a host of governance mechanisms or exert remote control through intermediaries, such as by contract and regulatory regimes. The challenge is clearly to organize and manage public agencies on a conductive basis, and thus public managers increasingly need to leave their agency offices while working with external partners.

In most cases the old is not necessarily replaced by the new, but the new exists alongside the old. For instance, despite the many ways to hear prerecorded music these days, we still own and use radios. Neighborhood organizations are as strong as ever, despite national interest associations and multinational or global nongovernmental improvement associations. The small owner-operated or limited partnership business can still be found on the streets of most towns, despite multinational corporations. Many formal organizations, including government agencies, exist alongside the newer, networked forms made up of parts of organizations. Governments still deliver many core services—police, fire, economic promotion, building regulation, and health and sanitary inspection—despite grants, contracting, and governments' other governance tools.

Is this a case of a need to dismantle governments and refine their missions? As Danny Hillis (2002, 276–77), an inventor and computer scientist, explains, governments have undergone deconstruction and externalization of governments, in the United States and on a global scale:

> I may get my defense from NATO and my trade laws from the WTO. I may get my post delivery from FedEx, my health insurance from a private carrier, and my education through a network of homeschoolers. Those are all functions that maybe I would have turned to the government for, but now I'm getting them from alternative sources. When you use alternative sources, that lets you shop for the best in each. In fact, I sort of like my American government's system of civil rights enforcement, but I don't much like their system of postal delivery. So I'll keep them for what they're good at, but I'll throw them away for what they're not good at. I don't think that nation-states are going to go away. What's going to happen is they're going to stop doing things that they're not good at. So they're going to do less; they're going to be less all-encompassing and less universal.
>
> This doesn't mean that there will be a world government. That's just reapplying the old model at a new scale. To me, the EEC (European Union) is very retro—it's that idea of trying to build a giant, omnipotent, nation-state on a larger scale. That's a silly idea. Having a common currency is a great idea, but I think having a new über-bureaucracy is a terrible idea.

This involves, he claims, understanding what government can and cannot do and making adjustments.

The previous chapters have been devoted to the problem of how to cope with those conductive changes in government in the presence of externalizing governments *and* bodies like networks. But government will not disappear in the era of network governance (McGuire and Agranoff 2010): "What governments have that networks don't have is legitimacy. If you're an agent of the state you have a uniform and a badge, you're trained, and you take an oath" (Sterling 2002, 281). Networks and most collaborative bodies do not have such powers, nor a legal system or accompanying rights. Because these structures have severe weaknesses, "it's sheer bohemian arrogance to think that networks are the future or that everything is going to be arranged like that."

The problem of the old and the new is how to get a handle on "the new world" where traditional means of control and organizing are not as self-evident. The old public bureaucratic model was once considered modern, an attitude of progress, because it got rid of more traditional forms of leadership selection and less structured organization. It ushered in the idea of control and the concept that things could only move in the direction in which one wanted them to go. That was the essence of Peter Drucker's (1974) magnum opus—*Management: Tasks, Responsibilities, Practices*—in which he identified a set of tasks designed to enhance performance. It was assumed that most of the work was within the agency—which took the raw inputs of law, money, people, rules, and audits—and at the other end were controlled services formed by managers. Raw inputs were to be pushed into the outputs that public managers wanted. This, conceptually, was about the exercise of power, based on legitimate authority. Managerial concerns were about how one managed with efficiency, while ordering the structure and the people to do the things managers decided they should.

The exponential changes related to conductive public agencies and network governance mean that the old and the new now together present a chaotic world of organization and outside organized activity. As Hillis (2002, 271) observes,

> It's a jungle out there, and you've just got to live in it. You're never going to understand it. You're never going to control it. Instead, you have to be responsive. You have to go with the flow. You have to make sure that when an opportunity arises you can take advantage of it. That's much more the attitude behind network economies and learning companies, the kind of agile organizational structures that are emerging. What's important about them is not that they're in control, but that they're able to adapt quickly, to redefine themselves. That's a different attitude about the world, and maybe its symbol is the Internet. There's nobody in charge of the Internet, there's no place to call up and say "It's not working," because it just kind of happens.

The world, he concludes, is moving from a symphony where everybody is working together under a conductor while the new world is jazz: "We are moving out of an age of control and entering an age of adaptability—out of an age of coherence into an age of combinatorial richness" (Hillis 2002, 272).

In this concluding chapter I try to extend the preceding ideas for adaptation in three ways. After an overview of the study of collaborative performance, it is demonstrated that successful outcomes do come from collaborative efforts. Managers do overcome the barriers and achieve results, although often they are not immediately apparent. A set of twelve minicases from the literature that demonstrate results are presented and provide a road map of more detailed reading and research into reviewing stories of collaborative results. Also, four different types of collaborative network outcomes to which administrators point are identified, as a means of explaining the depth of collaborative outcome.

Finally, an even dozen series of "ideas that you should know," concepts and practices that are important for contemplating positive results, are introduced from the literature. They include building capacity, achieving collaborative advantage, building a goal consensus, the intractability of collaborative performance, and many others. It is a sort of top ten–plus, in the same way that the Big Ten collegiate athletic conference now contains twelve universities, of good ideas about managing to collaborate.

COLLABORATIVE PERFORMANCE

Collaboration requires great commitment but can pay off in the long run. As was discussed previously in the book, Ansell and Gash (2008, 550) reviewed 137 cases and found that based on foundations of prior experience, initial trust, and perceptions of interdependence, participants can use facilitative leadership to combine face-to-face dialogue, further trust building, commitment to process, shared understandings, and intermediate outcomes (small wins, plans, fact-finding) into successful collaboration. Success can even come without a legal mandating of interaction or without highly elaborate structuring. One such example is the movement to safe construction, encouraged by the Federal Emergency Management Agency, as it promotes the adoption of stronger building codes through its financial assistance programs, provides technical support for building industry foundations and trade groups, and works with the insurance industry. Safe construction has been achieved through formal and informal partnerships, collaboration between government and industry, and "the cultivation of relationships based on shared responsibility within at least several networks of public, private, and nonprofit organizations" (Waugh 2004, 278–79). Among other forces, Waugh attributes success in safe construction to long-term development of relationships, broad participation, synergy and creativity lacking in hierarchical systems, leadership from the different sectors, and open and transparent processes.

Successful collaborative performance centers on the question of whether the interaction can lead to something that can be identified as adding value to some public undertaking. As Mark Moore (1995, 20) suggested, public managers seek to "discover, define and produce public value," extending discovery of means to focus on ends, becoming "important innovators in changing what public organizations do and how they do it." In a similar vein managers who collaborate in any form must "look out to the value of what they are producing," to paraphrase Moore.

In Bardach's (1998, 8, 11, 17) study of managing interagency action, he defined collaboration "as any joint activity by two or more agencies that is intended to increase public value by their working together rather than separately." From an administrative standpoint, he assumes that managers collaborating should create social value in the same way as its organizational counterparts do through differentiation and specialization. Collaboration results need to be assessed because any loss in efficiency due to political, institutional, or technical pressures diminishes public value. Consequently, he concludes that we should be impressed by the idea of collaboration only if it produces better organizational performance or lower costs than its alternatives. This means that the performance criteria may or may not include some measurable outcome. In many cases the outcomes can be further collaboration. For example, a multiagency study could lead to the funding and operation of a new joint program or new interactive knowledge base. Still others add longer-run collaborative value as a result of previous platforms of successful group processes.

It is also important to note that in hierarchical organizations, performance or value can be more easily attributed to effectiveness by analyzing success in achieving goals. This test almost always needs to be adapted with regard to networks and other collaborative activity. Klijn and Koppenjan (2000, 148) suggest that the goal achievement method has less credence with network processes because objectives are more autonomous, with no central authoritative coordinating actor. Moreover, each of several actors may have differing objectives. They further argue that the use of ex ante formulated objectives is usually untenable because actors adapt their perceptions and objectives interactively, responding to other parties and to the environment. Also, if certain parties do not participate in the interaction process, chances are high that their interests and preferences will not be represented in the derived solution. As a result, network results also need to be considered by the ex-post-satisfying criterion (Teisman 1992/1995, cited by Klijn and Koppenjan 2000), based on the subjective judgment of network actors. In the final analysis, along with considering the costs, actors must determine the benefits derived. Thus, both substantive and process elements need to be weighed.

A set of ex post yardsticks is often used in assessing network performance. Similar to the insightful evaluative framework of Provan and Milward (2001), broad areas of analysis—community, network, and organization/participant levels—are analyzed. Based on the logic of Axelrod (1984) that cooperation will produce outcomes more favorable to both parties than when they compete, collaboration efforts confront the collective problems of multiple constituencies, organization cultures, rules, processes, and so on. Nevertheless, Provan and Milward (2001, 416–17, 420) argue that the networks they studied must be judged by the communities they are trying to serve, their viability in the community in meeting organization partner expectations, and in those broader values that accrue to participant members and organizations. Performance is thus measured by the perceptions of participants with regard to how professional and organizational value is added by the network, how the network contributes to collective knowledge bases that are subsequently useful, and the specific joint projects that emanate from collective efforts. This is not the only form of performance measurement but rather one that appears to fit well with these flexible, adaptive, learning-oriented structures.

Indeed, a growing emphasis on collaborative performance, particularly through networks, is emerging in the public management literature. For example, Chen (2008, 641) compares process elements with five collaboration outcomes: goal achievement, quality of working relationships, broadening partners' views, increasing partner interactions, and equitable influences. Rethemeyer and Hatmaker (2008) link specific collaborative management behaviors to process "across policy, collaborative and fiscal networks within their home system as well as adjacent systems." One important work (Koliba, Meek, and Zia 2010) attempts to synthesize much of this governance network literature into midrange performance theory.

COLLABORATIVE PERFORMANCE IN PRACTICE

The different types of real-world results from collaborative processes are presented in boxes 9.1, 9.2, and 9.3. Each contains four case summaries from the literature on collaboration, ranging from long-term to more immediate results. Each is publicly available in longer report form, although they vary in terms of their propensity to explain the collaborative process. Of particular importance, they demonstrate results. Box 9.1 looks at four long-term cases, one on the years-long attempt to reduce chemical pollution in the Florida Everglades, one on the decades-long attempt to achieve a metropolitan perspective in Chicago-area transportation planning, another on the Philadelphia transitional workforce program, and one on the four-year effort by the State of Kansas to contract out its Medicaid waiver program for the frail elderly. Each demonstrates that some collaborative results do not occur rapidly but only through years of study, negotiations, accommodations, agreements, and testing that are often necessary to achieve any results. They also demonstrate that key stakeholders must be in the game for the long haul. Finally, they demonstrate that initial, gradual, small-scale reforms can begin a process that can be built upon later.

Some collaborative outcomes do occur in shorter time frames, but they still require a reasonable period of time to implement or their results are not immediate. Box 9.2 illustrates four cases: contracted integrated case management in a Wisconsin multicounty area; multisector family services and elderly housing in Rochester; regulatory, technical, and financial advice/assistance to Ohio small

Box 9.1   Long-Term Collaborative Results

- Between 1988 and 1993 the federal government, State of Florida, South Florida Water Management District, the sugar industry, and the environmental community were locked in protracted litigation and ultimately reached a settlement to mitigate wetlands degradation involving multiparty payments estimated at more than $1 billion (John 1994, chap. 5).
- Despite the existence of 272 municipal governments in the Chicago metropolitan area, transportation planning in the region has been able to achieve degrees of metropolitan perspectives through the leadership of a business link/network, Chicago Metropolis 2020, formed in 1959, the Metropolitan Planning Council, and the Metropolitan Mayor's Caucus. Together they "provide a forum for brokering compromises" (Weir, Rongerude, and Ansell 2005, 482).
- Philadelphia@Work is a highly successful performance contract for transitional work development for those persons who have not succeeded at other training programs. It is built on the long-term idea of market-skill development and established networks of relationships with private businesses of social services providers, and governmental agencies. More than 50 percent of its participants were able to secure and maintain market-rate jobs with benefits (Cohen and Eimicke 2008).
- Between 1996 and the early 2000s the State of Kansas received one of the earliest Medicaid waivers for home care for the frail elderly, which was developed in steps: (1) contracting out case management for those that needed daily living, meals, and home supports; (2) transferred authority from their social services to elderly departments; (3) retained its contract with Blue Cross and Blue Shield of Kansas as the state's Medicaid fiscal agent; (4) engaged in regional area agencies on aging training and performance monitoring; (5) established a reimbursement rate system; and (6) created the first waiting lists for home and community-based care (Johnston and Romzek 2000, 13–16).

towns regarding their water and wastewater problems; and negotiated measured-results self-cleanup of a toxic waste site by the city of Woodstock, Illinois. In these cases a less protracted set of processes was put into place, but nevertheless they required extensive multiparty negotiations and agreements, and the results were forthcoming on faster timelines than the long-term projects. Most important, each of the four cases points to something tangible—a program or agreed-on courses of action—that underlies collaborative success.

Other results or outcomes of collaboration can be almost immediate in impact, at least after agreements are made and actions are initiated. Box 9.3 presents four such cases, electronic benefits transfers for emergency victims, a streamlined federal aid application for Kansas rural development programs; shared goals, priorities, and work plans among multilevel governments in the Lake Tahoe watershed; and the use of virtual teams to develop alternative approaches to store nuclear waste at Yucca Mountain, Nevada. Each of these four cases demonstrates that to

Box 9.2   Intermediate Collaborative Results

- Fourteen Wisconsin counties have joined together to create a Family Partnership Initiative to provide integrated case management and services delivery, allowing for a scale that could meet needs that individual counties could not, by contract to a large nonprofit organization (Goldsmith and Eggers 2004, 66).

- The collaborative work with governments, foundations, clients, and the private sector of Family Services of Rochester, Inc., paid off generously despite the federal funding contraction of the 1980s: support from fourteen foundations totaling $775,000 for new program initiatives ranging from "Awareness Theater" for high-risk youth to a community-based "Enriched Housing" program for the elderly, client revenues from third-party payers for alcohol and mental health services, private-sector partnership contracts for employer counseling, and "purchased services" (federal–state–local) from the county welfare department to the tune of $1.6 million, matched by $350,000 in United Way subsidies (Liebschutz 1991, 167–68).

- The Small Communities Environmental Infrastructure Group is a nonchartered network of state, federal, local, educational, and service agencies whose staff administrators and professionals provide regulatory, technical, financial, and educational assistance for small government water/wastewater improvement projects. Since 1990 it has assisted more than 250 towns, particularly in understanding how to navigate through the federal, state, and private funding mazes (Agranoff 2003, 24).

- The City of Woodstock, Illinois, in collaboration with county and township governments and the State of Illinois, proposed and successfully negotiated, during a period of a year and one-half, with the Environmental Protection Agency a two-year, measured-results-based cleanup by city employees of a contaminated landfill as a money-saving substitute for the agency-based prescribed method, involving extensive monitoring and reporting (Agranoff and McGuire 2003, 70).

decide multiorganizationally, that is, to study, identify common problems, agree to courses of action, and jointly monitor results, can be achieved rapidly from an agreed-on course of action to implemented programming. They also demonstrate how various collaborative bodies can *operate* across organizational boundaries at the same time their organizational participants can work together to accomplish their own missions. These immediate efforts not only solve difficult cross-agency problems but also help serve the aims of the partner organizations.

These joint outcomes are not the only public benefits or values accrued, as illustrated by the twelve cases. Public managers have also pointed to three other, intangible collaborative process outcomes: (1) personal/professional benefits, (2) home agency gains, and (3) collaborative process outcomes. Among the personal and professional collaborative benefits identified were scientific and technical knowledge enhancement, exposure to different cultures and disciplines, enhanced ability

Box 9.3   Direct Collaborative Results

- Under the guidance of the Electronic Benefits Transfer (EBT) Council—composed of federal agencies, state agencies, merchants, payment networks, financial institutions, and other EBT providers (consultants, processors)— operating rules have been developed for electronic delivery of government benefits through a common framework, Quest, that has achieved interoperability across state programs and institutions (Stanton 2007, 30–31).

- The Kansas Federal-State Rural Development Council was able to streamline federal aid application processing when the Kansas Department of Commerce and Housing, two rural cooperative associations, and the state's certified development companies developed a single loan application based on the US Small Business Administration's Section 7(a) guaranty loan application (Radin et al. 1996, 189–90).

- The Tahoe Regional Planning Agency (California and Nevada) works with more than a dozen federal, state, and local governments, special authorities, and conservation associations to regulate, meet, set priorities, form shared goals and targets, develop joint work plans, monitor environmental conditions, and issue periodic reports on environmental indicators and process on programmatic indicators (Imperial 2004, 19).

- The US Department of Energy's (DOE) Radioactive Waste Management Project at Yucca Mountain, Nevada, employs virtual teams of research scientists, engineers, middle managers, clerical staff, and community relations experts working at their personal computers to come up with alternative approaches to store nuclear waste. The virtual teams link seven separate contract entities, two DOE offices, two prime contractors, and forty significant subcontractors, requiring collaboration of various specialists at scattered sites (DeMarie 2004, 150–51).

to engage in the negotiational and intergovernmental aspects of public management, and carryovers to other forms of cross-organizational engagement. Home agency benefits of collaboration included expansion of the agency's information base, access to different kinds of expertise, pooling and accruing of resources, sharing of the risks and costs of innovations, enhanced flexibility, and access to others' adaptive efficiencies. Finally, process outcomes identified included new forums for interagency processing, the ability to focus on multiagency/multiorganization processes, enhancing the knowledge quotient of those involved in collaborating, the ability to exchange a variety of resources, and the synergistic benefits of people working together on mutually identified problems. Each of these three helps create platforms upon which tangible outcomes can be reached, and thus constantly nurture and reinforce the human capital bases of the collaborative effort (Agranoff 2008, 329–31; see also Alter and Hage 1993, 36–37).

As mentioned above, results need to be considered by the ex-post-satisfying criterion. That is the case with regard to most of the results reported in boxes 9.1,

9.2, and 9.3. In this sense, with respect to the lead concepts from the insightful evaluative framework of Provan and Milward (2001), broad areas of analysis—community, network, and organization/participant levels—form a useful basis for understanding collaborative results.

A DOZEN IDEAS THAT YOU SHOULD KNOW FROM THE COLLABORATION LITERATURE

The collaborative management literature in the public sphere is growing by leaps and bounds. The bulk of it tends to focus on networks as a somewhat faddish thrust in the field. The network literature is broadly cast, whereby everything of a collaborative nature involves network as both a noun and a verb. As has been argued, many of these studies involve grants or contract arrangements, less permanent intergovernmental and lateral contacts across agencies and organizations, joint ventures and multilevel cooperation efforts, and even measured patterns of social/transactional interaction. These collaborative efforts go along with involvement in networks that more formally and permanently link parts of organizations to solve problems that are "difficult for the single organization" to solve. From the broader collaboration literature twelve useful ideas or additional "takeaways" that could well help in achieving success are offered. Although they are conceptual, they hold considerable practical implications: (1) coordination without hierarchy, (2) governing as governance, (3) reversing the logic of implementation, (4) power dependence, (5) interagency collaborative capacity, (6) polydiffusion, (7) managing activities that make a difference, (8) improving collaborative capacity, (9) joint learning, (10) structure as collaborarchy, (11) control in networks, and (12) challenges of accountability.

Coordination without Hierarchy

In his classic book *Collaboration without Hierarchy*, Donald Chisholm (1989) looked at collaborative management in the public transit system in the San Francisco Bay Area, which comprises functional interdependencies and a set of formally autonomous public agencies. Chisholm argues that in situations where components of an organizational system are functionally interdependent, the resulting uncertainty creates pressures for coordination. The parts affect one another, rather than the historic practice of consolidation and thus integration into a unitary whole, and the alternative is by linkage: "However, where formal organizational arrangements are absent, insufficient, or inappropriate for providing the requisite coordination (and I argue that they frequently are), informal adaptations develop to satisfy that need. The informal organization thus realized may be quite stable and effective, more so perhaps than formal hierarchical arrangements. Furthermore, because informal organization permits the continued existence of formally autonomous organizations in the face of mutual interdependence, it can achieve other values, such as reliability, flexibility, and representativeness, that would otherwise be precluded or substantially diminished under formal consolidation" (Chisholm 1989, 17–18).

The resulting process became a decentralized system of multiple independent organizations, held together by stable and informal mechanisms in an interagency context: regional planning, interactive operations and services, route interconnections, and transfer arrangements. This work was one of the first to explore the theoretical underpinnings of organizations maintaining their independence yet working together through coordinated operations.

Governing as Governance

Also at work for many years on the phenomenon of public work involving more than the bodies of governments is Jan Kooiman, whose work culminated in the book *Governing as Governance* (2003). His basic argument is that we must understand that contemporary governance involves public as well as private "governors"; it is a mix of all kinds of governing efforts by all manner of social-political actors, public as well as private; occurring between them at different levels, in different governing modes and orders. A governance view is thus broad in scope:

> The governance approach focuses on the interactions taking place between governing actors within social-political situations. These interactions give human actions their irreversible and unpredictable character as attempts are made toward understanding the diversity, complexity and dynamics of these situations. In doing so there is scope for influencing societal features that occur between the "modern" and the "post-modern." In this respect I find a kindred spirit in Toulman (1990), who has identified two philosophical traditions that contributed to modernity: one based upon the principle of rationality, the other based upon principles of humanism. I call a combination of elements taken from these two traditions "cross-modern;" elements of both traditions may, I believe, lead towards an improved governability in a broader sense. Pragmatic (meta) principles such as openness to difference, a willingness to communicate, and a willingness to learn are important criteria in coping with societal diversity, dynamics and complexity. Substantive criteria on which basis actors are willing and able to interact with each other and accept each other's boundaries are also needed. (Kooiman 2003, 7)

As a result, Kooiman argues that there has been an increase in the role of government as a facilitator and as a cooperating partner. Thus it is more appropriate to look at the changing role of the state, not its shrinking role.

Reversible Logic of Implementation

The complexity of carrying out intergovernmental programs that involve long chains of government agencies and nongovernmental organizations (NGOs) needs to be understood not only from a top-down (e.g., federal–state–local–NGO–client) but also in a form of reversible logic. As Richard Elmore (1985, 37) indicates, policymakers frame solutions using implements over which they exercise the greatest control, for example, program standards and funding rules; but on any given political or administrative level, "people have strong incentives to view the success of the policy mainly, or entirely, in terms of the implements they control, disregarding the fact that the overall success of the policy depends not on their implements alone but on the relationship between their implements and those at other levels." This brings up the need to reverse the top-down logic and map backward to entirely explain all the negotiations, trade-offs, and, most important, the role of the actors "down the line" who also shape policy and program:

> In order to address this question, we had to turn the system around and ask, first, what decisions policy must influence in order to have any effect, second, what the stakes of those decisions are for various target groups, third, how policy affects those decisions, fourth, which jurisdictional level has the closest proximity to those decisions, and finally, how policymakers can maneuver political jurisdictions into making explicit trade-offs among objectives and with variable local conditions.
>
> From the forward mapping perspective, the problem is finding a collection of implements that is likely to produce the effect that policymakers want. From the backward mapping perspective, the problem is finding a set of decisions that policy can influence and specifying how policy can tip those decisions in the desired direction. Forward mapping stresses the marginal influence that policy exercises over decisions by individuals and organizations. If we were to look at policy decisions only from the forward mapping perspective, we would consistently overestimate the degree of control policymakers exercise. Policymakers tend to see the world through the lens of the implements they control; they solve problems by applying parochial solutions. But the success of policy depends on more than choosing the correct combination of implements; it depends as well on conditions outside the control of policymakers and on decisions over which policy exercises only a marginal influence. In order to be good strategists, policymakers have to calculate the consequences of their actions from the point of view of the decisions they are trying to influence. This is the perspective of backward mapping. (Elmore 1985, 68–69)

Elmore thus offers important food for thought in the search for collaborative management by recognizing the important role that client-delivery agency, delivery agency intermediate program agent, and program agent-enabling-funding actors all have, and how they need to work interactively and sometimes interoperably to make programs work. Unfortunately, considerably more scholarly emphasis has been devoted to the top-down perspective at the expense of bottom-up.

Power Dependence

Within the scheme of governing it was once assumed in the United Kingdom that the Westminster model of parliamentary supremacy meant that higher-level governments controlled program agencies in the local governments. As the dispensers of rules and money, the lower-level governments were the agents that carried out policy. Others argued, however, that the locals had lots of discretion as the implementers that carried out policy. In practice, R. A. W. Rhodes (1997, 9) suggests that the two levels, as funder and recipient, are interdependent, embedded in various relationships with fluctuating discretion:

> It postulates that organizations depend on each other for resources and, therefore, enter exchange relationships. In this initial version of the model, central–local relations are a "game" in which both central and local participants maneuver for advantage. Each deploys its resources, whether constitutional-legal, organizational, financial, political or informational, to maximize influence over outcomes while trying to avoid becoming dependent on the other "players." It is a complex game, in which the various levels of government are interdependent but where the relationship between them is shifting from pluralistic bargaining to cooperation. . . . Power dependence is important for the differentiated polity organizing perspective because it provides the explanatory motor. It explains why different levels of government interact. It explains variations in the distribution of power within and between policy networks. It also replaces the zero-sum concept of power of the Westminster model with a relational concept which emphasizes resources, not personality, and the context of the relationships, not individual volition.

Rhodes also underscores the importance of various forms of intergovernmental negotiation (e.g., persuasion, bargaining, and power games): "A theory of bargaining needs to be wedded to an analysis of the interactions, appreciative systems, tactics and sub-processes that surround bargaining."

Interagency Collaborative Capacity

As was briefly identified above, as a result of reviewing more than forty cases of collaboration, Eugene Bardach (1998) introduces the concept of interagency collaborative capacity (ICC) as an essential ingredient in the successful craftsmanship of coordinative activity. ICC is developmental, in that it can start small and grow; it is general, in the sense that it applies to a range of activities; it is flexible, in that it involves different degrees of task difficulty; it is able to capture the link to value creation; and it implies quantity and quality (i.e., how much and how good):

> Interagency collaborative capacity (ICC), or sometimes "an ICC," when it is considered a virtual organization, is created by a process analogous to that of one or more craftsmen building a house. This craft metaphor is intended to emphasize that the process is integrative, creative, and purposive. The craft metaphor also suggests a number of craft-related concepts that will have an important role in my theoretical development and that are explicated in this chapter: materials, opportunity, purpose, smart practice, challenges, the vulnerability of the ICC and of various smart practices, craft skill and ability, and compensation and adaptation. Success in ICC construction is a function of the skill and purposiveness of craftsmen interacting with the quality of available materials and the craftsmen's ability to fashion protections against potentially destructive environmental forces such as personnel turnover and the erosion of political alliances. (Bardach 1998, 49)

Like the building of a house, collaborative craftpersons build on two platforms that lead to a third. As introduced in chapter 7 with regard to the federal government's stewardship contracting, the first contains creative opportunity, intellectual capital, an implementation network, and an advocacy group. The second involves building trust, acceptance of leadership, and a communication network. The third is built on the first two: improved steering capacity, an operating subsystem, and continuous learning. Each new capacity is a platform for the next one (Bardach 1998, 274).

Polydiffusion

Where do the good ideas come from? The idea of polydiffusion emanates from the work of Karen Mossberger (2000) on the spread of enterprise zones. It involves spreading of ideas collaboratively through both vertical and horizontal channels, from the US federal government to the states, as well as through the exchange of information between states, organizations in and between states, and through the press and other media. It is an important process of spreading attention and resources to a variety of organizations, who in turn have a propensity to take action:

> Naming other potential examples of intergovernmental polydiffusion requires little imagination. Intergovernmental networks have developed in a variety of issue areas, with state or professional organizations disseminating federal regulations or legislation, and state trends or "how-to" advice from exemplary practice. Employment and training policy has an intergovernmental character, for example. In this era of

devolution, many federal policy initiatives merely provide a general framework (like the federal enterprise zone legislation) and encourage states to devise their own means of implementing objectives. Interaction within a truly intergovernmental network flows logically from such a policy environment because of the demand for information from the states, and also the federal incentive to use information to exert some influence over policy direction. Welfare reform, the federal empowerment zones, and school-to-work programs leave policy design largely in the hands of the states. These, too, have generated conferences, information clearinghouses, web links, and publications from the federal government and professional organizations. States also have their own web sites so that making direct contacts between states is easier than ever. Today the volume and speed of information diffusion may dramatically eclipse the widespread circulation of information regarding enterprise zones. (Mossberger 2000, 193)

Mossberger concludes that the significance of polydiffusion enhances informed decision making by interacting parties and that the polydiffusion of information made the concept a familiar one among decision makers, promoting the use of the idea as a policy label. This work has been extended in other policy areas. Kathleen Hale's (2011) work on drug court policy diffusion demonstrates that states can achieve a greater degree of success in implementation by using the information relationships, tools, and processes that information networks provide.

Four Managing Activities That Make a Difference

Do the actions of a manager (or managers) contribute to the effectiveness of multiorganizational arrangements, and if so, how? This is a basic question asked by Michael McGuire (2002, 600) and identified in the previous chapter with regard to the process of Metro high school's network development. Rather than some form of spontaneous action or manual of ten-minute management, there is both an operational and strategic character to networks (and other collaborative endeavors) that depends on managerial action. The manager's behavior in conductive actions is important, particularly with regard to four concerns:

> One class of behaviors undertaken by network managers is referred to here as *activation*, which managers in the field suggest may be the most important activity of managing networks. I use the term "activation" to refer to a set of behaviors employed for identifying and incorporating persons and resources (such as funding, expertise, and legal authority) needed to achieve program goals. The single-organization parallel to activation would be personnel issues of staffing. Activating involves identifying participants for the network and including key stakeholders in the process. The skills, knowledge and resources of these potential participants must be assessed and tapped into. . . .

Other network management behaviors are employed to help frame the structure and the norms and values of the network as a whole. *Framing* is defined as the behaviors used to arrange and integrate a network structure by facilitating agreement on participants' roles, operating rules, and network values. Like activation, framing issued both during the formation of the network and when network effectiveness diminishes or is suboptimal. Network managers must arrange, stabilize, nurture, and integrate the network structure. Framing involves facilitating the internal structure and position of the participants, as well as influencing the operating rules and the norms of the network. . . .

Network managers also must induce individuals to make and keep a commitment to the network. *Mobilizing* behaviors are used to develop commitment and support for network processes from network participants and external stakeholders. Mobilization in this regard is a common and sometimes ongoing task for achieving network effectiveness. Managers build support by mobilizing organizations and coalitions and by forging an agreement on the role and scope of network operations. . . .

Managers must also employ *synthesizing* behaviors to create an environment and enhance the conditions for favorable, productive interaction among network participants. One critical behavior of the network manager is to build relationships and interactions that result in achieving the network purpose. The strategies of each network participant and the outcomes of those strategies are influenced by the patterns of relations and interactions that have developed in the network. (McGuire 2002, 602–3)

McGuire's four propositions are based in contingency logic as a way to test ideas—when, why, and how managers undertake these behaviors, as they strategically match behaviors within their governing contexts. Thus activation, mobilizing, framing, and synthesizing in relation to program objectives, resource allocations, garnering stakeholder support, resource allocation, and system maintenance are important ways to study the manager in collaborative undertakings, particularly within networks.

Improving Collaborative Capacity

The multistate assessment work of Stephen Page (2008) on measuring Bardach's capacity to collaborate addresses the problems of accounting for the collective action issues of catalyzing work across different organizational missions, mindsets, and bases of authority and accountability, which ensures that the various actors work together to add public value. His work involves human services programs, oriented to the McGuire network processes:

To address concerns about the accountability of interorganizational work, local collaborators and state officials can use outcomes and indicator data to drive and align the four network management activities of activating, framing, mobilizing, and synthesizing. Many of the states in my study made prominent use of outcomes and indicators to establish standards, rhetoric, incentives, and communication regarding local collaboration. Such network management activities helped local collaborators in the states build the capacity to manage for results across agencies and, in turn, legitimate their efforts to their stakeholders.

With regard to challenges of collective action, aligning network management activities tightly around outcomes and indicators enabled local collaboration to thrive. In states such as Georgia and Vermont, commitments to achieve broad outcomes and to use indicator data to measure progress toward those outcomes seemed to enhance local collaborators' willingness and ability to work together. In addition to evaluating interorganizational performance and enhancing collaborators' accountability, then using outcomes and indicator data as network management tools may also help make interorganizational collaboration not just more accountable and effective but also more viable. (Page 2008, 158)

Page (2008, 153–54) makes the case for the importance of government agencies in providing collaborative resources, guidance, discipline, and economies of scale in gathering and analyzing performance data, and of providing cross-site perspectives that worked. All his states altered the application of the four network processes over time. Regardless, the states were consistent in the network management activities they promoted while the states' approaches to rhetoric, standards, incentives, and communication modes varied considerably over time.

Joint Learning

The importance of learning together is captured by the work of Koppenjan and Klijn (2004, 10) in their book *Managing Uncertainties in Networks*. Joint action by interaction is seen in part as "searches where in public and private parties from different organizations (levels of) government and networks jointly learn about the nature of the problem, look at the possibility of doing something about it, and look at the characteristics of the strategic and institutional context within which the problem-solving develops." Cooperation, then, presupposes learning between actors, although it must be worked on:

> Since cooperation and learning behavior do not emerge spontaneously, it is necessary to support interaction around complex issues in network settings. We refer to strategies which are meant to further these interaction processes as network management. The literature on the network approach suggests network management is labor intensive and certainly not easy. It requires numerous skills, tacit knowledge of the network and negotiation skills since the adopted strategies are implemented in a situation where singular hierarchical relations are lacking. The role of the network

manager is one of mediator and stimulator of interaction and not one of central director. This role is not given a priori to one actor. In principle, this role can be fulfilled by several actors, sometimes by even more than one actor at the same time, both public and private. In addressing the central question of this book, namely, how uncertainties can be handled in dealing with complex societal issues, a great deal of attention is focused on identifying, analyzing and elaborating network management strategies used to initiate and support interaction and learning processes between the involved actors. (Koppenjan and Klijn 2004, 11)

The importance of learning in multiactor collaborative situations like in networks is needed to sort out the existence of diverging and sometimes conflicting perceptions, objectives, and institutions. It can be an important starting point in collaborative process.

Collaborarchy

If networks and other collaborative undertakings are nonhierarchical, what kind of structures are they? In his study of the internal operations of fourteen networks, Agranoff (2007, 83) found them not to be randomly organized or ad hoc but self-organized nonhierarchical entities (see table 7.1 in Agranoff 2007) that have some form of communication systems and distinct internal power structures, along with internal arrangements to learn and reach agreements. They are organized to facilitate joint learning, interactive process, and negotiated (nonhierarchical) agreements:

> Networks are self-managed collaborarchies. They are clearly not randomly or haphazardly organized or structured, nor do they work without definable processes. The most active and productive of our fourteen networks are those that are able to reach beyond their good cause; they are able to convene multiple delegates to produce concrete action. As with organizations, this takes more than a good idea and the right people; it also takes more than strong leadership. Participation must be transformed into energy through network structures and process. Managers in networks do this by borrowing on their experiences in their increasingly open, knowledge-seeking bureaucratic, and nonprofit organizations. Management in the collaborarchy is thus simultaneously similar to and different from management in hierarchical organizations. (Agranoff 2007, 123–24)

Drawing on ongoing experiences in their agencies and organizations in the postmodern era with their teams, task forces, and work groups and on the models provided by nonprofit organizations with boards and committees, collaborative structures are organized to facilitate the kind of knowledge-based, multi-interest, multidisciplinary problems that are so vexing they require structured joint action. Hence, they are not structureless, but "collaborarchies," to coin that term.

Control in Networks

As introduced by Kenis and Provan (2006, 228), control involves "the use of mechanisms by actors to monitor the actions and activities of organizational network to enhance the likelihood that the network-level goals can be attained." They suggest that control cannot be easily imported from knowledge on the control of organizations. However, control analysis is important for the understanding of performance being unique entities:

> From a practical point of view, the study of the control of networks is also important. In particular, for both government policy makers and funders (both government and foundations) it is imperative to understand better why networks succeed or fail and what the impact of control is for overall network performance. From the organizational literature we have learned that, in general, there is a relationship between control and performance. The direction of this relationship is often not apparent, however. For instance, tighter control may lead to positive network-level outcomes in some cases, but to weaker performance in others. Thus, a question of significant practical relevance is how the mechanisms and processes of controlling networks should be designed in order to have a positive effect on network performance and a negative effect on disruptive externalities. (Kenis and Provan 2006, 229)

Kenis and Provan identify five different types of controls: (1) *personal*, decisions made at the center or top and their review; (2) *formal-bureaucratic*, manuals or other attempts to standardize behavior; (3) *output*, measuring results against specified goals; (4) *cultural*, a system of norms or values to which participants conform; and (5) *reputational*, through monitoring of relational patterns. They then develop a set of propositions regarding the various controls, based on variation in size, reciprocal or sequential task interdependency, and low or high environmental uncertainty (Kenis and Provan 2006, 233).

Collaborative Advantage

When collaborative actions between public organizations and nonprofits successfully tackle social issues that would otherwise fall between the gaps, they have achieved what Chris Huxham and Siv Vangen call collaborative advantage. On the contrary, when the process is painful and slow progress and/or nonresults are forthcoming, the phenomenon of collaborative inertia has set in (see chapter 7). The problem is that too often the latter is the end result. Overcoming this result is a matter of theory and practice, reflecting on key themes:

> Our theory therefore describes collaboration in terms of a framework of theme labels constructed partly out of practitioner perceptions of key issues and partly out

of key issues that emerge across the practitioner-generated themes. The intention is to build up a picture for each theme, of the key issues that underlie the practice of collaboration. This means identifying and clarifying contradictions, tensions and difficulties in each theme area. . . .

Typical expressions from practitioners (which are mirrored in much of the research literature) on the subject of aims extol the virtues of having: "common aims"; "agreed aims"; "compatible aims"; "well-defined and tangible purpose"; "shared vision"; and/or "shared values." In contradiction to this, we paint a picture that argues that there *will* be a mass of different aims that individuals and organizations *will* be aiming to pursue through the collaboration, and that many of these will not be obvious because they will form parts of hidden agendas. Tensions arise concerning how far it is wise to bring these out into the open and about the extent to which, and level of detail in which, it is necessary to agree on aims before beginning to take some joint action. The theory recognizes that *managing* (rather than agreeing) aims is a central, continuous and inherently difficult aspect of collaboration practice, rather than a precursory task to be got out of the way so that the main business of getting on with the job can be accomplished. (Huxham and Vangen 2005, 33)

Other issues and themes explored include working processes, resources, communication and language, commitment and determination, culture, power, trust, compromise, accountability, democracy, and equality and risk (Huxham and Vangen 2005, 38). Collaborative advantage seeks to understand this complexity, convey it in a way that seems real, empower by legitimizing the pain and addressing isolation, and empower participants by providing conceptual handles that help practitioners find their way.

Challenges of Accountability

Performance monitoring and measurement are difficult under any circumstances. When it comes to public services that do not have tangible outputs, like garbage collection, they are extremely complicated. This is particularly the case with regard to public intergovernmental programs and other programs that involve external agents. With regard to measuring collaboration at the federal level, Beryl Radin (2006, 158) concludes that federal performance is complex and lacks data and because it "collides with strategies of devolution and a diminished federal role, because it puts the focus on federal agencies and assumes they have the ability to require the states and localities to follow their lead":

It is not easy to craft a strategy for performance measurement activity that addresses the tensions surrounding the intergovernmental systems. The approach that is taken must be sensitive to differences among policies and programs, differences among the players involved, the complexity of the worlds of both the federal and nonfederal agencies involved, and the level of goal agreement or conflict. One of the most vexing problems in the performance area involves the availability of "good" data—data that have been verified and can be believed to be valid by all parties to the relationship. The data problem cuts across all of the strategies. Few policy sectors have the tradition or past investment in the creation of good data systems that would allow one to know whether performance has actually been achieved. In addition, the experience with all of these efforts indicates how difficult it is to achieve a performance measurement system that focuses on outcomes. Part of the problem relates to the lack of control many agencies have over the achievement of program goals and the difficulty of linking program activities to results, even when those results can be measured. (Radin 2006, 179)

One cannot, Radin concludes, assume that agencies have the data or the authority to enforce performance measures, in great measure because "those who argue for more compliance-oriented federal government accountability are often those who also argue for a decreased federal role and increased autonomy for states in the way they expend the federal dollars" (Radin 2006, 158).

Clearly, many more concluding ideas about collaboration could be presented but are precluded by space concerns. For example, confirming Radin's conclusion regarding performance, in an interesting study in four metropolitan congestion management networks, Koliba, Campbell, and Zia (2011) found that while collaboration within these multisector networks was shaped by federal mandates, no uniform performance management system existed. Nevertheless, each used the collaborative process to develop their own databases of economic, environmental and health, and quality-of-life measures that drove planning action in the networks. Lee, Feiock, and Kai-Jo Fu (2012) found that local predispositions toward competition and cooperation with other entities were significant determinants of collaborative activities, and thus can be important building blocks of interorganizational network studies. In a related sense, Choi and Choi (2012) demonstrate the productive effects of collaborative partnerships between the police and cities and nongovernmental actors, and that such actions have an impact on the decrease in crime rates. Finally, it is well known that Elinor Ostrom (1990) has provided evidence that formal game theory models provide the possibility for understanding institutional arrangements that reinforce rules and ensure cooperation among parties. She found this to be the situation with regard to coordination and governance in situations of guarding and monitoring the rules related to common pool natural resource management. The dozen ideas presented here as takeaways are therefore just a start in developing more depth in the area of collaborative management. In this sense, it is a start on a basic reading list for additional exploration, for if these are issues that one should know about, one should know more about them.

CONCLUSION

When the world is so complicated, there are no simple solutions. The discussion above of having "common aims" brings this home. With multiple stakeholders and interests, Huxham and Vangen suggest that it is better to manage aims than to push ahead prematurely and forge agreement. That is what this volume intends to convey. Do not let the process steps or tips on how to organize or manage become a "cookbook" on how to proceed. Each successful endeavor is based on its unique context, stakeholders, vexing problems, opportunities, technology, politics, and many more forces. These must be considered, weighed, and applied along with the ideas contained here. In essence it involves "letting go—freeing actors to develop their own answers; 'letting it happen' is one response, alongside an emphasis on actors' individual sense-making activities as the basis of practice" (Fenwick and McMillan 2010).

Some manuals and other works on collaborative management will tell you not to engage in organized forms of collaborative management unless you absolutely have to. The problem with this advice is that increasingly in the governance era, one has no choice. Whether they involve a government program official, program worker, NGO officer, or program staff member, intergovernmental program links are so intertwined that it is impossible to avoid developing relationships. Moreover, occasional or dyadic/triadic links may sometimes work, but too often the problems and potential connections are more than occasional. For example, grants and contracts require reciprocal and continuing effort. Interoperable processes also require unavoidable, more extensive collaboration. As a result public agencies have become conductive. Increasingly, there is no alternative to collaborative management given the need to manage between and/or across as well as within.

A final word about the need to continue with "managing within" while one is crossing boundaries: Despite the growing interest in managing outside government, in what are called governance networks (Koliba, Meek, and Zia 2010), bureaucratic agency or public organizational management will not necessarily go away with externalization; but it will be changed by the need to work conductively across the boundaries, as Kooiman (2003) suggests above in this chapter. As Lipnak and Stamps (1994, 41) indicate, though networks may be the signature form of the information age, the industrial age's bureaucracy, the agricultural age's hierarchy, and the nomadic age's small groups still persist. Collaborative structures are not necessarily eclipsing the government agency in relative power and in their policy roles. They work with government agencies, present "overlays" on bureaucratic agencies' task environments, and are recognized statutorily as the final authority in most cases (McGuire and Agranoff 2010). Thus, rather than discussing the "end of bureaucratic management," the dialogue must shift to include adapted or conductive bureaucratic management along with collaborative management.

The Lower Platte River Corridor Alliance

The Lower Platte River Corridor Alliance is a consortium of three natural resource districts and seven state agencies in Nebraska, joined together in an effort to address natural resource management issues in the Lower Platte River Corridor area. With the passage of an interlocal agreement, the Lower Platte River Corridor Alliance was established in 1996. Members contribute to an administrative fund totaling $65,000 annually to support a coordinator's position for the Alliance, and agree to provide technical and other assistance within their authority to the coordinator. Quarterly meetings are convened to share progress reports on programs and projects of all involved.

The Alliance seeks to assist counties and communities spanning 100 river miles to become fully informed about the natural-resources impact of their decisions, and to promote consistent decision making across jurisdictions so as to promote natural-resources conservation in the river corridor area. The Alliance provides a forum for concerned, interested citizens and local elected officials to bring their different perspectives to the table and seek common solutions. The goals of the alliance are: to foster increased understanding of the Platte River's resources; to support local efforts to achieve comprehensive and coordinated land use to protect the long-term vitality of the river; and to promote cooperation among local, state, and federal organizations, private and public, to meet the needs of the many and varied interests in the river corridor. The Alliance furnishes easy access to relevant information on key issues and proposed projects, opportunities for dialogue and discussion for individuals wishing to influence the decision-making process, and a forum for consensus. Community participation is an integral part of this process. Opportunities for public involvement include river tours, a water quality golf tournament, stakeholder summit meetings, and regional planning workshops and charettes.

Source: Lower Platte River Corridor Alliance website, www.lowerplatte.org.

Lower Platte River
Regulatory Study Guide

Source: Scholz et al. (2000, iv–v).

Ten Challenges in Contract Management

1. Healthy levels of provider competition. Provides market incentives for strong performance at lowest possible cost. Potential loss of contract to more cost-effective competitors.
2. Resource adequacy. Reflects the capacity of the funder to fund staff and other expenses related to accurate cost projections, analysis of contractor capacity and training for new contract staff.
3. In-depth planning for contractor performance measurement. Facilitates evaluation of provider performance and cost-effectiveness.
4. Intensive training for contract management staff. Often requires retooling and reinvesting in conversion of service delivery staff to service oversight.
5. Evaluation of contractor staff capacity. Funders must ensure that contractor has the capability to staff-up adequately in a timely fashion so as not to compromise performance.
6. Evaluation of contractor financial management capacity. Funders access the potential of contractors to manage the financial side of service delivery.
7. Theoretical integrity of the rationale for contracting. Does the undertaking meet the social problem or program need? Other than for economy and efficiency reasons, a policy reform based on a flawed rationale is probably doomed.
8. The political strength of client advocacy groups. Their influence with officials (e.g., legislators) can lead to situations where contract managers' enforcement authority is undercut.
9. The complexity of subcontractor relationships. Effective implementation in human services arenas normally requires cooperation, if not integration of services, among separate contractors, making accountability more difficult.
10. Risk shifting to the contractor. In programs like managed care, where prepaid or capitated payments are involved, the contractors are exposed to losses that cannot be covered by agreed-on payments; consequently, contractors resist expensive clients or cut back on higher-paid staff.

Source: Summarized by permission from "Effective Contract Implementation and Management," Barbara S. Romzek and Jocelyn Johnston (2002).

Explicit Knowledge Management Activities

Type of Activity	Type of Agency	Example/Use
Intranet	State communications connections	State agency communication system; allows field offices and state headquarters to be in interactive electronic contact and builds selected bodies of management information.
Listservs of discussion groups	Economic development	Quadrennial plan regional groups; broken down by areas of economic development interest (manufacturing, value-added agriculture, services), first step in plan development.
Databases	Transportation planning	Accident frequency and location within the metropolitan area; one input into project/plan development.
Corporate (network) libraries	Economic development agency	Catalogues of independent economic/business listings, and how to access them; library provides access by web links to virtually any business ranking service, related studies, plans.
Virtual organizations	State office of rural development	Value-Added Agricultural Partnership, a nonformally organized group of funders/researchers/entrepreneurs that explores data and information and tries to produce new knowledge.
Information portals	State data center	Access by Internet to various web uses by nongovernmental organizations and state agencies for planning and decision making.
Electronic archiving	State geographic council	Ortho-infrared mapping of the state to the one meter square, a variable for public agency use, for example, in transportation, natural resource, agriculture, other planning/programming.
Knowledge maps	Transportation planning	Locational targeting of existing freight terminals, public transport stops, green trails, handicapped access, and so on, for planning purposes.
Decision support systems	Transportation planning	Travel Demand Forecasting Model; use of current measurable travel habits with projected employment/population estimates for needs-based decisions.
Chief knowledge officer	State communications connections	Head of program also serves as chief information/knowledge officer for state department of administration; uses state agency interactively generated data, information to develop usable knowledge.

Source: Compiled by the author.

Tacit Knowledge Management Activities

Type of Activity	Type of Agency	Example/Use
Sharing best practices	State geographic council	Biannual/state geographic information system (GIS) conference; sharing among three GIS tiers: (1) expert, technically involved; (2) administrator/manager; (3) novices, contemplating GIS use.
Informal mentoring	State department of the environment	Field-based watershed coordinators work with landowners, local government officials, others to disseminate degradation and conservation knowledge, including river basin studies.
Formal mentoring	Community development department	Community visitation teams work with small towns on their community development challenges together to write a formal plan.
Task force/work group	State department of economic development	Special study of the problem of "business succession" in rural, small towns, that is, the closing of local businesses when the current entrepreneur retires or otherwise closes the business; for planning and policy purposes.
Electronic decision support group work	State vocational rehabilitation	Using university electronic work laboratory to develop proposed program revisions.
Discussion groups	Rural state economic development agency	Organized focus groups to prepare state rural economic development strategy.
Expert interviews	State geographic council	Presentations/questions of vendor-experts at meetings to demonstrate latest GIS technology.
Apprenticeships	State department of environment	A series of plan coordinators are university interns or new graduates who primarily fund and blend research and plan programs from a variety of federal and state resources.
Training programs	State water resource board	Operational, conservation, and regulatory compliance workshops for small water company managers and technicians.
Cultural change	State office of rural development	Cooperative development center tries to create natural atmosphere of sharing of informational staff.
Fostering collaboration	Developmental disabilities state agency	Rather than petitioner and petitioned, the state division works together with two state-level peak interest groups and a host of nongovernmental organization providers to share information, create program knowledge, and guide the program's future.

Source: Compiled by the author.

Twenty-Two Public Values Contributed by Networks

Problem identification information exchange
1. Convening stakeholders.
2. Issue discussion.
3. Identification of existing agency actions.
4. Identification of possible solutions.

Identification of extant technologies
5. From external situations.
6. Provide venues for informational data exchange.
7. Creation of technical task forces/work groups.

Adaptation of technology
8. Location of existing technologies.
9. Interactively create adaptations for multiagency use.
10. Legal and financial adjustments.

Implementation of knowledge infrastructures
11. Information and communications technology improvements inside the network.
12. Establish knowledge management processes.
13. Information and communications technology improvements for activities outside the network.

Capacity building
14. Outreach
15. Educating individual partners.
16. Enhancing agency capabilities.

Reciprocal programming/joint strategy
17. Knowledge-driven agreements.
18. Negotiated solutions.
19. Regularized interagency transactions.

Joint policymaking
20. Knowledge-driven decisions.
21. Consensus-oriented decision processes.
22. Regularized agency transactions.

Source: Agranoff (2007, chap. 8).

Alternative Dispute Resolution Processes

1. Negotiation: Principled or interest-based negotiation is sometimes considered a form of dispute resolution, and these skills are fundamental to all the remaining third-party processes. Disputants negotiate directly and attempt to untangle interpersonal and substantive issues, focus on interests not rights or positions, promote creative problem solving, and use principles rather than power to reach agreement.

2. Conciliation: An agency attempts to negotiate a private settlement generally between two private parties to a dispute subject to the agency's jurisdiction. For example, the Civil Rights Act of 1964 (commonly known as Title VII) mandates conciliation for disputes regarding discrimination in employment based on race, sex, or other status. This term is also sometimes used to mean mediation.

3. Facilitation: A neutral third party, the facilitator structures group discussions toward a voluntary settlement, asking pointed questions and using collaborative bargaining techniques. This process is more commonly used in multiparty issues or for large groups.

4. Mediation: This is assisted negotiation, in which a neutral third party attempts to help parties reach mutual agreement. Sometimes the mediator uses shuttle diplomacy, in which the parties separately and mostly in confidence communicate their interests, goals, and concerns. The mediator identifies a range of possible settlements, but has no power to impose a solution or decide the case. This process is widely used in environmental and public policy conflict resolution.

5. Fact-finding: This is a form of advisory arbitration where a neutral third party conducts an informal evidentiary hearing to narrow the disputed facts.

6. Mini-trials: A form of advisory arbitration where a neutral third party conducts a more formal but still abbreviated evidentiary hearing and advises on disputed questions of law.

7. Arbitration: Private adjudication, where a neutral third party conducts an informal adjudicatory hearing on all disputed issues of fact and law, and renders an award or decision on all issues. Arbitration may be voluntary or mandatory and may be advisory or binding.

8. Ombudsperson program: This is the use of an in-house neutral third party to assist people in handling conflict. The ombudsperson can help refer employees or citizens to the appropriate dispute resolution process, can engage in conflict coaching, and can help manage the variety of agency processes.

Source: Summarized by permission from "Legal Frameworks for Collaboration in Governance and Public Management," Lisa Blomgren Bingham (2008, 252–53).

Milestones in Metro School's Development

- Initial contacts by Battelle, Ohio State University (OSU), and small schools association staff.
- Development of a proposal for a mathematics and science high school; $200,000 grant from Gates Foundation/Coalition for Essential Schools (CES).
- Retreat in Tacoma at CES meeting to work on the details of the operation, governance, space, learning modes, and early college. Leadership also designated.
- Educational Council, through its sixteen superintendents, agrees to take on the small school as one of its projects.
- Space and build out, gathering of financial/donated resources by major partners, school district exchange principles/tax base support, and technical assistance commitments.
- Public announcement, mobilization of public official and community leadership support.
- Partnership steering group formed out of partner and leadership cadre.
- Curricular task forces comprised of teachers, industry representatives, university faculty, other experts design courses of study in all areas, from arts and humanities to biological and physical sciences.
- Enlistment of learning sites at area museums, laboratories, research centers, libraries, industry, and public agencies.
- Full-time faculty of fourteen recruited, plus doctoral students, student teachers, and tutors.
- School opens, freshman class of 100 enters representing on a district student population ratio basis, from all sixteen school districts.
- Two years later, nearly 90 of the initial class begin classes as both high school juniors and OSU students.
- Three years later, class of 100 enters, Metro at full complement of 400 students, 200 at its facility on the OSU campus, 200 at OSU.

Source: Summarized from Hunter et al. (2008).

References

ACIR (Advisory Commission on Intergovernmental Relations). 1962. *Alternative Approaches to Governmental Reorganization in Metropolitan Areas*. Report A-11. Washington, DC: ACIR.

Agger, Annika, Eva Sorenson, and Jacob Torfing. 2008. "It Takes Two to Tango: When Public and Private Actors Interact." In *Civic Engagement in a Network Society*, edited by Kaifeng Yang and Erik Bergrud. Charlotte: Information Age.

Agranoff, Robert. 1986. *Intergovernmental Management: Perspectives from Problem Solving in Six Metropolitan Areas*. Albany: State University of New York Press.

———. 1991. "Human Services Integration: Past and Present Challenges in Public Administration." *Public Administration Review* 51 (November–December): 426–36.

———. 1995. "The Iowa State Rural Development Council." In *Intergovernmental Partnerships and Rural Development: State Rural Development Council in Sixteen States*, edited by Beryl Radin. Washington, DC: National Rural Development Partnership.

———. 1998. Partnerships in Public Management: Rural Enterprise Alliances. *International Journal of Public Administration* 21 (11): 1533–75.

———. 2003. *Leveraging Networks: A Guide for Public Managers Working across Organizations*. Washington, DC: IBM Center for the Business of Government.

———. 2007. *Managing within Networks: Adding Value to Public Organizations*. Washington, DC: Georgetown University Press.

———. 2008. "Collaboration for Knowledge: Learning from Public Management Networks." In *Big Ideas in Collaborative Public Management*, edited by Lisa Bingham and Rosemary O'Leary. Armonk, NY: M. E. Sharpe.

———. 2009. "Intergovernmental Management by Network: Lessons from Mental Retardation/Developmental Disabilities Programs, Federal to Local." Paper presented at Annual Meeting of the American Political Science Association, Toronto, September 3–6.

———. 2011. "Collaborative Public Agencies in the Network Era." In *The State of Public Administration: Issues, Challenges, and Opportunities*, edited by Donald C. Menzel and Harvey L. White. Armonk, NY: M. E. Sharpe.

Agranoff, Robert, and Michael McGuire. 2000. "Administration of State Government Rural Development Policy." In *Handbook of State Government Administration*, edited by J. J. Gargan. New York: Marcel Dekker.

———. 2001. "Big Questions in Public Network Management Research." *Journal of Public Administration Research and Theory* 11 (3): 295–326.

———. 2003. *Collaborative Public Management: New Strategies for Local Governments*. Washington, DC: Georgetown University Press.

———. 2005. "The Olmstead Decision, The ADA and Federal-State Relations." Paper prepared for 2005 Annual Meeting of American Political Science Association, Washington, September 1–4.

———. 2004. "Another Look at Bargaining and Negotiating in Intergovernmental Management." *Journal of Public Administration Research and Theory* 14 (4): 498–525.

Agranoff, Robert, and Alex N. Pattakos. 1979. *Dimensions of Services Integration*. Rockville, MD: Project SHARE.

Agranoff, Robert, and Mete Yildiz. 2007. "Decision-Making in Public Management Networks." In *Handbook of Decision-Making*, edited by Göktuğ Morçöl. Boca Raton, FL: Taylor & Francis.

Alter, Catherine, and Jerald Hage. 1993. *Organizations Working Together*. Newbury Park, CA: Sage.

Alvesson, Mats, and Stanley Deetz. 1996. "Critical Theory and Postmodernism Approaches to Organizational Studies." In *Handbook of Organization Studies*, edited by Stewart R. Clegg, Cynthia Hardy, and Walther Nord. London: Sage.

Ansell, Chris, and Alison Gash. 2008. "Collaborative Governance in Theory and Practice." *Journal of Public Administrative Research and Theory* 18 (4): 543–72.

Argullol, Enric, Robert Agranoff, Maria Aguirre, Francis Delpérée, Jacques Frémont, Scott Greer, Antonio Hernández, Winfred Kluth, Katy LeRoy, Francesco Merloni, Peter Pernthaler, Cheryl A. Saunders, José María Serna, Urs Thalmann, and Carles Viver i Pi-Sunyer. 2004. *Federalismo y autonomía*. Barcelona: Ariel.

Ashford, Douglas E. 1988. "Decentralizing Welfare States: Social Policies and Intergovernmental Politics." In *The Dynamics of Institutional Change: Local Governmental Reorganization in Western Democracies*, edited by Bruno Dente and Francesco Kjellberg. London: Sage.

Ashkenas, Ron, Dave Ulrich, Todd Jick, and Steve Kerr. 2002. *The Boundaryless Organization*. San Francisco: Jossey-Bass.

Axelrod, Robert. 1984. *The Evolution of Cooperation*. New York: Basic Books.

Bacow, Adela F. 1995. *Designing the City: A Guide for Advocates and Public Officials*. Washington, DC: Island Press.

Barber, Benjamin. 1983. *The Logic and Limits of Trust*. New Brunswick, NJ: Rutgers University Press.

Bardach, Eugene. 1998. *Getting Agencies to Work Together*. Washington, DC: Brookings Institution Press.

Barrett, Katherine, and Richard Greene. 2010. "New Revenue, New Concerns: Contingency Fee Contracts Are Becoming Hot, but Have Their Limits." *Governing* 23 (6): 46–47.

Beam, David R., and Timothy J. Conlan. 2002. "Grants." In *The Tools of Government*, edited by Lester M. Salamon. New York: Oxford University Press.

Behn, Robert D. 2001. *Rethinking Democratic Accountability*. Washington, DC: Brookings Institution Press.

Bikson, Tora K., and Constantijn W. A. Panos. 1999. *Citizens, Computers and Connectivity*. Santa Monica, CA: RAND Corporation.

Bingham, Lisa Blomgren. 2008. "Legal Frameworks for Collaboration in Governance and Public Management." In *Big Ideas in Collaborative Public Management*, edited by Lisa Blomgren Bingham and Rosemary O'Leary. Armonk, NY: M. E. Sharpe.

Bingham, Lisa B., Tina Nabachi, and Rosemary O'Leary. 2005. "The New Governance: Practice and Processes for Stakeholder and Citizen Participation in the Work of Government." *Public Administration Review* 65 (5): 547–58.

Bingham, Lisa B., and Rosemary O'Leary, eds. 2008. *Big Ideas in Collaborative Public Management*. Armonk, NY: M. E. Sharpe.

Bingham, Lisa Blomgren, Rosemary O'Leary, and Christine Carlson. 2008. "Frame Shifting: Lateral Thinking for Collaborative Public Management." In *Big Ideas in Collaborative Public Management*, edited by Lisa Blomgren Bingham and Rosemary O'Leary. Armonk, NY: M. E. Sharpe.

Blanco, Ismael, and Ricard Gomá. 2002. "Proximidad y participación: Marco conceptual y presentación de experiencias." In *Gobiernos locales y redes participativas*, edited by Ismael Blanco and Ricard Gomá. Barcelona: Ariel.

Booher, David E. 2005. "A Call to Scholars from the Collaborative Democracy Network." *National Civic Review* 94 (3): 640–67.

———. 2008. "Civic Engagement as Collaborative Complex Adaptive Networks." In *Civic Engagement in a Network Society*, edited by Kaifeng Yang and Erik Bergrud. Charlotte: Information Age.

Borins, Sandford F. 2012. "Making Narrative Count: A Narratological Approach to Public Management Innovation." *Journal of Public Administration Research and Theory* 22 (1): 165–89.

Boyte, Harry C. 1989. *Common Wealth: A Return to Citizen Politics*. New York: Free Press.

Braddock, David, and Richard E. Hemp. 2004. *Developmental Disabilities Services in Indiana: 2004 Progress Report*. Report prepared for INARF/Arc/Governor's Planning Council/Indiana University IIDC. Indianapolis: Association of Rehabilitation Facilities of Indiana.

Braddock, David, Richard Hemp, and Mary C. Rizzolo. 2004. "State of the States in Developmental Disabilities: 2004." *Mental Retardation* 24 (5): 356–70.

Bradley, Valerie J. 2009. Personal correspondence, April 22.

Brody, Ralph. 1982. *Problem Solving: Concepts and Methods for Community Organizations*, 2nd ed. New York: Human Sciences Press.

Brown, L. David. 1983. *Managing Conflict at Organizational Interfaces*. Reading, MA: Addison-Wesley.

Brown, Trevor L., and Matthew Potoski. 2004. "Managing the Public Service Market." *Public Administration Review* 64 (6): 656–68.

Brown, Trevor L., Matthew Potoski, and David Van Slyke. 2006. "Managing Public Service Contracts: Aligning Values, Institutions and Markets." *Public Administration Review*, 66 (3): 323–31.

———. 2008. "Simple and Complex Contracting." *PA Times*, July 2008, 5.

Bryer, Thomas A. 2009. "Explaining Responsiveness in Collaboration: Administrator and Citizen Role Perceptions." *Public Administration Review* 69 (2): 271–83.

Bryer, Thomas A., and Jerry L. Cooper. 2007. "Challenges in Enhancing Responsiveness in Neighborhood Governance." *Public Performance and Management Review* 31 (2): 191–214.

Bryson, John M., and Barbara C. Crosby. 1992. *Leadership for the Common Good*. San Francisco: Jossey-Bass.

———. 2008. "Failing into Cross-Sector Collaboration Successfully." In *Big Ideas in Collaborative Public Management*, edited by Lisa Blomgren Bingham and Rosemary O'Leary. Armonk, NY: M. E. Sharpe.

Bryson, John M., Barbara C. Crosby, and Melissa M. Stone. 2006. "The Design and Implementation of Cross-Sector Collaborations." *Public Administration Review* 66 (6): 44–55.

Bryson, John M., Barbara C. Crosby, Melissa M. Stone, and Emily O. Saunoi-Sandgren. 2009. *Designing and Managing Cross-Sector Collaboration: A Case Study in Reducing Traffic Congestion*. Washington, DC: IBM Center for the Business of Government.

Buchanan, Mark. 2002. *Small World: Uncovering Nature's Hidden Networks*. London: Weidenfeld & Nicholson.

Campbell, Andrew, and Michael Gould. 1999. *The Collaborative Enterprise*. Reading, MA: Perseus Books.

Castellani, Paul J. 2000. "Administration of Developmental Disabilities Services in State Government." In *Handbook of State Government Administration*, edited by John J. Gargan. New York: Marcel Dekker.

———. 2005. *From Snake Pits to Cash Cows: Politics and Public Institutions in New York*. Albany: State University of New York Press.

Castells, Manual. 1996. *The Rise of the Network Society*. Oxford: Blackwell.

Chen, Bin. 2008. "Assessing Interorganizational Networks for Public Service Delivery." *Public Performance and Management Review* 31 (3): 348–63.

Chisholm, Donald. 1989. *Coordination without Hierarchy: Informal Structures in Multiorganizational Systems*. Berkeley: University of California Press.

Chisholm, Rupert F. 2001. "Bringing About Change in a Public School System: An Interorganizational Network Approach." In *Getting Results through Collaboration: Networks and Network Structures for Public Policy and Management*, edited by Myrna P. Mandell. Westport, CT: Quorum Books.

Choi, Cheon Geun, and Sang Ok Choi. 2012. "Collaborative Partnerships and Crime in Disorganized Communities." *Public Administration Review* 72 (2): 228–39.

Chrislip, David D., and Carl E. Larson. 1994. *Collaborative Leadership*. San Francisco: Jossey-Bass.

Cigler, Beverly A. 2001. "Multiorganization, Multisector, and Multicommunity Organizations: Setting the Research Agenda." In *Getting Results through Collaboration: Networks and Network Structures for Collaboration*, edited by Myrna B. Mandell. Westport, CT: Quorum Books.

Circles. 2010. "An Innovative Model to End Poverty." Available at www.movethemountain.com.

Clegg, Stewart R. 1990. *Modern Organizations: Organization Studies in the Postmodern World*. London: Sage.

Clegg, Stewart R., and Cynthia Hardy. 1996. "Conclusion: Representations." In *Handbook of Organization Studies*, edited by Stewart R. Clegg, Cynthia Hardy, and Walter Nord. London: Sage.

Cohen, Stephen, and William Eimicke. 2008. *The Responsible Contract Manager*. Washington, DC: Georgetown University Press.

Cooper, Terry L., Thomas A. Bryer, and Jack W. Meek. 2006. "Citizen-Centered Collaborative Public Management." *Public Administration Review* 66 (6): 76–88.

Cross, Rob, Andrew Parker, Laurence Prusak, and Stephen Bargotti. 2001. "Knowing What We Know: Supporting Knowledge Creation and Sharing in Social Networks." *Organizational Dynamics* 30 (2): 100–120.

Davenport, Thomas H. 2005. *Thinking for a Living: How to Get Better Performance and Results from Knowledge Workers*. Boston: Harvard Business School Press.

Davenport, Thomas H., and Laurence Prusak. 2000. *Working Knowledge: How Organizations Manage What They Know*. Boston: Harvard Business School Press.

Dayton City Manager's Office. 1983. "A Senior Services Strategy for Dayton." In *Human Services on a Limited Budget*, edited by Robert Agranoff. Washington, DC: International City Management Association.

DeHoog, Ruth Hoogland. 2002. "Purchase-of-Service Contracting." In *The Tools of Government*, edited by Lester M. Salamon. New York: Oxford University Press.

DeMarie, Samuel M. 2004. *Virtual Teams to Manage Complex Projects*. In *Collaboration: Using Networks and Partnerships*, edited by John M. Kamensky and Thomas J. Burlin. Lanham, MD: Rowman & Littlefield,

Denters, Bas, and Lawrence E. Rose. 2005. "Towards Local Governance?" In *Comparing Local Governance*, edited by Bas Denters and Lawrence E. Rose. London: Palgrave.

Drucker, Peter F. 1974. *Management: Tasks, Responsibilities, Practices*. New York: Harper & Row.

———. 2001. *The Essential Drucker: Selections from the Management Works of Peter F. Drucker*. New York: HarperCollins.

Economist. 2009. "On-Line Social Networking." February 28, 85–86.

———. 2010a. "Briefing: Social Innovation." August 14, 55–57.

———. 2010b. "The Wiki Way." September 25, 82.

———. 2011. "Building with Big Data." May 28, 74.

Edner, Sheldon, and Bruce D. McDowell. 2002. "Surface Transportation Funding in a New Century: Assessing One Slice of the Federal Marble Cake." *Publius: The Journal of Federalism* 32 (1): 7–24.

Eisinger, Peter K. 1988. *The Rise of the Entrepreneurial State*. Madison: University of Wisconsin Press.

Elazar, Daniel J. 1962. *The American Partnership: Intergovernmental Cooperation in the Nineteenth-Century United States*. Chicago: University of Chicago Press.

———. 1984. *American Federalism: A View from the States*, 3rd ed. New York: Harper & Row.

Elmore, Richard F. 1985. "Forward and Backward Mapping: Reversible Logic in the Analysis of Public Policy." In *Policy Implementation in Federal and Unitary Systems*, edited by Kenneth Hanf and Theo A. J. Toonen. Dordrecht: Martinus Nijhoff.

Emerson, Kirk, Tina Nabatchi, and Stephen Balogh. 2012. "An Integrative Framework for

Collaborative Governance." *Journal of Public Administration Research and Theory* 22 (1): 1–29.

Esmark, Anders. 2007. "Democratic Accountability and Network Governance." In *Theories of Democratic Network Governance*, edited by Eva Sorenson and Jacob Torfing. Houndsmills, UK: Palgrave Macmillan.

Fenwick, John, and Janice McMillan. 2010. "Public Policy and Management in Postmodern Times." In *Public Management in the Postmodern Era*, edited by John Fenwick and Janice McMillan. Cheltenham, UK: Edward Elgar.

Ferguson, Ronald F., and Sara E. Stoutland. 1999. "Reconceiving the Community Development Field." In *Urban Problems and Community Development*, edited by Ronald F. Ferguson and William T. Dickens. Washington, DC: Brookings Institution Press.

Fernandez, Sergio. 2009. "Understanding Contracting Performance: An Empirical Analysis." *Administration and Society* 41 (1): 67–100.

Fisher, Roger, and Scott Brown. 1988. *Getting Together: Building Relationships As We Negotiate*. New York: Penguin.

Fisher, Roger, William Ury, and Bruce Patton. 1991. *Getting to Yes*, 2nd ed. New York: Penguin.

Font, Joan, Núria Font, and Joan Subirats. 2002. "Las Agendas 21 locales: La Experiencia de Barcelona en perspectiva comparada." In *Gobiernos locales y redes participativas*, edited by Ismael Blanco and Ricard Gomá. Barcelona: Ariel.

Forester, John. 1999. *The Deliberative Practitioner: Encouraging Participatory Planning Processes*. Cambridge, MA: MIT Press.

———. 2009. *Dealing with Differences: Dramas of Mediating Public Disputes*. New York: Oxford University Press.

Fountain, Jane E. 1994. "Trust as a Basis for Interorganizational Forum." Paper presented at conference of Network Analysis and Innovations in Public Programs, University of Wisconsin–Madison, October.

Franz, Roger, and Alex N. Pattakos. 1996. "Economic Growth and Evolution: The Intuitive Connection." In *Intuition at Work*, edited by Roger Franz and Alex N. Pattakos. San Francisco: New Leaders Press.

FSSA (Family and Social Services Administration). 1998. *A Proposal for Person-Centered Planning for Persons with Developmental Disabilities*. Indianapolis: State of Indiana.

Fung, Archon. 2006. "Varieties of Participation in Complex Governance." *Public Administration Review* 66 (S1): 66–75.

GAO (US Government Accountability Office). 2004. *Homeland Security: Federal Leadership and Intergovernmental Cooperation Required to Achieve First Responder Interoperable Communications*. Report GAO-04-470. Washington, DC: US Government Printing Office.

———. 2006. *Results-Oriented Government: Practices That Can Help Enhance and Sustain Collaboration among Federal Agencies*. Report GA006-15. Washington, DC: US Government Printing Office.

———. 2009. *Metropolitan Transportation Planning Organizations: Options to Enhance Transportation Planning Capacity and Federal Oversight*. Report GAO-09-868. Washington, DC: US Government Printing Office.

Gazley, Beth. 2008. "Intersector Collaboration and the Motivation to Collaborate: Toward Integrated Theory." In *Big Ideas in Collaborative Public Management*, edited by Lisa Blomgren Bingham and Rosemary O'Leary. Armonk, NY: M. E. Sharpe.

Gettings, Robert M. 2003. "Building a Comprehensive Quality Management Program: Organizing Principles and Primary Operating Components." In *Quality Enhancement in Developmental Disabilities*, edited by Valerie J. Bradley and Madeleine H. Kimmich. Baltimore: Paul H. Brookes.

Goldsmith, Stephen, and William D. Eggers. 2004. *Governing by Network*. Washington, DC: Brookings Institution Press.

Goodnow, Frank J. 1900. *Politics and Administration*. New York: Macmillan.

Goss, Sue. 2001. *Making Local Governance Work: Networks, Relationships and the Management of Change*. Basingstoke, UK: Palgrave.

Gray, Barbara. 1989. *Collaborating: Finding Common Ground for Multiparty Problems*. San Francisco: Jossey-Bass.

Grodzins, Morton. 1966. *The American System*, edited by Daniel J. Elazar. Chicago: Rand McNally.

Haas, Peter M. 1992. "Introduction: Epistemic Communities and International Policy Coordination." *International Organization* 46 (1): 1–35.

Hale, Kathleen. 2011. *How Information Matters*. Washington, DC: Georgetown University Press.

Hayes, Catherine, Linda Joyce, and Elizabeth Couchoud. 2003. "Federal Policy and Practice in Transition: A Look Ahead at the ICF/ID Program." In *Quality Enhancement in Developmental Disabilities*, edited by Valerie J. Bradley and Madeleine H. Kimmich. Baltimore: Paul H. Brookes.

Herranz, Joaquim, Jr. 2008. "The Multisectoral Trilemma of Network Management." *Journal of Public Administration Research and Theory* 18 (1): 1–32.

Hillis, Danny. 2002. "Unbundling and Reassembling Governments." In *What's Next? Exploring the New Terrain for Business*, edited by Eamonn Kelly, Peter Leyden, and Members of the Global Business Network. New York: Basic Books.

Himmelfarb, Gertrude. 1998. "Second Thoughts on Civil Society." In *Community Works: The Revival of Civil Society in America*, edited by E. J. Dionne Jr. Washington, DC: Brookings Institution Press.

Holbeche, Linda. 2005. *The High Performance Organization*. Amsterdam: Elsevier.

Honadle, Beth W. 1981. "A Capacity-Building Framework: A Search for Concept and Purpose." *Public Administration Review* 41:575–80.

Hood, Christopher. 1991. "A Public Management for All Seasons?" *Public Administration* 69 (1): 3–19.

Human, Sherrie E., and Keith G. Provan. 2000. "Legitimacy Building in the Evolution of Small-Firm Multilateral Networks: A Comparative Study of Success and Demise." *Administrative Science Quarterly* 45 (2): 327–65.

Human Services Research Institute. 2005. *Status Report: Litigation Concerning Home and Community Services for People with Disabilities*. Tualatin, OR: Human Services Research Institute. www.hsri.org/index.asp?id=news.

Hunter, Monica, Robert Agranoff, Michael McGuire, Jill Greenbaum, Janice Morrison,

Maria Cohen, and Jing Liu. 2008. *Metro High School: An Emerging STEM Community.* Report for Grant 420038AC-07. Columbus: PAST Foundation/Battelle Center for Mathematics and Science Education Policy.

Huxham, Chris, and Siv Vangen. 2005. *Managing to Collaborate: The Theory and Practice of Collaborative Advantage.* London: Routledge.

Hyneman, Charles S. 1950. *Bureaucracy in a Democracy.* New York: Harper and Brothers.

Imperial, Mark J. 2004. *Collaboration and Performance Management in Network Settings: Lessons from Three Watershed Governance Efforts.* Washington, DC: IBM Center for the Business of Government.

INARF (Indiana Association of Rehabilitation Facilities). 2005. "Maintaining 317 as the Indiana *Olmstead* Response." Indianapolis: INARF.

Ingram, Helen. 1977. "Policy Implementation through Bargaining: The Case of Federal Grants-in-Aid." *Public Policy* 25 (4): 499–526.

Innes, Judith. 2004. "Consensus Building: Clarifications for the Critics." *Planning Theory* 3 (1): 5–21.

Innes, Judith, and David E. Booher. 1999. "Consensus-Building and Complex Adaptive Systems: A Framework for Evaluating Collaborative Planning." *Journal of the American Planning Association* 65 (4): 412–23.

Jenkins, William O. 2006. "Collaboration over Adaptation: The Case for Interoperable Communications in Homeland Security." *Public Administration Review* 66 (3): 319–22.

John, DeWitt. 1994. *Civic Environmentalism: Alternatives to Regulation in States and Communities.* Washington, DC: Congressional Quarterly Press.

John, Peter. 2004. "Strengthening Local Leadership? More Than Mayors." In *British Local Government into the 21st Century*, edited by Gerry Stoker and David Wilson. Houndsmill, UK: Palgrave Macmillan.

Johnston, Jocelyn M., and Barbara Romzek. 2000. *Implementing State Contracts for Social Services.* Washington, DC: IBM Center for the Business of Government.

———. 2010. "The Promises, Performance, and Pitfalls of Government Contracting." In *The Oxford Handbook of American Bureaucracy*, edited by Robert F. Durant. New York: Oxford University Press.

Kamieniecki, Sheldon, Robert O'Brien, and Michael Clarke. 1985. "Intergovernmental Cooperation in Environmental Policy-Making." Paper presented at Annual Meeting of the American Political Science Association, New Orleans, August 21–September 1.

Kathi, Pradeep Chandra, and Terry L. Cooper. 2005. "Democratizing the Administrative State: Connecting Neighborhood Councils and City Agencies." *Public Administration Review* 65 (5): 559–67.

Keleman, Steven J. 2002. "Contracting." In *The Tools of Government*, edited by Lester M. Salamon. New York: Oxford University Press.

Kenis, Patrick, and Keith G. Provan. 2006. "The Control of Public Networks." *International Public Management Journal* 9 (2): 227–47.

Kickert, Walter J. M., and Joop F. M. Koppenjan. 1997. "Public Management and Network Management: An Overview." In *Managing Complex Networks*, edited by Walter J. M. Kickert, Erik-Hans Klijn, and Joop F. M. Koppenjan. London: Sage.

Kilduff, Martin, and Wenpin Tsai. 2003. *Social Networks and Organizations*. Thousand Oaks, CA: Sage.

Klijn, Erik-Hans. 2001. "Rules as Institutional Context for Decision-Making in Networks." *Administration in Society* 33 (3): 133–64.

———. 2003. "Governing Networks in the Hollow State: Contracting Out, Process Management, or a Combination of the Two?" *Public Management Review* 4 (2): 149–65.

Klijn, Erik-Hans, and Joop F. M. Koppenjan. 2000. "Public Management and Policy Networks: Foundations of a Network Approach to Governance." *Public Management* 2 (2): 135–58.

———. 2007. "Governing Policy Networks." In *Handbook of Decision-Making*, edited by Göktuğ Morcöl. Boca Raton, FL: Taylor & Francis.

Koliba, Christopher, Erica Campbell, and Asim Zia. 2011. "Performance Management Systems of Congestion Management Networks: Evidence from Four Cases." *Public Performance and Management Review* 34 (4): 520–48.

Koliba, Christopher, Jack Meek, and Asim Zia. 2010. *Governance Networks: Public Administration Policy in the Midst of Complexity*. New York: Taylor & Francis.

Kooiman, Jan.. 2003. *Governing as Governance*. London: Sage.

Koppenjan, Joop F. M., and Erik Hans Klijn. 2004. *Managing Uncertainties in Networks*. London: Routledge.

Lakin, K. Charlie, Robert Doljanac, Soo-Young Byen, Roger Stancliffe, Sarah Taub, and Giuseppeina Chiri. 2008. "Choice-Making among Medicaid HCBS and ICF/MR Recipients in Six States." *American Journal on Mental Retardation* 113 (5): 325–42.

Lakin, K. Charlie, Robert Prouty, and Kathryn Coucouvanis. 2007. "HCBS Recipients Are Increasingly Likely to Live with Parents or Other Relatives." *Intellectual and Developmental Disabilities* 45 (5): 359–61.

Lax, David A., and James K. Sebenius. 1986. *The Manager as Negotiator: Bargaining for Cooperation and Competitive Gain*. New York: Free Press.

Lee, In-Won, Richard C. Feiock, and Kai-Jo Fu. 2012. "Competitors and Cooperators: A Micro-Level Analysis of Regional Economic Development Collaboration Networks." *Public Administration Review* 72 (2): 253–62.

Liebschutz, Sarah F. 1991. *Bargaining under Federalism*. Albany: State University of New York Press.

Lin, Alice P. 2007. *The Implementation of Local Management Entities in North Carolina*. Report prepared for Division of Mental Health, Developmental Disabilities, and Substance Abuse Services. Raleigh: North Carolina Department of Health and Human Services.

Lipnack, Jessica, and Jeffrey Stamps. 1994. *The Age of the Network*. New York: John Wiley and Sons.

Loughlin, John. 2001. "Introduction: The Transformation of the Democratic State in Western Europe." In *Subnational Democracy in the European Union*, edited by John Loughlin. Oxford: Oxford University Press.

Man, Joyce Y. 2001. "Effects of Tax Increment Financing on Economic Development." In *Tax Increment Financing and Economic Development: Uses, Structures, and Impacts*, edited by Craig L. Johnson and Joyce Y. Man. Albany: State University of New York Press.

Mandell, Myrna P. 2001. "The Impact of Network Structures on Community-Building Efforts: The Los Angeles Round Table for Children Community Studies." In *Getting Results through Collaboration: Networks and Network Structures for Public Policy and Management*, edited by Myrna P. Mandell. Westport, CT: Quorum Books.

———. 2008. "New Ways of Working: Civic Engagement through Networks." In *Civic Engagement in a Network Society*, edited by Kaifeng Yang and Erik Bergrud. Charlotte: Information Age.

Mandell, Myrna P., and Toddi A. Steelman. 2003. "Understanding What Can Be Accomplished through Interorganizational Innovations: The Importance of Typologies, Content and Management Strategies." *Public Management Review* 5 (2): 197–224.

Margolis, Mac. 2010. "Your Pass to Good Government." *Daily Beast*, August 16. www .thedailybeast.com/newsweek/2010/08/16/how-e-government-is-empowering -citizens-worldwide.html.

Martin, Roscoe C. 1963. *Metropolis in Transition: Local Government Adaptation to Changing Urban Needs*. Report of US Housing and Home Finance Agency. Washington, DC: US Government Printing Office.

———. 1965. *The Cities and the Federal System*. New York: Atherton Press.

Matthews, David. 1994. *Politics for People*. Urbana: University of Illinois Press.

McGuire, Michael. 2002. "Managing Networks: Propositions on What Managers Do and Why They Do It." *Public Administration Review* 62 (5): 426–33.

———. 2009. "The New Professionalism and Collaborative Activity in Local Emergency Management." In *The Collaborative Public Manager*, edited by Rosemary O'Leary and Lisa B. Bingham. Washington, DC: Georgetown University Press.

McGuire, Michael, and Robert Agranoff. 2010. "Networking in the Shadow of Bureaucracy." In *Oxford Handbook of American Bureaucracy*, edited by Robert F. Durant. New York: Oxford University Press.

———. 2011. "The Limitations of Public Management Networks." *Public Administration* 89 (2): 265–84.

McGuire, Michael, and Chris Silvia. 2008. "Does Leadership in Networks Matter?" Paper presented at Annual Meeting of the American Political Science Association, Boston, August 29–September 1.

Meier, Kenneth J., and Laurence J. O'Toole Jr. 2003. "Public Management and Educational Performance: The Impact of Managerial Networking." *Public Administration Review*, 3 (6): 689–99.

Metzenbaum, Shelley H. 2008. "From Oversight to Insight: Federal Agencies as Learning Leaders in the Information Age." In *Intergovernmental Management in the 21st Century*, edited by Timothy J. Conlan and Paul L. Posner. Washington, DC: Brookings Institution Press.

Mintzberg, Henry. 1983. *Structure in Fives: Designing Effective Organizations*. Englewood Cliffs, NJ: Prentice Hall.

Moore, Mark H. 1995. *Creating Public Value: Strategic Management in Government*. Cambridge, MA: Harvard University Press.

Morgan, Gareth. 1993. *Images of Organization*. London: Sage.

Moseley, Casandra. 2010. *Strategies for Supporting Frontline Collaboration: Lessons from Stewardship Contracting*. Washington, DC: IBM Center for the Business of Government.

Mossberger, Karen. 2000. *The Politics of Ideas and the Spread of Enterprise Zones*. Washington, DC: Georgetown University Press.

Nalbandian, John. 1999. "Facilitating Community, Enabling Democracy: New Roles for Local Government Managers." *Public Administration Review* 59 (3): 187–97.

NCSL (National Conference of State Legislatures). 2003. *The State's Response to the Olmstead Decision: How Are States Complying?* Report prepared by Wendy Fox-Grage, Donna Fulkener, and Jordan Lewis. Washington, DC: NCSL. www.ncsl.org/programs/health/forum/olmsreport.htm.

Neu, C. Richard, Robert H. Anderson, and Tora K. Bikson. 1999. *Citizens, Computers and Connectivity*. Santa Monica, CA: RAND Corporation.

Newell, Sue, Maxine Robertson, Harry Scarbrough, and Jacky Swan. 2002. *Managing Knowledge Work*. Houndsmills, UK: Palgrave.

Newsweek. 2009. "Future of Newspapers." October 19, 18.

Nohria, Nitin. 1992. "Information and Search in the Creation of New Business Ventures: The Case of the 128 Venture Group." In *Networks and Organizations: Structure, Form, and Action*, edited by Nitin Nohria and Robert Eccles. Boston: Harvard Business School Press.

Olmstead v. L.C. and E.W. (1999). 28 CFR §35130 (b)(7), (d)(c)-1.

Olsen, Johan P. 2006. "Maybe It Is Time to Rediscover Bureaucracy." *Journal of Public Administration Research and Theory* 16 (1): 1–24.

Ostrom, Elinor. 1990. *Governing the Commons: The Evolution of Institutions for Collective Action*. Cambridge: Cambridge University Press.

O'Toole, Laurence J. 1997. "Treating Networks Seriously: Practical and Research-Based Agendas in Public Administration." *Public Administration Review* 57 (1): 45–52.

Padovani, Emanuele, and David W. Young. 2012. *Managing Local Governments: Designing Management Control Systems That Deliver Value*. Milton Park, UK: Routledge.

Page, Stephen. 2008. "Managing for Results across Agencies: Building Collaborative Capacity in the Human Services." In *Big Ideas in Collaborative Public Management*, edited by Lisa Blomgren Bingham and Rosemary O'Leary. Armonk, NY: M. E. Sharpe.

Pasternack, Bruce A., and Albert Viscio. 1998. *The Centerless Corporation*. New York: Simon & Schuster.

Perrow, Charles. 1986. *Complex Organizations: A Critical Essay*. New York: Random House.

Peters, B. Guy. 1996. *The Future of Governing: Four Emerging Models*. Lawrence: University Press of Kansas.

Polanyi, Michael. 1962. *Personal Knowledge*. Chicago: University of Chicago Press.

Polanyi, Michael, and Herbert Prosch. 1975. *Meaning*. Chicago: University of Chicago Press.

Pressman, Jeffrey L. 1975. *Federal Programs and City Politics: The Dynamics of the Aid Process in Oakland*. Berkeley: University of California Press.

Prouty, Robert W., Kathryn Alba, Naomi L. Scott, and Charlie Lakin. 2008. "Where People Lived While Receiving Services and Supports from State Developmental Disabilities Programs in 2006." *Intellectual and Developmental Disabilities* 46 (1): 82–85.

Provan, Keith G., and Patrick Kenis. 2008. "Modes of Network Governance: Structure,

Management and Effectiveness." *Journal of Public Administration Research and Theory* 18 (2): 229–52.

Provan, Keith G., and H. Brinton Milward. 1991. "Institutional-Level Norms and Organizational Involvement in a Service-Implementation Network." *Journal of Public Administration Research and Theory* 1 (4): 391–417.

———. 1995. "A Preliminary Theory of Interorganizational Effectiveness: A Comparative Study of Four Community Mental Health Systems." *Administrative Science Quarterly* 40 (1): 1–33.

———. 2001. "Do Networks Really Work? A Framework for Evaluating Public Sector Organizational Networks." *Public Administration Review* 61 (4): 414–23.

Prueller, Isabella. 2006. "Trends in Local Government in Europe." *Public Management Review* 8 (1): 7–30.

Radin, Beryl A. 2006. *Challenging the Performance Movement*. Washington, DC: Georgetown University Press.

Radin, Beryl A., Robert Agranoff, C. Gregory Buntz, Ann O'M. Bowman, Barbara Romzek, and Robert Wilson. 1996. *New Governance for Rural America: Creating Intergovernmental Partnerships*. Lawrence: University of Kansas Press.

Radin, Beryl A., and Paul Posner. 2010. "Policy Tools, Mandates, and Intergovernmental Relations." In *Oxford Handbook of American Bureaucracy*, edited by Robert F. Durant. New York: Oxford University Press.

Rethemeyer, R. Karl, and Deneen M. Hatmaker. 2008. "Network Management Reconsidered: An Inquiry into Management of Network Structures in Public Sector Service Provision." *Journal of Public Administration Research and Theory* 18 (4): 617–46.

Rhodes, R. A. W. 1997. *Understanding Governance: Policy Networks, Governance, Reflexivity and Accountability*. Buckingham, UK: Open University Press.

Riccucci, Norma. 2005. *How Management Matters: Street-Level Bureaucrats and Welfare Reform*. Washington, DC: Georgetown University Press.

Rimmerman, Craig A. 2005. *The New Citizenship: Unconventional Politics, Activism, and Service*, 3rd ed. Boulder, CO: Westview Press.

Roberts, Johnnie L. 2009. "PeytonPlace.com." *Daily Beast*, October 2. www.thedailybeast.com/newsweek/2009/10/02/peytonplace-com.html.

Romzek, Barbara S., and Jocelyn Johnston. 2002. "Effective Contract Implementation and Management." *Journal of Public Administration Research and Theory* 12 (3): 423–53.

Rosenbaum, Sara, Alexandria Stewart, and Joel Teitelbaum. 2002. "Defining 'Reasonable Pace' in the Post-Olmstead Environment." Washington, DC: Center for Health Services Research and Policy, George Washington University.

Rosenbaum, Sara, and Joel Teitelbaum. 2004. *Olmstead at Five: Assessing the Impact*. Washington, DC: Kaiser Commission on Medicaid and the Uninsured.

Ross, Doug, and Robert E. Friedman. 1991. "The Emerging Third Wave: New Economic Development Strategies." In *Local Economic Development: Strategies for a Changing Economy*, edited by R. Scott Fosler. Washington, DC: International City/County Management Association.

Rossi, Robert J., Kevin Gilmartin, and Charles W. Dayton. 1982. *Agencies Working Together: A Guide to Coordination and Planning*. Beverly Hills, CA: SAGE.

Sabel, Charles F. 1992. "Studied Trust: Building New Forms of Cooperation in a Volatile Economy." In *Industrial Districts and Local Economic Regeneration*, edited by Werner Sengenberger and Frank Pyke. Geneva: International Institute for Labor Studies.

Saint-Onge, Hubert, and Charles Armstrong. 2004. *The Conductive Organization*. Amsterdam: Elsevier.

Salamon, Lester M. 1995. *Partners in Public Service*. Baltimore: Johns Hopkins University Press.

———. 2002. "The New Governance and the Tools of Public Action." In *The Tools of Government*, edited by Lester M. Salamon. New York: Oxford University Press.

Sancton, Andrew. 2002. "Metropolitan and Regional Governance." In *Urban Policy Issues*, edited by Edmund P. Fowler and David Siegel. Don Mills, ON: Oxford University Press.

Sawyer, Keith. 2007. *Group Genius: The Creative Power of Collaboration*. New York: Basic Books.

Schambra, William A. 1998. "All Community Is Local: The Key to America's Civic Renewal." In *Community Works: The Revival of Civil Society in America*, edited by E. J. Dionne Jr. Washington, DC: Brookings Institution Press.

Schapp, L., and Mark. J. W. van Twist. 1997. "The Dynamics of Closedness in Networks." In *Managing Complex Networks*, edited by Walter J. M. Kickert, Erik-Hans Klijn, and Joop F. M. Koppenjan. London: Sage.

Scholz, Gordon P., J. David Aiken, Sharon L. Gaber, and Thomas C. Huston. 2000. *Public Policy Study for the Lower Platte River Corridor Region*. Lincoln: Department of Community and Regional Planning, University of Nebraska–Lincoln.

Schorr, Lisbeth B. 1988. *Within Our Reach*. New York: Anchor Press.

Schrage, Michael. 1995. *No More Teams: Mastering the Dynamics of Creative Collaboration*. New York: Doubleday.

Seidman, Harold. 1986. *Politics, Position and Power*, 4th ed. New York: Oxford University Press.

Senge, Peter M. 1990. *The Fifth Discipline: The Art and Practice of the Learning Organization*. New York: Doubleday.

Shapek, Raymond. 1981. *Managing Federalism: Evolution and Development of the Grant-in-Aid System*. Charlottesville, VA: Community Collaborators.

Shogren, K. A., V. J. Bradley, S. C. Gomez, M. H. Yeager, R. L. Schalock, W. S. Borthwick-Duffy, W. H. Bontix, D. L. Coulten, E. P. Craig, Y. LaChapelle, R. A. Luckasson, A. Reeve, M. E. Snell, S. Spreot, M. J. Tasse, J. R. Thompson, M. A. Verdigo, and M. L. Wehmeyer. 2009. "Public Policy and the Enhancement of Desired Outcomes for Persons with Intellectual Disability." *Intellectual and Developmental Disabilities* 47 (4): 307–19.

Skocpol, Theda. 1995. *Social Policy in the United States: Future Possibilities in Historical Perspective*. Princeton, NJ: Princeton University Press.

Skowronek, Stephen, 1982. *Building a New American State: The Expansion of National Administrative Capacities 1877–1920*. Cambridge: Cambridge University Press.

Smith, Steven R., and Helen Ingram. 2002. "Policy Tools and Democracy." In *The Tools of Government*, edited by Lester M. Salamon. New York: Oxford University Press.

Smith, Steven R., and Michael Lipsky. 1993. *Non-Profits for Hire: The Welfare State in the Age of Contracting*. Cambridge, MA: Harvard University Press.

Snape, Stephanie. 2004. "Liberated or Lost Souls: Is There a Role for Non-Executive Coun-
cilors?" In *British Local Government into the 21st Century*, edited by Gerry Stoker and
David Wilson. London: Palgrave.

Snyder, William M., Etienne Wenger, and Xavier de Sousa Briggs. 2003. "Communities of
Practice in Government: Leveraging Knowledge for Performance." *Public Manager* 32
(4): 17–23.

Solo, Paula, and George Pressberg. 1998. "Beyond Theory: Civil Society in Action." In
Community Works: The Revival of Civil Society in America, edited by E. J. Dionne Jr.
Washington, DC: Brookings Institution Press.

Sorenson, Eva, and Jacob Torfing, eds. 2007. *Theories of Democratic Network Governance*.
Basingstoke, UK: Palgrave-Macmillan.

Stanton, Thomas H. 2007. *Delivery of Benefits in an Emergency: Lessons from Hurricane
Katrina*. Washington, DC: IBM Center for the Business of Government.

Sterling, Bruce. 2002. "Preparing for the Long Term." In *What's Next? Exploring the New
Terrain for Business*, edited by Eamonn Kelly and Peter Leyden. New York: Basic Books.

Stewart, Alexandria, Marisa Cox, Joel Teitelbaum, and Sara Rosenbaum. 2003. *Beyond
Olmstead and Toward Community Integration: Measuring Progress and Change*. Washington, DC: George Washington University Medical Center.

Stoker, Gerry, and Karen Mossberger. 1994. "Urban Regime Theory in Comparative Perspective." *Environment and Planning C: Government and Policy* 12 (2): 195–212.

Stone, Clarence N. 1989. *Regime Politics*. Lawrence: University Press of Kansas.

———. 2005. "Civic Capacity: What, Why, and from Whence." In *The Public Schools*, edited
by Susan Fuhrman and Marvin Lazerson. New York: Oxford University Press.

Stone, Clarence N., Kathryn Doherty, Cheryl Jones, and Timothy Ross. 1999. "Schools and
Disadvantaged Neighborhoods: The Community Development Challenge." In *Urban
Problems and Community Development*, edited by Ronald F. Ferguson and William T.
Dickens. Washington, DC: Brookings Institution Press.

Strauss, Anselm L. 1993. *Continual Permutations of Action*. Hawthorne, NY: Aldine de
Gryther.

Sundram, Clarence J. 2003. "Foreword." In *Quality Enhancement in Developmental Disabilities*, edited by Valerie J. Bradley and Madeleine H. Kimmich. Baltimore: Paul H.
Brookes.

Tapscott, Don. 2009. *Grown Up Digital: How the Net Generation Is Changing Your World*.
New York: McGraw-Hill.

Tapscott, Don, and Anthony D. Williams. 2006. *Wikinomics: How Mass Collaboration
Changes Everything*. New York: Portfolio.

Tarrow, Sidney. 2005. *The New Transnational Activism*. Cambridge: Cambridge University
Press.

Teisman, Geert R. 1992/1995. *Complexe Besluitvorming: Een Pluricentrisch Perspectief op
Besluitvorming over Ruimtelijke Investeringen*. The Hague: VUGA.

Thomas, Craig W. 1998. "Maintaining and Restoring Public Trust in Government Agencies
and Their Employees." *Administration and Society* 30 (2): 166–94.

———. 2003. *Bureaucratic Landscapes: Interagency Cooperation and the Preservation of Bio-
diversity*. Cambridge, MA: MIT Press.

Thompson, Ann Marie, and James M. Perry. 2006. "Collaboration Process: Inside the Black Box." *Public Administration Review* 66 (56): 20–32.

Thompson, Frank J., and Courtney Burke. 2008. "Federalism by Waiver: Medicaid and the Transformation of Long-Term Care." Paper prepared for Annual Meeting of American Political Science Association, Boston, August 28–September 1.

Thompson, James D. 1967. *Organizations in Action*. New York: McGraw-Hill.

Toulmin, S. 1990. *Cosmopolis*. Chicago: University of Chicago Press.

Tsoukas, Hardimos. 2005. *Complex Knowledge*. Oxford: Oxford University Press.

Turner, Bryan S. 1990. "Periodization and Politics in the Postmodern." In Bryan S. Turner (ed.), *Theories of Modernity and Postmodernity*. London: Sage.

Urban Institute. 2010. *National Survey of Nonprofit-Government Contracting and Grants*. Washington, DC: Urban Institute.

Vandeventer, Paul, and Myrna Mandell. 2007. *Networks That Work*. Los Angeles: Community Partners.

Van Slyke, David. 2007. "Agents or Stewards: Government Nonprofit Service Contracting Relationship." *Journal of Public Administration Research and Theory* 17 (2): 157–87.

Wagenaar, Hendrik. 2004. "'Knowing the Rules: Administrative Work as Practice." *Public Administration Review* 64 (6): 643–55.

Walters, Jonathan. 2011. "Help for the Helpers: Nonprofits Deliver the Lion's Share of Health and Human Services." *Governing* 24 (8): 32–35.

Walzer, Michael. 1998. "The Ideal of Civil Society: The Path to Social Reconstruction." In *Community Works: The Revival of Civil Society in America*, edited by E. J. Dionne Jr. Washington, DC: Brookings Institution Press.

Watts, Ronald L. 1999. *Comparing Federal Systems in the 1990s*, 3rd ed. Kingston, ON: Institute of Intergovernmental Relations, Queen's University.

Waugh, William L., Jr. 2004. "Leveraging Networks to Meet National Goals: FEMA and the Safe Construction Networks." In *Collaboration: Using Networks and Partnerships*, edited by John Kamensky and Thomas J. Burlin. Lanham, MD: Rowman & Littlefield.

Waugh, William L., Jr., and Gregory Streib. 2006. "Collaboration and Leadership for Effective Emergency Management." *Public Administration Review* 66 (6) (Supplement): 131–40.

Wedel, Kenneth R. 1983. "Purchase of Service Contracting in Human Services." In *Human Services on a Limited Budget*, edited by Robert Agranoff. Washington, DC: International City Management Association.

Weiner, Myron. 1990. *Human Services Management: Analysis and Applications*, 2nd ed. Belmont, CA: Wadsworth.

Weir, Margaret, Jane Rongerude, and Christopher K. Ansell. 2005. "Collaboration Is Not Enough: Virtuous Cycles of Reform in Transportation Policy." *Urban Affairs Review* 44 (4): 482.

Wenger, Etienne. 2000. "Communities of Practice: The Key to Knowledge Strategy." In *Knowledge and Communities*, edited by Eric L. Lesser, Michael A. Fontaine, and Jason A. Slusher. Boston: Butterworth-Heinemann.

Wheatley, Margaret J. 1999. *Leadership and the New Science: Discovering Order in a Chaotic World*, 2nd ed. San Francisco: Berrett-Koehler.

Williams, Walter. 1980. *Government by Agency: Lessons from the Grants-in-Aid Experience.* New York: Academic Press.

Windhoff-Héntier, Andriene. 1992. "The Internationalization of Domestic Policy: A Motor of Decentralization." Paper prepared for European Consortium for Political Research Joint Sessions, Limerick, Ireland.

Wise, Charles R. 2006. "Organizing for Homeland Security after Katrina: Is Adaptive Management What's Missing?" *Public Administration Review* 66 (3): 302–18.

Wolf, Thomas. 1999. *Managing a Nonprofit Organization in the Twenty-First Century.* New York: Simon & Schuster.

Wolfensberger, Wolf. 1972. *Normalization.* Toronto: National Institute on Mental Retardation.

Wondolleck, Julia M., and Steven L. Yaffee. 2000. *Making Collaboration Work.* Washington, DC: Island Press.

Wright, Deil S. 1988. *Understanding Intergovernmental Relations*, 3rd ed. Belmont, CA: Wadsworth.

Zuboff, Shoshana, and James Maxim. 2002. *The Support Economy.* New York: Penguin.

Index